E-LEARNING – ORGANIZATIONAL INFRASTRUCTURE AND TOOLS FOR SPECIFIC AREAS

Edited by **Elvis Pontes, Anderson Silva, Adilson Guelfi** and **Sérgio Takeo Kofuji**

E-Learning – Organizational Infrastructure and Tools for Specific Areas
Edited by Elvis Pontes, Anderson Silva, Adilson Guelfi and Sérgio Takeo Kofuji

Published by InTech

Janeza Trdine 9, 51000 Rijeka, Croatia

Publishing Process Manager Ivona Lovric

Technical Editor Teodora Smiljanic

Cover Designer InTech Design Team

Additional hard copies can be obtained from orders@intechopen.com

E-Learning – Organizational Infrastructure and Tools for Specific Areas,
Edited by Elvis Pontes, Anderson Silva, Adilson Guelfi and Sérgio Takeo Kofuji
p. cm.
ISBN 978-953-51-0053-9

For EU product safety concerns:
IN TECH d.o.o., Prolaz Marije Krucifikse Kozulić 3, 51000 Rijeka, Croatia,
info@intechopen.com or visit our website at intechopen.com.

Meet the editors

Elvis Pontes is professor at the University Estácio de Sá, at the Universidade Paulista, and at SENAC. He applied for Ph.D. at the University of São Paulo, holds MSc from the Institute of Technological Research of São Paulo; MBA from the Institute of Energy and Nuclear Researches; BSc from the Technological Institute of Osasco.

Anderson Aparecido Alves da Silva applied for PhD at the University of São Paulo (USP), Electrical Engineering Postgraduate Program. He holds MSc from the Institute of Technological Research of São Paulo (IPT), MBA from the Alvares Penteado's Foundation, and technological degree from the Educational Institute of Osasco. Currently he is full time professor at the Paulista University.

Adilson Guelfi holds PhD in Electric Engineering from the University of São Paulo. He is professor and researcher at the Institute of Technological Research of São Paulo, technical manager of the first Brazilian laboratory for testing and verifying the compatibility of systems, devices and equipments for the Brazilian Public Key Infrastructure standards.

Sérgio Takeo Kofuji holds Bachelor Degree in Physics from the University of São Paulo (1985), Masters in Electrical Engineering from the University of São Paulo (1988) and Ph.D. in Electrical Engineering from the University of São Paulo (1995). He is currently Professor RiDP Polytechnic School of the University of São Paulo.

Contents

Preface

For many decades education in the form of courses by correspondence or TV has been an interesting alternative for those who do not have enough free time to study, or for those who live far from a school, or those unable to attend classes due to some physical or medical restriction. Over the years, many students have benefitted from this way of apprenticeship, developing skills and enhancing expertise in sectors as diverse as health, engineering, human sciences, zoology, and architecture, among others.

With the advent of the Internet the increasing demand of long-distance courses went through a period of fantastic expansion. A specific term was associated with the technology for long-distance education: e-learning.

The term e-learning is associated with all kinds of knowledge transferred by electronic means, with the purpose of teaching or learning. It also includes handling tools which improve the instruction process. Technology development, mainly for telecommunications and computer systems, was a key factor for the interactivity and, thus, for the expansion of e-learning.

In addition to the on-line interaction among students and teachers, the interaction process has brought other benefits such as conferences with multiple users, collaborative work, and the possibility of sharing, sending, and receiving work material (files such as texts, pictures, and programs) in real time. Actually, these technological advances create new challenges such as the need for new methodologies that can explore the full potential of interaction between students and teachers, and the development of new tools which allow the best use of technological resources for learning purposes. This is an excellent opportunity for teachers and practitioners to improve their work.

This book is divided into two parts, presenting some proposals to deal with e-learning challenges, opening up a way of learning about and discussing new methodologies to increase the interaction level of classes and implementing technical tools for helping students to make better use of e-learning resources.

In the first part, the reader may find chapters mentioning the required infrastructure for e-learning models and processes, organizational practices, suggestions, implementation of methods for assessing results, and case studies focused on pedagogical aspects that can be applied generically in different environments. The second part is related to tools that can be adopted by users such as graphical tools for engineering, mobile phone networks, and techniques to build robots, among others. Moreover, part two includes some chapters dedicated specifically to e-learning areas like engineering and architecture.

Professor Elvis Pontes,
Professor Anderson Silva,
Professor Adilson Guelfi and
Professor Sérgio Takeo Kofuji
Department of Electrical Engineering
Polytechnic School
University of São Paulo (USP)
Brazil

Part 1

E-Learning Organizational Infrastructure

1

Factors that Influence Academic Teacher's Acceptance of E-Learning Technology in Blended Learning Environment

Snježana Babić
Polytechnic of Rijeka, Business Department, Rijeka, Croatia

1. Introduction

The idea of distance learning as the concept of learning at one's own pace independent of time and place, originated in 19th century. The Open University of United Kingdom, which introduced blended learning in 1969, had the crucial role in introducing the distance learning into the higher education. The term e-learning (electronically supported learning) was introduced in 1995, and its most common definition is: learning and teaching using information and communications technology, or more broadly, e-learning technology.

Blended model of learning combines different models of learning and teaching: in traditional classroom (which provides e-learning technologies) and virtual learning environment. Virtual Learning Environment (VLE) is a component or subsystem of the Managed Learning Environment (MLE), where students and teachers take part in different types of online interaction, and whose focus is on managing and facilitating the learning process while providing the required resources. The commonly used synonym for VLE is Learning Management System (LMS). MLE includes various information systems and processes of the higher education, and together with VLE they make a part of virtual campus (The Joint Information System Committee [JISC], 2011).

One of the definitions of virtual campus is: "...refers to a specific format of distance education and on-line learning in which students, teaching staff and even university administrative and technical staff mainly 'meet' or communicate through technical links" (benchmarking of Virtual Campuses [BENVIC], 2011).

Higher education teacher can find the service of using VLE at certain institutions, which can use the service developed within the institution or at the university level. In practice, most commonly used are commercial software packages (integrated set of tools for communication, knowledge evaluation, collaboration, monitoring and other) such as WebCT and Blackboard, and among Open Source packages, Moodle and Claroline.

Introducing e-learning into higher education institution brings about changes on organizational, economical and technical level, however, the practice shows that e-learning has been introduced into such institutions in various ways which resulted in different quantity and quality of the education processes using e-learning technology. To improve the effectiveness of e-learning, the need occurred for developing the quality management system in the field of e-learning (Kermek et al., 2007). Those standards are: ISO/IEC 19796-

1:2005 (Information Technology - Learning, Education and Training - Quality Management, Assurance and Metrics - Part 1: General Approach, 2005) which provides a framework for quality management and consists of reference model describing the education processes and subprocesses in e-education, and ISO/IEC 19796-3:2009 (Information Technology - Learning, Education and Training - Quality Management, Assurance and Metrics - Part 3: Reference methods and metrics, 2009) which extends the previous reference framework by providing methods and metrics required to implement quality management and quality assurance systems for stakeholders designing, developing or utilizing e-learning technology. Processes related to e-education are compared to the software development process, where the basis for quality standards is taken from the domain of software engineering (Kermek et al., 2007). Based on this, Marchall & Mitchell (2004) defined E-learning maturity model for estimating the organization's level of maturity relating to the e-education processes and their improvement. The improvement of education processes depends on the development of capabilities in all their elements, from the institution in charge to the every single individual involved in the educational system, and in this case it is important to emphasize teacher competences.

On the other hand, the quality and usability of the virtual learning environment are the key influencers on the learning outcome, i.e., student satisfaction. The usability of the e-learning technologies, as the main element of the e-learning success, includes pedagogical and technical usability. Pedagogical usability refers to the support in the process of teaching and learning, while technical usability refers to the interaction between the user and the computer (Melis et al., 2003). Due to the mentioned facts, to create a virtual learning environment, apart form the teacher as an expert in a certain field of study, a team of experts is required: multimedia experts, programmers, administrators, instructional designers and similar experts. However, the practice shows that often teachers are the ones who perform many different roles themselves.

With regards to the complexity of the proper use of e-learning in teaching, the results of the research indicate the slow manner of teachers accepting e-learning. For that reason, a question is being asked: *Which factors influence the higher education teacher's acceptance of e-learning?*

Numerous authors have researched many factors from different aspects, they have monitored introducing e-learning as an innovation diffusion in organization, introducing and accepting new information system, communication between human and the machine, psychology, pedagogy, reengineering the education/business process and other. During the research they have used existing theories and models of technology and innovation acceptance.

Keller (2009) approaches the teacher's acceptance of VLE as an innovation diffusion from the aspect of organizational learning, while Nanayakkara and Whiddett (2005) group factors as individual, organizational and system factors. Argawal (2000) defines the following categories of factors related to the personal acceptance of the information technology in organizations: personal differences, situational factors, social influence, organizational factors, beliefs and attitudes. Osika and Buteau (2009) monitor acceptance of the e-learning technology through motivational factors, which they group as intrinsic factors (beliefs, sense of competence, anxiety) and extrinsic factors (institutional factors).

In professional development individual's commitment to the quality of his or her work is shown through the change in attitudes and values, development of skills and competences, and using certain tools and instruments which results in quality work (Ehlers, 2007). Baia (2009) confirmed the influence of the factor commitment to pedagogical quality on technology acceptance, which is influenced by: belief about learning technologies, academic title and years of work experience.

Competence perception and confirmation of the initial expectation (attitude) influence the teacher's satisfaction through perception of usefulness, where the attitude related to the teacher's education (Ø. Sørebø & A. M. Sørebø, 2008) is the confirmation of the initial expectation.

The following pages contain the overview of the most commonly used theories and models of accepting technology and innovation, as well as key responsibilities of teachers in blended learning process for better understanding of the concept of higher education teacher competence in the field of e-learning. Furthermore, categories of factors have been singled out in which there is an overview of those factors which, as found in recent studies, showed connection with teacher's accepting e-learning technology. The conclusion contains the categories with key factors which can aid future researchers in defining theoretic models as the foundation for future empirical researches.

2. Education process in blended learning environment and the teacher competence concept

To describe a teaching scenario in any form of e-learning and in different educational environments, a reference model ISO/IEC 19796-1 can be used, which includes the complete life-long learning cycle. The model is a framework consisting of two parts: generic process model and generic descriptive model. Generic process model is divided into 7 basic processes and 38 subprocesses, and the following is the description of the basic processes (Pawlowski, 2006):

Needs Analysis: identification and description of requirements, demands, and constraints of an educational project

Framework Analysis: identification of the framework and the context of an educational process

Conception /Design: conception and design of an educational process

Development /Production: realization of concepts

Implementation: description of the implementation of technological components

Learning Process: realization and use of the learning process

Evaluation/Optimization: description of the evaluation methods, principles, and procedures

There are numerous instructional design models (systematic approach to analysis, design, development, implementation and evaluation of the study material for learning according to the set learning outcomes, following the analysis of student needs) which teachers can use to design different education processes in blended form. Some of the instructional design models are: Dick and Carey, rapid prototyping, Knirk and Gustafson and others, among which the most commonly used in higher education is ADDIE (Analyze, Design, Develop, Implement, Evaluate) model.

Academic teachers most frequently use their own non-standardised models, and very often use the virtual learning environment only for access to study material. In practice, the search for the best blended learning model in a particular context boils down to combining the advantages and disadvantages of traditional teaching activities and technology-mediated activities (Fig. 1) (Rothery et al., 2008).

Fig. 1. Searching for the best blended learning model (Rothery et al., 2008).

The quality of the education process is one of the factors responsible for students achieving success. Creating the blended learning environment is not easy and it requires teachers to redefine the existing competences and develop new ones, during which is essential to understand the concept of the quality of e-education.

Numerous definitions of competence concept have been published, and according to Weinert (2001) it "...is a specialized system of abilities, proficiencies, or skills that are necessary to reach a specific goal". From this definition, it can be inferred that the concept of personal e-competence of the higher education teacher includes: teacher's ability to implement e-learning in his or her education process, as well as ability to adopt new competences for implementing e-learning in the education process.

With the aim of defining the concept of e-competence, numerous authors used the general competence concept, developed by Weinert (2001), as their basis. Its central idea is the learning process which together with practical experience develops new knowledge and skills that change values and form a certain attitude. Weinert (2001) emphasizes the importance of the experience and explains that competences can be learned and developed through practical values. The foundation for action lies in: attitude, knowledge and skills, and great importance is put on action competence which includes "available cognitive, motivational and social requirements for successful learning or performing an action".

Based on the mentioned general competence concept, Schneckenberg (2007) defined the e-competence concept applicable to all levels, from institution, group, to every stakeholder in higher education environment. The concept assumes knowledge, skills and attitude as the basis for performance, which can be looked at from the aspect of pedagogical, technical, organizational and sociocultural dimension, and the action competence can be seen through four core competences: subject matter, methodology, social competence and personal competence. It is important to emphasize that the teacher's personal competence for e-learning application cannot be defined without identifying situational variables in specific education scenarios which are determined by the following elements (Schneckenberg, 2007): pedagogical model (set of methods for optimum realization of communication between teacher, content and student), choice of e-learning technology, student competences for using ICT in learning activities and the characteristics of the education content, i.e., the course. Education scenario is performed in specific context with specific characteristics, therefore the more specific and less specific education contexts are the key elements of the aforementioned competence model. Assuming that a competent person will not apply and develop his or her competences unless motivated, the motivation component is of crucial importance and it can be intrinsic (teacher's personality, attitude and values) and extrinsic (situational and institutional factors).

Taking into consideration the same general competence concept in organization (Weintert, 2001) and the fact that e-learning is introduced into education to improve the education quality (dependent of the desire for quality performance of all the stakeholders in the educational system), Ehlers (2007) defined the concept of competence as "quality literacy". Thus he describes the ability of education stakeholders to improve in quality while emphasizing the importance of professionalism as the crucial component in quality development. He looks at the "quality literacy" concept through four dimensions of competence which lead to professionalism and quality development on all levels: quality knowledge, quality experience, quality innovation and quality analysis. "Quality literacy" is the competence concept which, besides knowledge and skills, includes: the responsibility of the stakeholders towards the surroundings, i.e., professionalism in the field of quality development in e-education.

3. Theories and models of accepting technology and innovation

With the aim of understanding the factors which influence teachers accepting the e-learning technology, different existing theories and models have been used, and this paper mentions only the ones used frequently in recent studies.

The model of accepting technology has its foundations in the theory of social psychology, developed by Fisbein and Ajzen (1975) as Theory of Reasoned Action (TRA) which points out key factors influencing the behavioral intent: attitude toward behavior and subjective norm; if users have the intention of accepting technology, they will do so, but under the strong influence of the environment.

In his Theory of Planned Behavior (TPB) model, Ajzen (1991) later added the factor of perceived behavioral control to the factors attitude toward behavior and subjective norm, which stems from the self-efficacy theory and is a condition for change in behavior.

One of the first models of accepting technology, and most commonly used in the research is Technology Acceptance Model (TAM) (Fig. 2) developed by Davis (1989), according to which the user's attitude towards technology is mainly influenced by the following factors: perceived usefulness and perceived ease of use. According to Davis (1989), perceived usefulness is defined as "the prospective user's subjective probability that using a specific application system will increase his or her job performance", while perceived ease of use is defined as "degree to which the prospective user expects the target system to be free of effort".

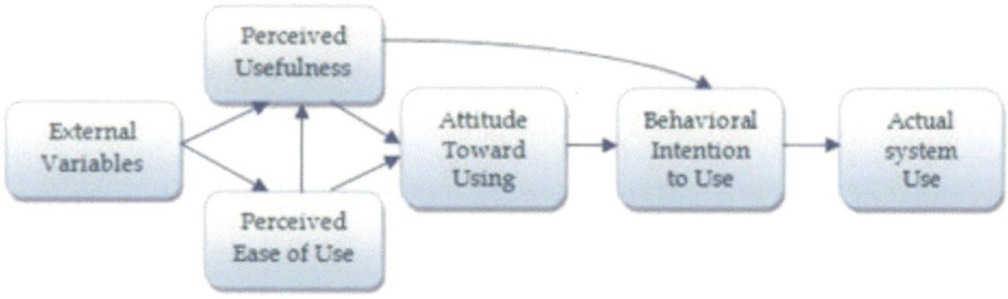

Fig. 2. Technology Acceptance Model (TAM) developed by Davis (1989).

TAM model was later updated by its author adding numerous factors, and so have other authors; Venkatesh and Davis (2000) developed TAM2 model in which the TAM model is upgraded with the processes of cognitive influence: job relevance, output quality and result demonstrability, and the processes of social influence: subjective norm, voluntariness and image, which influence the perceived usefulness.

The next important model, very often used in the field of e-learning, was developed by Venkatesh et al. (2003) as Unified Theory of Acceptance and Use of Technology (UTAUT), according to which the following four factors influence the user's technology acceptance: performance expectancy, effort expectancy, social influence and facilitating conditions. The model emphasizes the importance of four moderators: age, gender, experience and voluntariness of use, as individual differences between users towards technology acceptance.

From the aspect of diffusing new ideas and innovations, according to Rogers (1995), four main elements have a direct influence: innovation, communication channels, time and social system. In Innovation Diffusion Theory (IDT) Rogers (1995) defined five steps through which the user goes through when deciding about accepting new technology: knowledge, persuasion, decision, implementation and confirmation. In the phase of persuasion about positive characteristics of the product/service, the user is influenced by: relative advantage, compatibility, complexity, trialability and observability. According to the decision-making about innovation acceptance, Rogers (1995) groups the users as following: innovators, early adopters, early majority, late majority and laggards (Fig. 3).

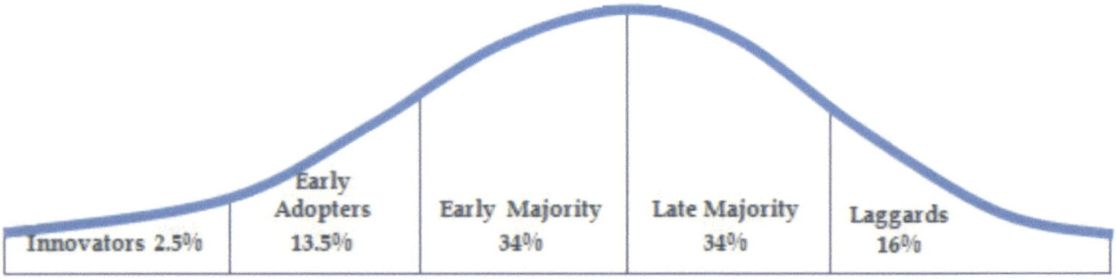

Fig. 3. Rogers Innovation Adoption Curve (Rogers, 1995).

Among early and late adopters (Fig. 3) there are systematic differences in three areas: socioeconomic, personality variables, communication behavior, and other characteristics: previous practice, wants and needs, innovativeness and social norms.

Based on Rogers' theory (1995), Moore and Benbasat (1991) developed a model for measuring user's perception of information technology's characteristics as innovation. The model was applied in the field of adopting information systems, and it consists of the following: relative advantage, compatibility, trialability, ease of use (replacement for: complexity (Rogers, 1995)), visibility and result demonstrability (replacement for: observability (Rogers,1995)), image and voluntariness.

4. Factors that influence academic teacher's acceptance of e-learning technology

What follows are the factors connected to the academic teacher's acceptance of e-technology, grouped in several categories.

4.1 Teacher competence (knowledge and skills)

Certain knowledge and skills encourage changes in individual's values and attitudes which influence the user's behavior, as well as belief about self-efficacy.

The main prerequisite for the use of e-learning technology is: computer literacy, and the lack of computer knowledge is closely related to computer anxiety and the level of perceived usefulness of e-learning technology (Liu, 2005). Computer literate person is more likely to experiment with new software. Therefore, the level of experience in working with e-learning system (LMS) is the powerful motivator in teacher's adoption of e-learning (Gautreau, 2011). It is well known that after having accepted the e-learning system, it is used on different levels. Renzi (2008) proved the existence of differences in competences between certain groups of teachers. Teachers who create virtual learning environments according to the instructional design principles transform their way of teaching. Knowledge and skills from using the instructional design model, i.e., designing the education scenario, are related to the following factors: formal education, teacher's experience and perceived technology usefulness (Renzi, 2008).

E-moderating is the key teacher competence influencing the success of the online part of the lessons, and which (according to Salmon (2000)) refers to: knowledge and skills of online moderating and online mentoring. On the organizational level of e-learning, besides the pedagogical and technical dimension of the teacher competence, Shenckenberg (2008) points out the importance of the sociocultural and organizational dimension of the competence profile when adopting e-learning. In this case, sociocultural dimension refers to the teacher's readiness to adopt new knowledge from the field of e-learning, as well as communication and sharing of knowledge within certain networks, and the competence profile of academic teachers in organizational dimension includes taking part in deciding about implementation of e-learning at institutional level, working in interdisciplinary teams on solving problems due to the complexity of education using e-learning technology and managing e-learning projects which are a part of university's e-learning strategy (Shenckenberg, 2008).

4.2 Attitude and values

In the process of accepting innovation in teaching, teacher's belief about the usefulness of the innovation plays one of the main roles and it encourages changes in the curricula (Colorado & Eberle, 2009). Teacher's attitude and values are important motivational factor in developing and applying e-learning competence.

There have been many researches about teacher's attitude towards e-learning technology: positive (confirmation) or negative (anxiety) (Mihhailova, 2006). Less researches are oriented towards beliefs which form certain values and attitudes (Agarwal, 2000). Researches have shown that users' behavior is influenced by different beliefs or e-learning technology attributes, and according to Moore and Benbast (1991) they are: relative advantage, compatibility, trialability, ease of use, result demonstrability, observability. Most frequently confirmed attributes are: ease of use and usefulness (Gibson et al., 2008; Renzi, 2008; Keller, 2009).

Ozkan and Findik (2010) confirm the importance of the e-learning technology compatibility attribute in relation to the differences in certain academic departments, where the difference has been confirmed. Kundu et al. (2010) confirm the importance of compatibility attribute through the following obstacles in accepting e-learning technology: integration with other systems in organization, incompatibility in technology use and existing work practice, the problem of integrating technology and existing practice in traditional classrooms. Moscinska and Rutkowski (2011) confirm the attributes: flexibility and "user-friendly" which influence the acceptance and use of e-learning systems, and present technical characteristics of the e-learning system.

It is well known that different beliefs about the value of e-learning encourage teachers to apply e-learning technology on different levels (Renzi, 2008). The perception of e-learning usefulness is formed under the influence of intrinsic and extrinsic factors, and numerous authors list: belief in institution's competitiveness, increased number of enrolled students (Osika et al., 2009), facilitated student cooperation in educational context (Lofstrom & Nevgi, 2008), communication and additional support for students, distribution of study material, the ease of administration, the value of collaborative online work (Keller, 2009), belief in information sharing, automated activities of the learning process, value of social learning as an important part of learning in general (Renzi, 2008). Successful pedagogical use of e-learning technology depends on teacher's attitude towards technology Mihhailova, 2006). Research results show that teacher's attitude has been studied more from the technical and less from the pedagogical aspect (Mahdizadeh et al., 2008).

4.3 Teacher's personality

Teacher's personality is a powerful intrinsic motivational factor which influences e-learning technology acceptance. It represents a set of characteristics which make every teacher unique in education process and it is strongly influenced by the surroundings.

The most commonly studied teacher's features are: self-efficacy and anxiety, more often approached from the technical aspect. Computer anxiety is closely connected to the teacher's attitude, author suggests the possibility of understanding computer self-efficacy as a construct of perceived ease of use (Timothy, 2009). Malik et al. (2010) mention teacher's organizational commitment as an important factor in quality teaching process and Baia (2009) confirmed the influence of commitment to the pedagogical quality on the e-learning technology acceptance.

Teacher's personality is evident through teaching and learning style applied in the education process and which includes certain teaching methods and techniques, and represents a mechanism responsible for quality conveyance of the educational content influencing the student success (Grasha, 1994). Changes in the teacher's belief, attitude and values influence the teaching style. Lucas & Wright (2009) predicts the possibility of connection between teaching style and the attitude towards the use of e-learning technology. Dugas (2006) determined a slight connection of teaching style and the degree of innovation with accepting e-learning technology.

Apart from the teacher's personality, great importance lies in the demographic and situational variables. The experience with LMS and computer experience are strong motivators in teachers' acceptance of e-learning (Gautreau, 2011). In his research Timothy (2009) did not find significant link between attitude, age and gender, which contradicts the hypothesis by Houtz and Gupta, Cully et al. (Timothy, 2009), he found a significant difference in the attitudes of the female computer users. However, Marwan and Sweeney (2010) point out to a significant connection between gender, department and academic title with the teacher's attitude towards e-learning technology. Academic title and years of work experience influence the commitment to the pedagogical quality which influences acceptance of e-learning technology (Baia, 2009).

4.4 Characteristics of students and the field of study

While creating virtual learning environment the choice of e-learning technology depends on pedagogical model, and its choice is influenced by: field of study characteristics and characteristics of the students, which both represent situational factors.

Kanuka (2006) stresses out the importance of the following factors: value and culture within certain discipline, understanding unique problems within each field of study as crucial elements when designing learning environment. Keller (2009) proved that the culture within the discipline represents the obstacle of e-learning application. Before using the virtual learning environment, reasons for the use of e-learning technology need to be defined, where, according to Rebman Jr et al. (2004), certain physical educational activities require classical approach in a traditional classroom. Knowledge is hierarchically organized and therefore it is essential to define learning outcomes within each course using knowledge taxonomy, and based on the outcomes define educational strategies and student activities (Donnelly, 2005). Numerous models of instructional design can be found in literature, however, Donnelly (2005) emphasizes that teachers mostly use non-systemized personal models because the planning of the educational structure requires: time, commitment and careful systematic approach. One characteristic of the study object (any segment of the digital study material) is: multiple use in different educational contexts; however, Parrish (2007) brings up the problem of intellectual property which limits the distribution of the study objects. Learning happens in predictable patterns that can me modeled using algorithms, which influences the development of the intelligent tutoring systems (Parrish, 2007).

Student characteristics can act as motivators for application and development of e-learning in teaching, and student capabilities (Osika et al., 2009) can be an obstacle in using e-learning technology in teaching. Each student has his or her own learning style and there are various instruments that can measure those styles (Grasha, 1994). A very important student characteristic is motivation; a motivated student shows greater interest in information, the quality of information, confidence when accessing information and technology, satisfaction in work (Kumarawadu, 2011). Colorado and Eberle (2009) conclude that the level of student self-regulated learning is related to demographic data: gender, status, certify cates, completed degree of education and characteristics of the self-regulated learning: learning strategy, critical thinking, knowledge sharing, asking for help, where students who have graduated have a higher level of self-regulated learning.

On the other hand, the number of students in virtual classrooms and complexity of education scenario influence the success of virtual learning process (Salmon, 2000). Perception of student characteristics can be a part of the construct: facilitating circumstances (Ø. Sørebø & A. M. Sørebø, 2008).

4.5 Acquiring knowledge and skills

The lack of knowledge about e-learning technology and the lack of skills influence the successful integration of e-learning in higher education institutions. New knowledge and skills, together with experience, encourage the change in existing value system, and finally they become attitudes influencing the teacher's behavior in the education process. On the

other hand, the attitudes and values of other important people in a certain environment also have significant influence on developing behavior.
Formal education in the field of pedagogy influences the level of e-learning application in the education process (Renzi, 2008). Learning is a process which can be realized in different ways using current e-learning technology at various life-long learning centers, organized by different institutions. On the other hand, Samarawickrema and Stacey (2007) point out the importance of learning and support from the experienced colleagues and experts via formally organized networks, as well as informal group networks, within and outside the university, i.e., through different learning communities. Support and encouragement from the colleagues within the network are the strong motivators for the experimenting with e-learning technology and teacher's eagerness and interest for introducing innovation into the education process. Keller and associates (2009) also confirm the importance of the colleague support, as well as expert help in accepting and applying e-learning, which is closely connected to the lack of time needed to invest in acquiring new pedagogical and technological competences (Keller et al., 2009). Organizational learning is strongly and reciprocally connected with individual learning. Learning is a continuous process which can be encouraged by: personal, situational and institutional motivational factors, therefore it is essential to understand their influence. Gautreau (2011) confirms the importance of teacher's personal motivation to attend the course about applying e-learning in education process, which strongly influences the successful integration of e-learning system in education process.

4.6 Institutional factors

Institutional factors belong to a group of extrinsic motivational factors influencing academic teacher's acceptance of e-learning technology. Numerous study results indicate that factors which influence academic teachers differ depending on the current phase of e-learning introduction into the academic institution in question. One of the key factors is the capacity and reliability of the ICT infrastructure (Nanayakkera & Whiddett, 2005). In practice, teachers frequently list the following conditions as obstacles: access to the computer classroom, number of computers in a classroom, computer network, Internet (access and speed) (Osika et al., 2009). After solving the problem of infrastructure, there are other negative factors that influence e-learning application. Thus, perceived adequacy of support (e.g. technical, pedagogical, personnel), as facilitating circumstance, has an important impact on applying e-learning in education (Timothy, 2009). Availability of information about the manner of applying e-learning technology in education process can positively influence teacher's adoption of e-learning (Kundi et al., 2010).
Since introduction of e-learning technology into academic institutions causes changes in structure, policies and organizational culture, it also brings about changes in organizational learning. Keller (2009) proved that organizational culture has the strongest impact on e-learning technology integration by academic teachers through the level of organizational learning, thus the expected effort and observability have stronger connection with the lower level of organizational learning, while social influence and facilitating circumstances relate to the higher level of organizational learning. The author suggests that the teacher's attitude towards education quality needs to be examined. Numerous authors confirmed that institutional strategy is an important obstacle in adopting e-learning (Keller, 2009; Marwan & Sweeney, 2010; Samarawickrema & Stacey, 2007). Teacher's academic freedom and

organizational culture of teaching also represent obstacles in in e-learning acceptance (Keller, 2009).

After accepting e-learning technology, teachers still point out the following obstacles in its use: work overload, question of property, required resources, professional growth and management (Marwan & Sweeney, 2010). The academic institution's management has a great role in introducing and developing e-learning. Gautreau (2011) confirms the importance of adequate support and training factors, but also proves that reward and encouragement system and recognition of accomplishments are very important motivational factors in teachers adopting and developing e-learning.

However, even after removing many of the aforementioned obstacles, numerous study results indicate that time is the crucial factor that needs to be invested when changing to blended learning model, and it is connected to acquiring new knowledge, adjusting and implementing the course material to e-learning system, as well as to the lack of time for the requirements of the scientific research (Samarawickrema & Stacey , 2007).

5. Conclusion

Numerous authors have tried to understand the problem of academic teachers accepting e-learning technology by discovering and confirming the influence of many factors studied from different aspects, while using existing theories and models of innovation acceptance (as well as their combination) as basis for empirical research. Study results frequently confirm the factors: usefulness and ease of use of the e-learning technology. Authors have in different ways adapted the constructs from the existing theories and models, in which greater significance was given to the technical aspect of the e-learning technology, and not so much to the pedagogical aspect, which will only later gain more significance. Also, researches include more institutional factors and less situational ones (such as field of study characteristics and student characteristics) which represent important extrinsic motivational factors influencing the teachers when creating virtual learning environments. The researches are increasingly focused on the personality of teachers, as an intrinsic motivational factor, after certain institutional obstacles have been removed with the aim of creating encouragement measures for developing and applying e-learning. The training has been singled out as a separate category regarding that, apart from the required ICT infrastructure, acquiring new knowledge and skills is one of the essential factors in adopting e-learning. Learning through experience influences the creation of new values which become attitudes that have a strong impact on teacher's behavior towards e-learning technology. Therefore, the attitude and values are singled out as a separate category as well, linking together certain factors that influence them.

Because of the manner of academic teaching process, the most commonly used is blended learning model where teacher chooses the e-learning technology based on certain elements stated in this paper. The practice has shown that creating a blended learning environment is not easy and that teachers have problems in many stages of designing the virtual learning environment, from the analysis of the course requirements, analysis of the student requirements, application of instructional design model, e-learning technology use, not understanding the concept of the quality of e-learning process and many other factors. Based on existing study results in the field of academic teacher's accepting e-learning technology, the figure 4 shows intrinsic and extrinsic motivational factors which can serve as a foundation for theoretical models in the future empirical researches.

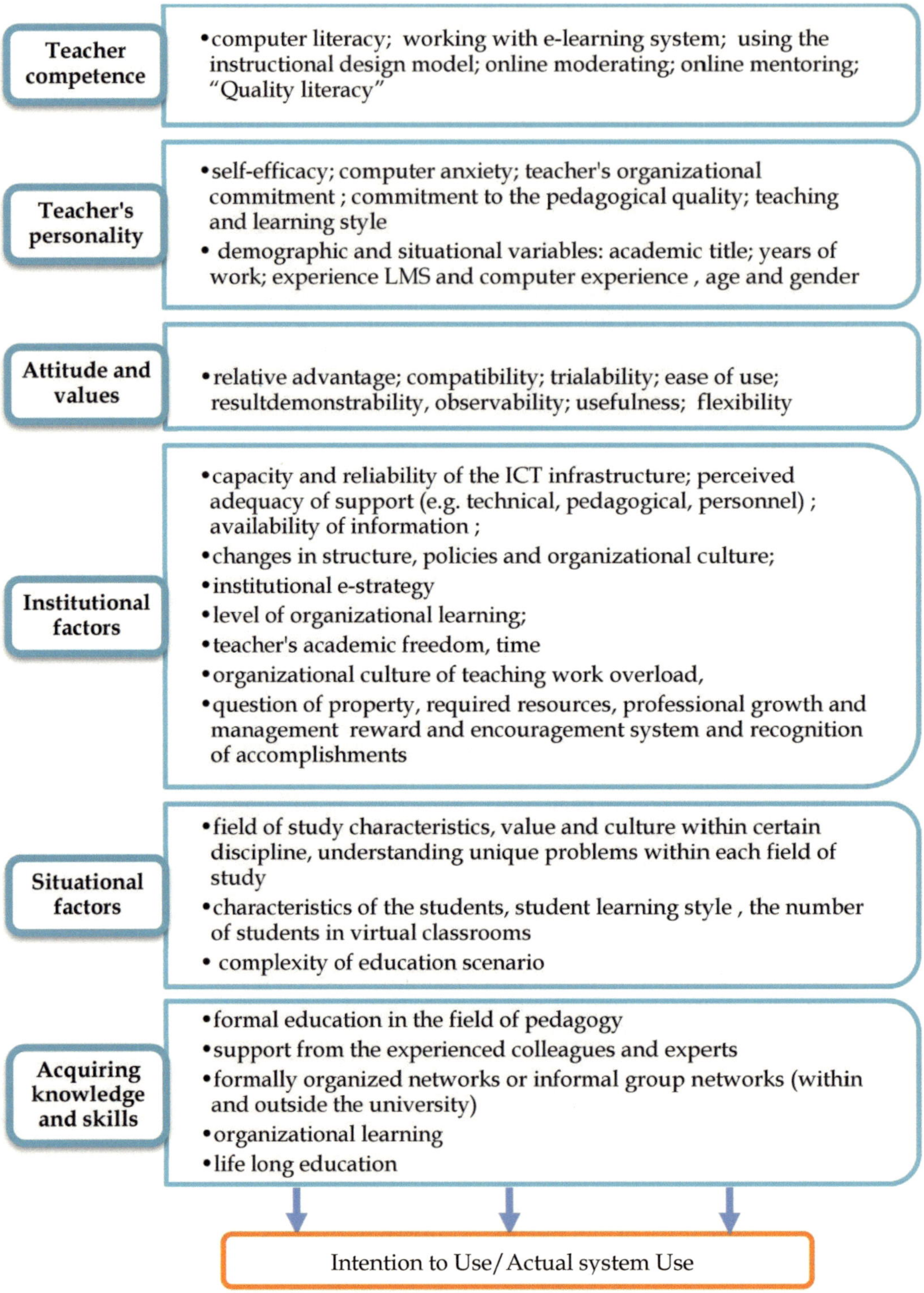

Fig. 4. Factors that influence academic teacher's acceptance of e-learning technology.

6. References

Agarwal, R. (2000). Individual Acceptance of Information Technologies, *in R. W. Zmud (Ed.), Framing The Domains of IT Management: Projecting the Future Through the Past, Cincinnati*, OH: Pinnaflex Press, 85-104.

Ajzen, I.(1991). The Theory of Planned Behaviour, *Organizational Behavior and Human Decision Processes*, 50(2), 179-211.

Baia, P. (2009). The Role of Commitment to Pedagogical Quality: The Adoption of Instructional Technology in Higher Education, *Study by Albany College of Pharmacy and Health Studies*, ERIC: ED504055

Benchmarking of Virtual Campuses BENVIC, URL: http://www.benvic.odl.org/indexpr.html [14/7/2011]

Colorado, J. & Eberle J. (2009). The Relationship of Student Demographics and Academic Performance in an Online Learning Environment. In T. Bastiaens et al. (Eds.), *Proceedings of World Conference on E-Learning in Corporate*, Government, Healthcare, and Higher Education 2009 (pp. 2469-2474). Chesapeake, VA: AACE

Davis, F. D. (1989). Perceived Usefulness, Perceived Ease of Use, and User Acceptance of Information Technology, *MIS Quarterly*, 13(3), 319-340.

Donnelly, R . & Fitzmaurice M. (2005). Designing Modules for Learning. In G. O'Neill, S. Moore & B. McMullin (Eds.) *Emerging Issues in the Practice of University Learning and Teaching* (pp. 99-110). Dublin: AISHE/HEA

Dugas, C. A. (2006). Adopter Characteristics and Teaching Styles of faculty Adopters and Nonadopters of a Course management System. *Disseration*. Indiana State University. Loetud

Ehlers, U. D. (2007). Quality Literacy – Competencies for Quality Development in Education and e-Learning, *Technology & Society* , 10 (2), 96-108.

Fishbein, M. & Ajzen I. (1975). Belief, attitude, intention and behavior: an introduction to theory and research, *Addison-Wesley*, Reading MA: Addison-Wesley

Gautreau, C. (2011). Motivational Factors Affecting the Integration of a Learning Management System by Faculty, California State University Fullerton, *The Journal of Educators Online*, Volume 8, Number 1, January 2011

Gibson, S.; Harris, M. & Colaric, S. (2008). Technology acceptance in an academic context: faculty acceptance of online education. *Journal of Education for Business*, 83(6), 355-359.

Grasha, A. F. (1994). A matter of style: The teacher as expert, formal authority, personal model, facilitator, and delegator. *College Teaching*. 42, 142-149.

ISO/IEC 19796-1:2005, Information Technology – Learning, Education, and Training – Quality Management, Assurance and Metrics– Part 1: General Approach

ISO/IEC 19796-3:2009, Information technology – Learning, Education and Training – Quality management, assurance and metrics—Part 3: Reference methods and metrics

Kanuka, H. (2006). Instructional design and e-learning: A discussion of pedagogical content knowledge as amissing construct, *The e-Journal of Instructional Science and Technology*, 9(2).

Keller, C. ; Lindh, J. ; Hrastinski, S. ; Casanovas, I. & Fernandez, G. (2009). The impact of national culture on e-learning implementation: A comparative study of an Argentinean and a Swedish University. *Educational Media International*, 46(1), 67-80.

Keller, C. (2009). User Acceptance of Virtual Learning Environments: A Case Study from Three Northern European Universities. *Communications of the Association for Information Systems*: Vol. 25, Article 38.

Kermek D. ; Orehovački T. & Bubaš G. (2007) Procjena i unapređenje kvalitete u e-obrazovanju, Stručno-znanstveni skup "E-obrazovanje", Zbornik radova / Bubaš, Goran ; Kermek, Dragutin (ed). - Varaždin : Fakultet organizacije i informatike, 169-177

Kumarawadu, P. (2011). Motivation of online learners: Review of practies and emering trend, Sri Lanka Institute of Information Technology, URL: http://www2.uca.es/orgobierno/ordenacion/formacion/docs/jifpev5-doc5.pdf [14/7/2011]

Kundi, G. ; Nawaz, A. & Khan, S. (2010) The predictors of success for e-learning in higher education institutions (HEIs) In N-W.F.P, Pakistan, *JISTEM Journal Of Information Systems And Technology Management*, 7(3), 545-578.

Liu, C. C. (2005). The Attitudes od University Teachers to adopt Information Technology in Teaching, *Information Technoloogy Journal*, 4 (4), 445-450.

Lofstrom, E. & Nevgi, A. (2008). University teaching staffs' pedagogical awareness displayed through ICT - facilitated teaching, *Interactive Learning Environments*, vol. 16, p.2, pp. 101-116(16).

Lucas, S. & Wright, V. (2009). Who Am I? The influence of teacher beliefs on instructional technology incorporation. *The Journal on Excellence in College Teaching*, 20(3), 77- 95.

Mahdizadeh, H. ; Biemans, H. & Mulder, M. (2008). Determining Factors of the Use of E-Learning Environments by University Teachers, *Computers & Education*, 51, 142-154.

Malik, M.E. ; Nawab, S. ; Naeem, B. & Danish, R.Q. (2010). Job Satisfaction and Organizational Commitment of University teachers in Public Sector of Pakistan, *International Journal of Business and Management*, 5(4).

Marshall, S. & Mitchell, G. (2004). Applying SPICE to e-learning: An e-learning maturity model?, Sixth Australasian Computing Education Conference (ACE 2004), Dunedin. U: R. Lister i A. Young (ur.) *Conferences in Research and Practice in Information Technology*, vol. 30., 185-191.

Marwan, A. & Sweeney, T. (2010). Teachers' perceptions of educational technology integration in an Indonesian polytechnic, *Asia Pacific Journal of Education*, Volume 30, Number 4, 463-476(14).

Melis, E. ; Weber, M. & Andrès, E. (2003). Lessons for (Pedagogic) Usability of eLearning Systems. *World Conference on E-Learning in Corporate, Government, Healthcare, & Higher education*. (1), 281-284.

Mihhailova, G. (2006). E-learning as internationalisation strategy in higher education: Lecturer's and student's perspective. *Baltic Journal of Management*, 1 (3), 270-284.

Moore, G. & Benbasat, I. (1991). Development of an Instrument to Measure the Perceptions of Adopting an Information Technology Innovation. *Information Systems Research*, (2:3) 192-222.

Moscinska, K. & Rutkowski, J. (2011).Barriers to introduction of e-learning: A case study In: *Global Engineering Education Conference (EDUCON)*, 2011 IEEE, Amman, 4-6 April, 460 – 465.

Nanayakkara, C. & Whiddett, D. (2005). A model of user acceptance of e-learning technologies: A case study of a Polytechnic in New Zealand, *4th International*

Conference on Information Systems Technology and its Application (ISTA'2005), Palmerston North, New Zealand, GI.

Osika, E. R. ; Johnson, R.Y. & Buteau, R. (2009).Factors influencing faculty use of technology in online instruction: A case study. *Online Journal of Distance Learning Administration*. 12(1)0

Ozkan, S. & Fındık, D. (2010). Work in Progress - Learning Management Systems Acceptances of Instructors from Various Departments: Empirical Investigation. Middle East, 26-28.

Pawlowski, J. M. (2006): ISO/IEC 19796-1: How to Use the New Quality Framework for Learning, Education, and Training. White Paper, Essen, Germany, 2006.

Parrish, P. E. (2007). Learning with Object. In Shank P, Carliner S (Eds), The e-learning Handbook: Past Promise, Present Challenges (pp. 215-241), San Francisko, CA:Pfeiffer

Rebman, C. ; Cegielski, C. & Kitchens, F. (2004). Web-Based Instructional Course Development: Lessons Learned and a Proposed Model, *Journal of Informatics Education Research*, (6:2), Summer 2004.

Renzi, S. (2008). Differences in University Teaching after Learning Management System Adoption: An Explanatory Model Based on Ajzen's Theory of Planned Behavior. *PhD Thesis*, University of Western Australia

Rogers, E. M. (1995). Diffusion of Innovations, 4thed. New York, Free Press

Rothery, A.; Cilia, J.; Stenalt, M. H. & Dupuis, M. (2008). E-Learning Snapshots 2008. *EUNIS2008*, Aarhus University, Denmark, 2008.

Salmon, G. (2000) *E Moderating- The Key to Teaching and learning Online.* London: Taylor & Francis Books Ltd

Samarawickrema, G. & Stacey, E. (2007). Adopting Web-Based Learning and Teaching: A case study in higher education, *Distance Education*, 313 - 333.

Schneckenberg, D. (2008). Educating Tomorrow's Knowledge Workers: The concept of eCompetence and its application in international higher education *Amsterdam: Eburon Academic Publishers.*

Schneckenberg, D. (2007). Competence Reconsidered - Conceptual Thoughts on eCompetence and Assessment Models for Academic Staff. *In: U. Bernath & A. Sangra (Eds.),* ASF Series, Vol. 13, 17-34.

Sørebø, Ø. & Sørebø, A. M. (2008). Understanding e-learning satisfaction in the context of university teachers. *Proceedings of World Academy of Science, Engineering and Technology*, Bangkok

The Joint Information Systems Committee (JISC), URL: http://www.jiscinfonet.ac.uk/InfoKits/effective-use-of-VLEs/intro-to-VLEs/introtovle-intro/index_html [14/7/2011]

Timothy, T. (2009). Modelling technology acceptance in education: A study of pre-service teachers. *Computers & Education*, 52(2), 302-312.

Venkatesh, V. & Davis, F. D. (2000).A theoretical extension oft he technology acceptance model: four longitudinal field studies. *Management Science*, 46(2): 186-204.

Venkatesh, V. ; Morris, M. G.; Davis, G. B. & Davis, F. D. (2003). User Acceptance of Information Technology: Toward a Unified View, *MIS Quarterly*, 27(3), 425-47.

Weinert, F. E. (2008).Concept of Competence: a conceptual definition. In: D. S. Rychen & L. H. Salganik (Eds.). Defining and Selecting Key Competencies, p46. Seattle, WA: Hogrefe &Huber). 2001.

2

Towards Economical E-Learning Educational Environments for Physically Challenged Students

Amir Zeid et al.*
American University of Kuwait
Kuwait

1. Introduction

The World Health Organization defines Disability as follows: "Disabilities is an umbrella term, covering impairments, activity limitations, and participation restrictions. Impairment is a problem in body function or structure; an activity limitation is a difficulty encountered by an individual in executing a task or action; while a participation restriction is a problem experienced by an individual in involvement in life situations. Thus disability is a complex phenomenon, reflecting an interaction between features of a person's body and features of the society in which he or she lives[1]." Disabilities could be natural or could happen due to accidents. Technology could be used to create new software/hardware tools to help the disabled to participate in a creative collaborative educational environment.

In this chapter, we introduce two economically feasible solutions to aid physically challenged young students. They want they do (TWTD) is a simple system to help young students with hand disabilities interact with computers using web-camera and set of markers. The solution has been tested in some local schools and the results are promising [9]. Section 3 will introduce more details about version 2 of TWTD.

Autistic Touchless Board (ATB) is a system to help autistic children interact with computers with their hands. The system teaches autistic kids basic math and skills by projecting the problems on any surface (walls could be used) and the students interact by pointing to the wall without the need for extra tools. Section 4 will introduce more details about the design of ATB.

The rest of the chapter will be organized as follows:

- Section 2 will include the frameworks used to develop the e-learning environments.
- Sections 3,4 will include the two main developed environments. Each one will include the following points:
    - Problem
    - Solution

* Sarah S. Sakit, Noor A. Al-AbdulRazzaq, Mariam M. Al-Tattan, Fatima S. Sakit, Abrar Amin, Mariam Al-Najdi and Aisha Al-Rowaished
American University of Kuwait, Kuwait

    - Technologies used
    - Assessments and possible extensions
- Section 5 will conclude and provide directions for future research

2. Technologies adopted

In this section we will include the frameworks used to develop the main e-learning environments.

2.1 Touchless as an alternative

Touchless is an SDK that allows users to create and experience multi-touch applications. Touchless started as Mike Wasserman's college project at Columbia University. The main idea: to provide the same functionality of a multi-touch environment using cheap hardware and open-source software. All the user needs is a camera, which will track coloured markers defined by the user. Touchless is released free and open-source to the world under the Microsoft Public License (Ms-PL) on CodePlex [2]. Figure 1 is a snapshot of the major classes of the touchless SDK [2]. We modified the touchless SDK to support different types of disabilities. The details will be introduced in sections 3 and 4.

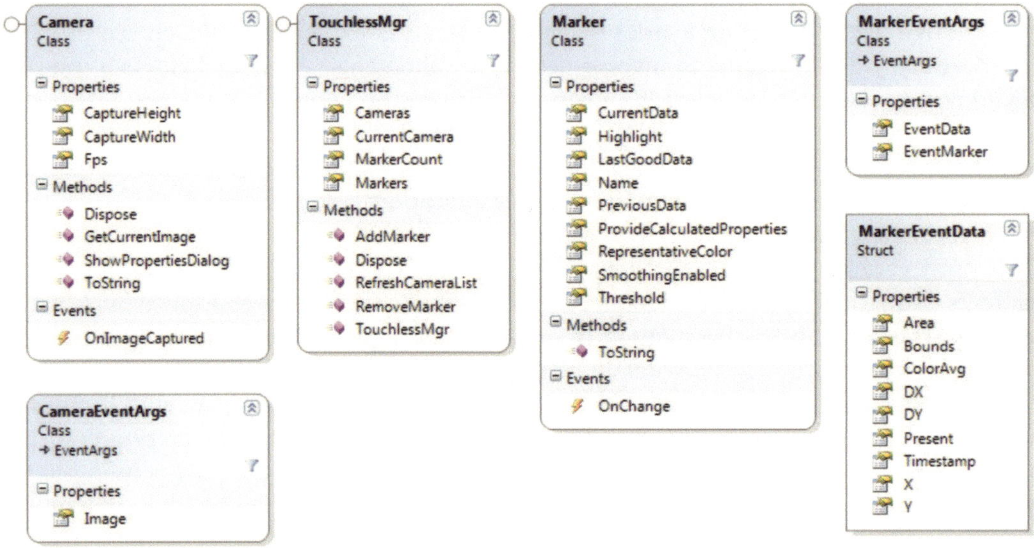

Fig. 1. Class diagram of touchless SDK [2].

2.2 Possible solutions

The following are some possible solutions to ease the interaction with computers for the physically impaired:

- Software utilities that consolidate multiple or sequential keystrokes.
- Mouth sticks, head sticks, or other pointing devices.
- Trackballs or other input devices provide an alternative to a mouse.
- Keyboard emulation with specialized switches that allow the use of scanning or Morse code input.

- Speech input and output.
- Word prediction software.

Our proposed solutions could be categorized as alternative to pointing devices.

3. TWTD

They want they do (TWTD) is educational software that uses markers and web-camera as a method of interacting with computers (to replace the mouse). The markers are defined according to the level of disability. The users then get educated using computers in different subjects. The aim of this solution is to help physically challenged students who were not able to use computers to get educated in a creative way. Also the solution is economically feasible since it only requires a web-cam and a layer of software for interactions. There are several products that target the same problem. TWTD (since it used touchless SDK) remains by far more economically feasible [9].

We implemented TWTD [9] as a proof of concept that creative solutions may help in educating physically challenged students with minimal resources. We already tried TWTD at special purposes schools in Kuwait to test the first version of the software. What we are presenting in this chapter is version 2 of TWTD.

3.1 Problem in details

TWTD was developed mainly for people who suffer different kinds of hand disabilities. After survying special needs schools in Kuwait, we identified the following problems:

- Students with hand disabilities are facing many difficulties to access computers.
- In Kuwait, there are many schools for the disabled. However, most students with hand disabilities are exempted from activities that involve computer usage.
- The only other option to dedicate teachers or helpers to help students use the computers.

3.2 Solution

We developed TWTD which is an economical educational tool with the following features:

- TWTD provides educational tools for Basic Mathematics, Science, Shapes, Colors and Basic English.
- TWTD adopts the curriculum of Ministry of Education in Kuwait
- TWTD is an educational software that uses markers and web-cam as a method of interacting with computers.

3.3 Use cases

Figure 2 depicts the main users of TWTD. Students can view tutorials and solve tests and exercises. Teachers can add and edit subjects, tutorials and exercises.

3.4 TWTD design

Figure 3 depicts the main layers of TWTD. In TWTD version 2, the databases were hosted on the cloud using Microsoft Azure cloud to accommodate larger databases and more subjects.

How touchless SDK was modified?

We modified touchless SDK to comply with hand disabilities. The original library has 3 markers. We customized the library to use two markers instead [9].

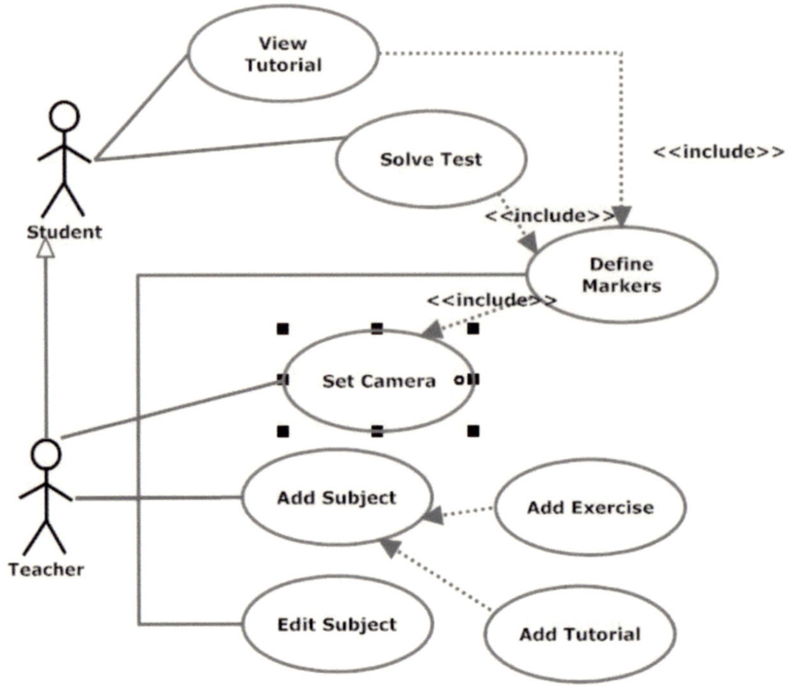

Fig. 2. Use Case Diagram for TWTD.

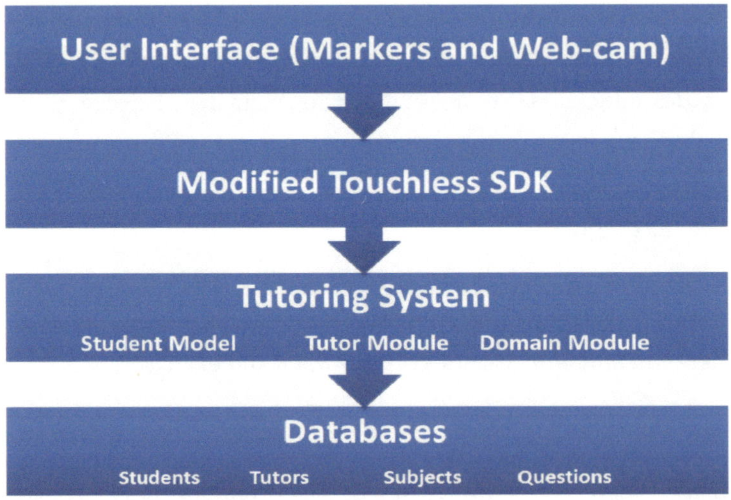

Fig. 3. Architecture Diagram of TWTD.

Figure 4 depicts the main classes of TWTD. The main classes are following PLITS [3] (a pattern language for constructing intelligent tutoring system). The details of using PLITS in developing TWTD are discussed in details in [9].

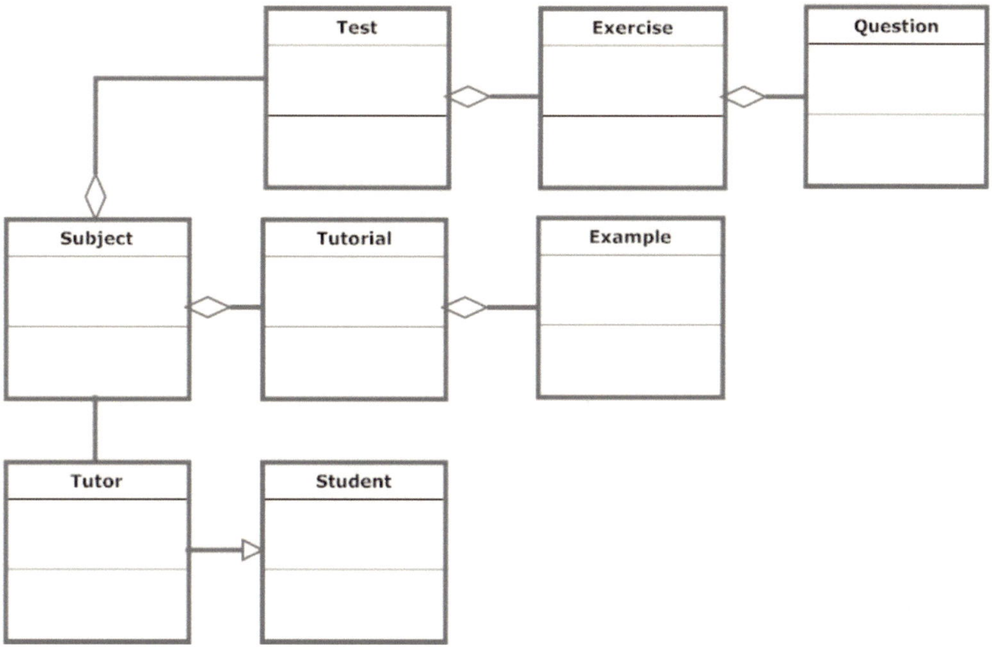

Fig. 4. Class Diagram of TWTD.

3.6 Using TWTD 2

Figure 5 depicts a snapshot of a handicapped student starting to use TWTD version 2. The markers are attached to the remains of the user's arms. In the figure the user is about to choose a given lesson out of the different options: English, Math, Shapes, Science). The applications are mainly what public schools offer in Kuwait.

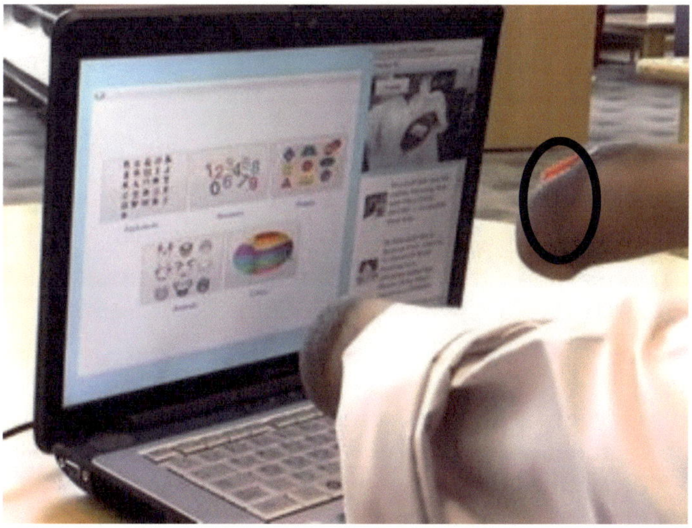

Fig. 5. Setting up markers.

Figure 6 depicts a user interacting with the English application. In the upper right corner of the screen the user can see himself. The user can check his score at the end of the exercises. The figure also includes the Mathematics module where students have to match numbers to figures.

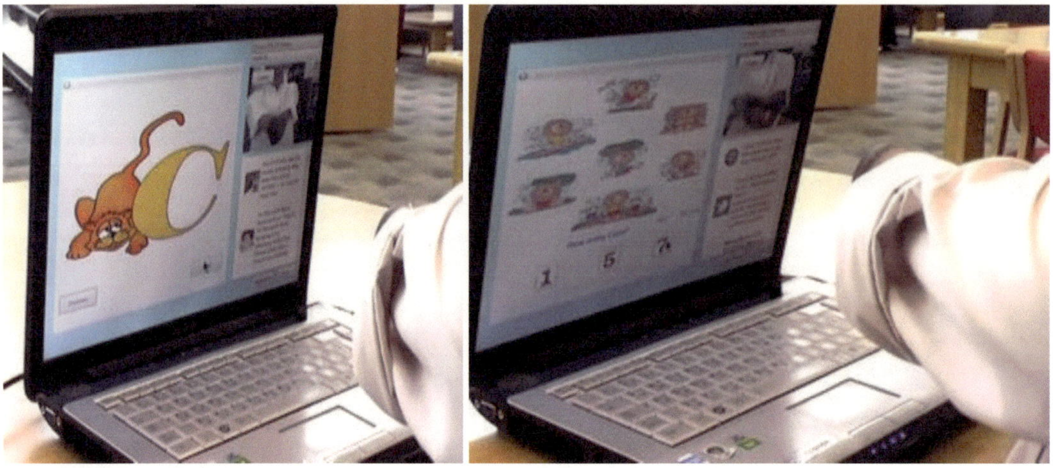

Fig. 6. Using TWTD.

3.7 Used technologies

TWTD was developed using the following technologies:

- Visual Studio 2008 Professional (Using the C# language)
- MS SQL
- Windows Azure

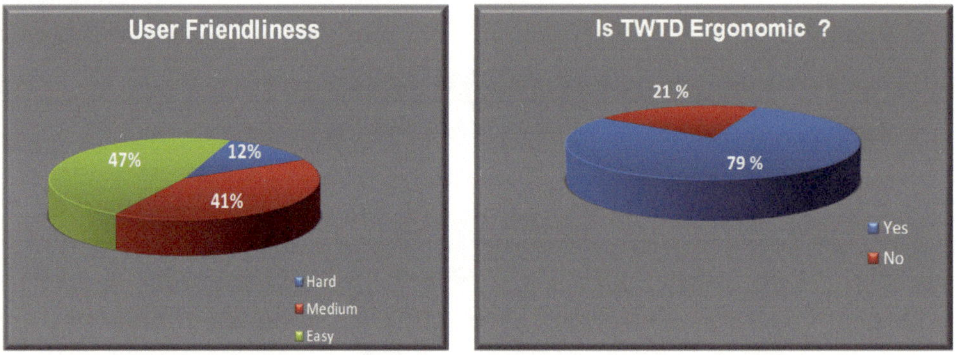

Fig. 7. Assessments of TWTD.

3.8 Assessments

Figure 7 depicts the results of the assessment experiments we carried out. The results of initial testing with 25 students show that 88% of the users indicated that using TWTD was east to medium. 79% confirmed that it is ergonomic.

Assistive technology has the potential to enhance the abilities and, bypass or compensate for barriers that disabilities make. TWTD addresses the potential of assistive technologies as it relates to specific disabilities and life tasks. For children with disabilities in public school classrooms, assistive technologies are their tools to extend their physical, social and communicative abilities.

3.9 Similar work

While the total cost of TWTD does not exceed the price of the web-camera. Other similar products are far more expensive.

Microsoft surface

Microsoft Surface is a multi-touch computer that responds to natural hand gestures and real-world objects, helping people interact with digital content in a simple and intuitive way. Surface also sees and interacts with objects placed on the screen, allowing users to move information between devices like mobile phones or cameras. Although the product is not available for widespread purchase, it is relatively expensive.

HeadMouse Extreme

HeadMouse Extreme replaces the standard computer mouse for people who cannot use or have limited use of their hands when controlling a computer or augmentative communication device. The HeadMouse captures the movements of a user's head then translates it directly into proportional movements of the computer mouse pointer. This device works just like a computer mouse, with the mouse pointer being moved by the motion of the users head. This device cost around $1000 [6].

EyeTech TM2

The EyeTech TM2 replaces the standard computer mouse which allows the user with physical disability to place the mouse pointer anywhere on the screen by simply looking at the desired location.

EyeTech TM2 is program that uses a webcam set on the computer monitor that focused on one eye. EyeTech TM2 software Eye tracking is the process of measuring either the point of gaze or the motion of an eye relative to the head.Mouse clicks are done with either a slow eye blink, eye gaze or a Hardware switch (toe click, finger click, etc). The device costs around $6,500 [7].

Jouse 2

The Jouse2 is an advanced joystick-operated USB mouse that is controlled with user's mouth. The user moves the joystick with his/her mouth, cheek, chin or tongue to shift the mouse cursor wherever she/he wants. The further the user moves the joystick, the faster the cursor shifts. The user can perform right-click, left-click and double-click actions with the sip and puff switches built into the Jouse2. The device costs around $1500 [8].

4. ATB

4.1 Problem

Autism is defined by the Autism Society Of America (ASA) as: " a complex developmental disability that typically appears during the first three years of life and is the result of a neurological disorder that affects the normal functioning of the brain, impacting development in the areas of social interaction and communication skills. Both children and adults with autism typically show difficulties in verbal and non-verbal communication, social interactions, and leisure or play activities. Also, children with such syndrome may harm themselves if they use new tools. According to teachers in the Autism center in Kuwait, a 13-year old autistic child swallowed 64 magnetic pieces while interacting with some lessons at the Autism center. It is not advised to have any tool around autistic children, which makes the educational process even harder.

Latest statistics show that about 1% of children is diagnosed with autism. An estimated 1.5 million individuals in the U.S. and tens of millions worldwide are affected by autism. Government statistics suggest that autism is increasing annually. There is not established explanation for this increase, although improved diagnosis and environmental influences are two reasons often considered. Other research efforts noted that males are more vulnerable than girls. Current estimates indicate that in the United States alone, about 1.5% of young males are diagnosed with autism[10].

Studies in the United States during the 1990s have estimated prevalence rates of autism to be 2.0-7.0 per 1,000 children, an over tenfold increase compared to the 1980s. This suggests that autism is being identified and diagnosed much more in the community in recent years [11].

Autistic children suffer in both social and educational activities, according to a new study in the journal Neurology. In a recent study children with mild autism was compared to normal children regarding how to form words from letters. It was found that autistic children faced difficulty in forming words [12].

Autism is considered to be one of the most difficult developmental disabilities in the world. Parents of autistic children have hard time understanding their child and helping them to learn. Autistic children can't use any tools in their learning process as they can easily hurt themselves. As a result, teaching Autistic children involves many risks and concerns about children's safety. The learning material for autistic children is limited due to these constraints. Therefore, we aimed to provide a solution that consists of a projector and camera to help them learn in a new, safe and interesting way whether they're at home or at school. The students do not interact with the projector and the camera, rather they use their fingers to interact with a projected image of the screen.

Technology could be used to help autistic children by providing economically feasible solutions. In this section, we design a solution for autistic children to help them learn in a safe, creative and economically feasible method.

4.2 Solution

ATB is a solution that helps Autistic children in their education process by enabling them to interact with the computer in a safe and secure way without using any tools. The child will be able to control computer applications through the projected screen on the wall using their fingertips only. In addition, we provide autistic children with educational applications that are designed to suit their educational needs. The applications teach basic math and matching.

4.3 Use cases

Users can interact with the system using the traditional mouse clicks events. The user can drag, click, switch between applications, open and close applications. The teacher could use the system similar to the child and also could do more by:

- Activating the system
- Defining markers
- And Setting Calibration Points

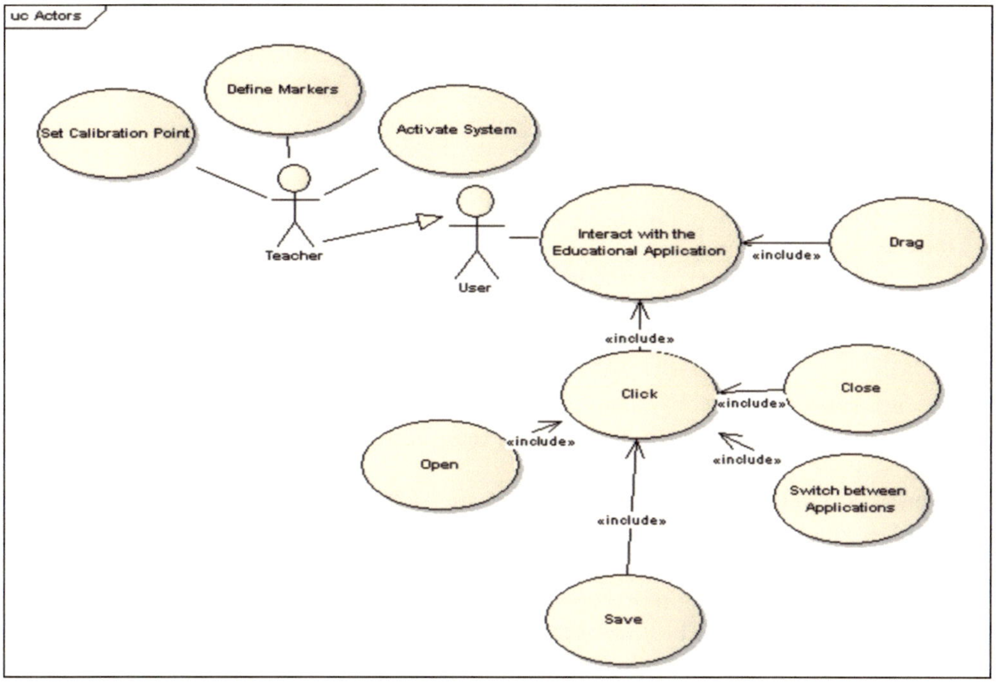

Fig. 8. Use Cases of ATB.

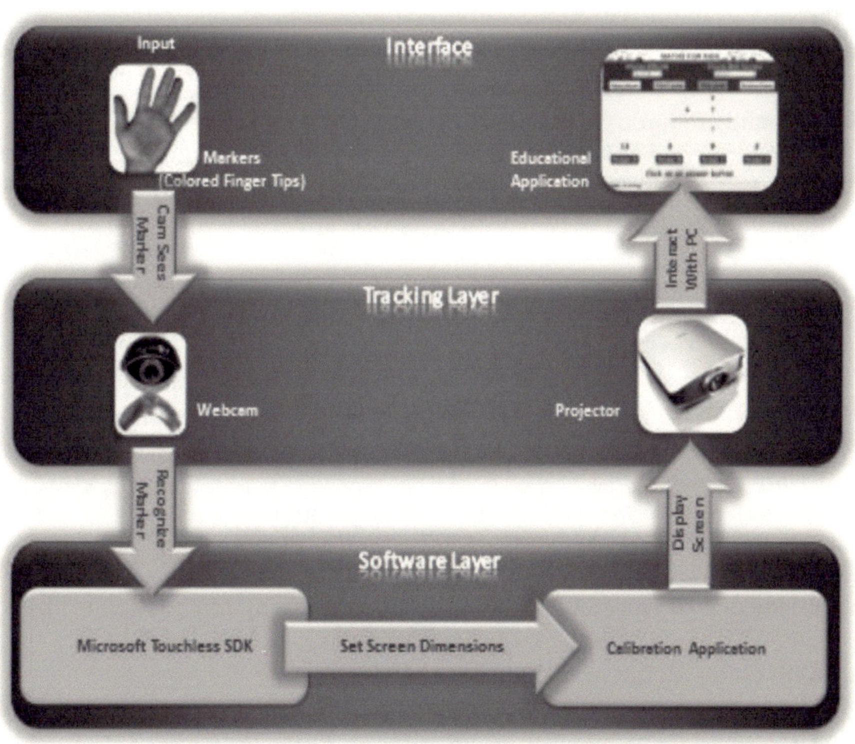

Fig. 9. Architecutre Diagram of ATB.

4.4 ATB design

ATB mainly consists of three layers (Figure 9). The layers are: interface layer, tracking layer and software layer.

a. Interface Layer

The interface Layer consists of the PC desktop or the educational application. The user shall interact directly with the PC through the hand gestures to form different marker events (i.e. click, drag…etc.)

b. Tracking Layer

This layer is the middle layer. It consists of the projector and the webcam. It helps convert the whiteboard to an electronic touch-screen, where any program can be controlled through hand gestures. The webcam will track the hand gestures through detecting pre-defined colors.

c. Software layer

This is the bottom layer, which consists of the Calibration Applications and Microsoft Touch-less SDK.

- Calibration Application: It is software to measure the dimension of the PC's screen and represent it on the whiteboard through the projector. The main idea is to calibrate the resolution of the pc screen to the dimensions of the white board.
- Modified Touchless SDK: In this application we modified the click action to accomodate the interaction method. The code was modified so that the click event is generated if the user holds his hands/markers over an object (on the wall or screen) for around 2 seconds. The advantage of this method is that it is fairly simple.

How Touchless was modified?

We added the calibration application to interact with touchless SDK for better performance. The main purpose is to calibrate the resolution of the screen and the virtual display. The application is mainly to improve the accuracy of the markers interactions.

Figure 10 depicts the main classes of ATB. The first set of Classes includes the following classes: ActivateSystem, Marker, and CalibrationPoints. In the ActivateSystem class, the user (teacher or admin) can startSystem and EndSystem. While in the Marker class, the teacher can DefineMarker or add NewMarker. Moreover, the teacher or admin can setCalibrationPoints in the class CalibrationPoints. However, the class CalibrationPoints is aggregated to the class Marker; that is, if the user didn't define a Marker, he or she can't setCalibrationPoints. Also, the class Marker is aggregated to the class ActivateSystem. The teacher can't defineMarker or add newMarker without Activating the system first.

The second set of Classes includes three classes which are: Subject, Lesson, and Test. In the Subject class the user (Autistic User) can chooseSubject or close the Application. While in the Lesson class the user can start NewLesson, OpenLesson (open a previous lesson), SaveLesson, and CloseLesson. In the Test class, the user can start NewTest, RepeatTest (repeat a previous test), and check the TestScore. Also, the class Test is aggregated to the class Lesson, and the class Lesson is aggregated to the class Subject. That is, the user can't take a test if there is no lesson, and the user can't take a lesson if there is no subject.

4.5 Using ATB

Figure 11 depicts the sequence diagram of calibration process. The user "StartSystem()" to start the ATB System. After that, the admin should select "defineMarker" to define a new Marker. After defining a Marker, the admin or the teacher should carefully set the calibration points through selecting "SetCalibrationPoints()". This will set the dimensions of the whiteboard. Doing this process will convert the whiteboard to a smart interactive board. As a result, the user or the admin can interact with the whiteboard through hand gestures. So, he or she can run the Educational Applications to "chooseSubject()".

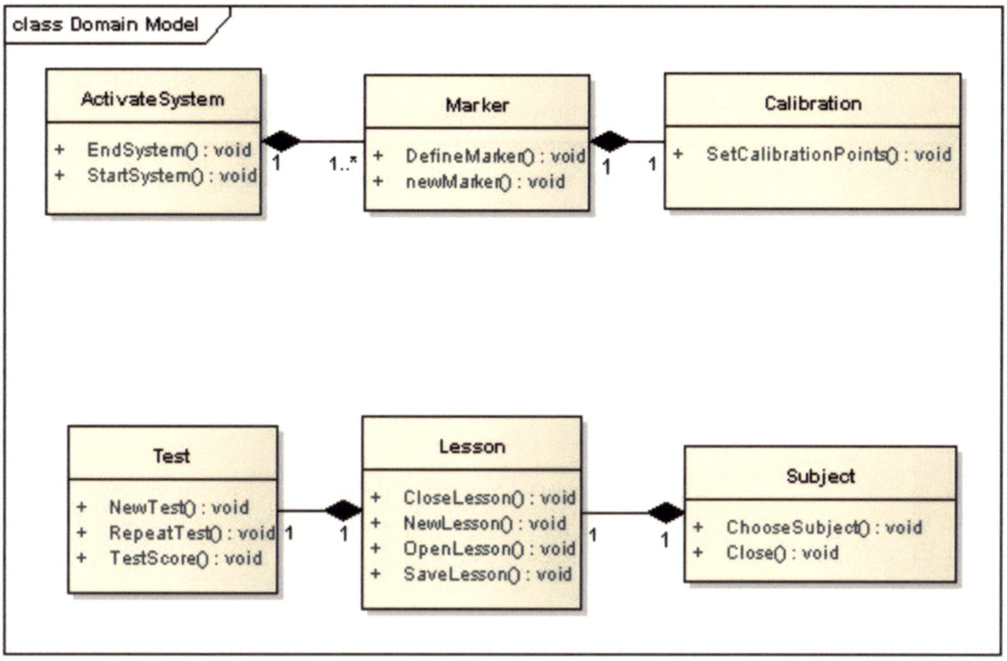

Fig. 10. Class diagram of ATB.

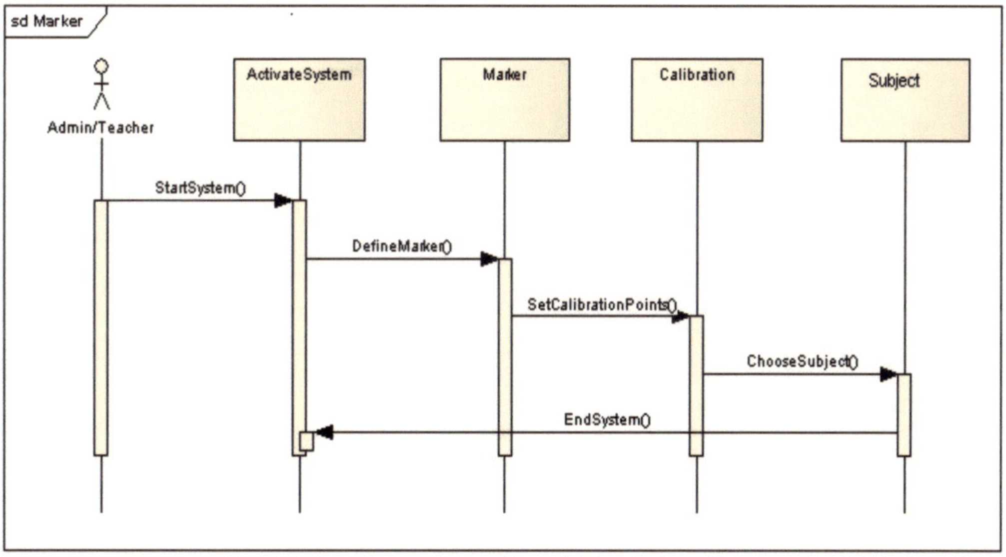

Fig. 11. Sequence Diagram of using ATB.

The educational programs

Figure 12 depicts user sequence diagram for user solving a question in a test. The user shall "ChooseSubject()" to choose between the Educational Applications (Math Application or the Voice Recognition Application). Then, the user can start a "NewLesson()" where he/she can learn new subject. After finishing the lesson, the user can "SaveLesson()" and "CloseLesson()". After learning the lesson, the user can start a "NewTest()" to test his/her abilities. Users can "RepeatTest()" to repeat previous test. If the user finishes the test, he or she can view "TestScore()" and end the Educational Applications through using "Close()".
The educational programs are html applications that are addressed to Autistic children age 8 to 10. There are two Math programs, one in Arabic and the other in English. The Math program allows the children to choose the difficulty of the math problems, and choose the math function: adding, subtracting, multiplying, random adding and subtracting, or random adding, subtracting and multiplying. This program keeps track of the scores the child achieved and his or her speed. Figure 13 shows a user using the mathematics lessons with her bare hands as a pointer.

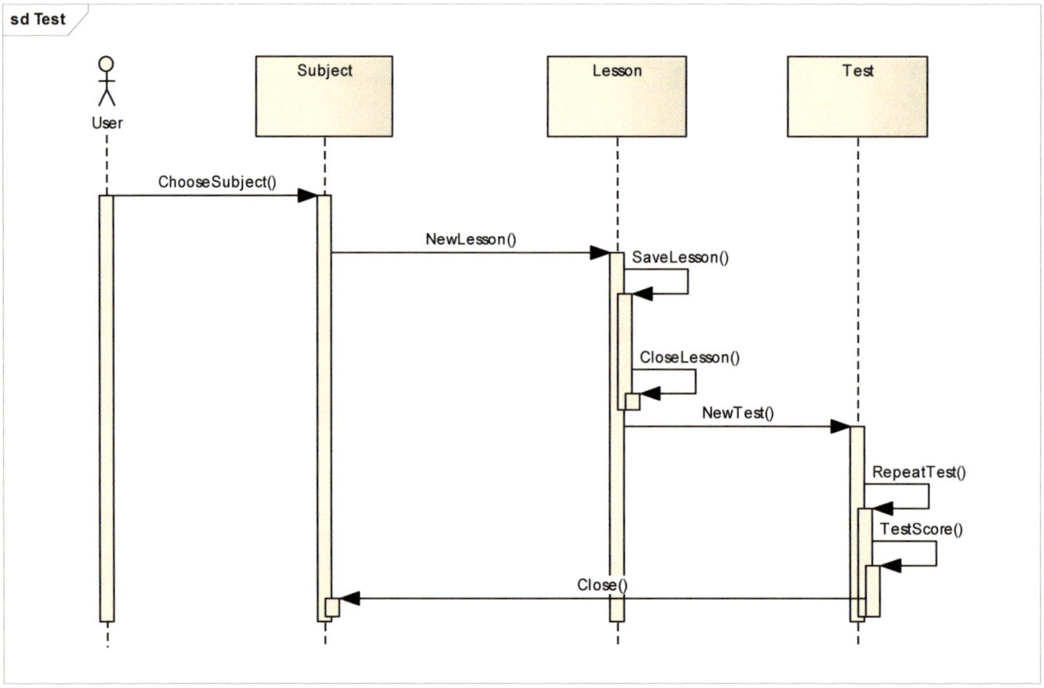

Fig. 12. Sequence Diagram for solving a question in a test.

In Figure 14 another educational application is shown, the child can see different animals' pictures and by pointing to the image they will hear the animal voice. In tests, the child will hear the animal voice, and will see different images of different animals. So, he will aim to choose the appropriate image. The scores and speed will be stored with the child's name.

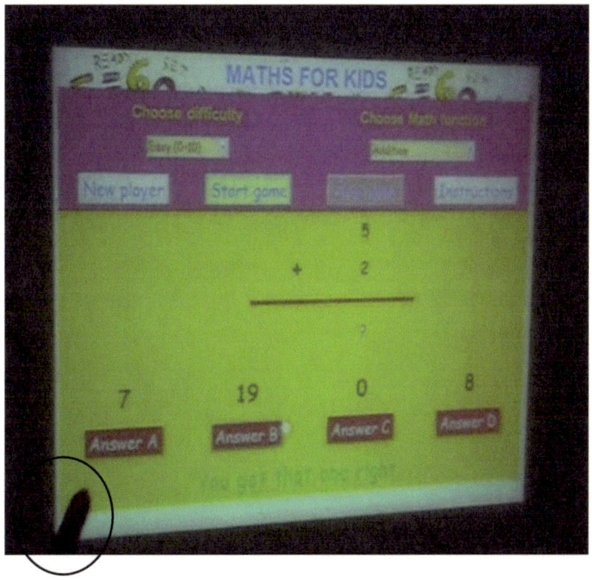

Fig. 13. Using ATB.

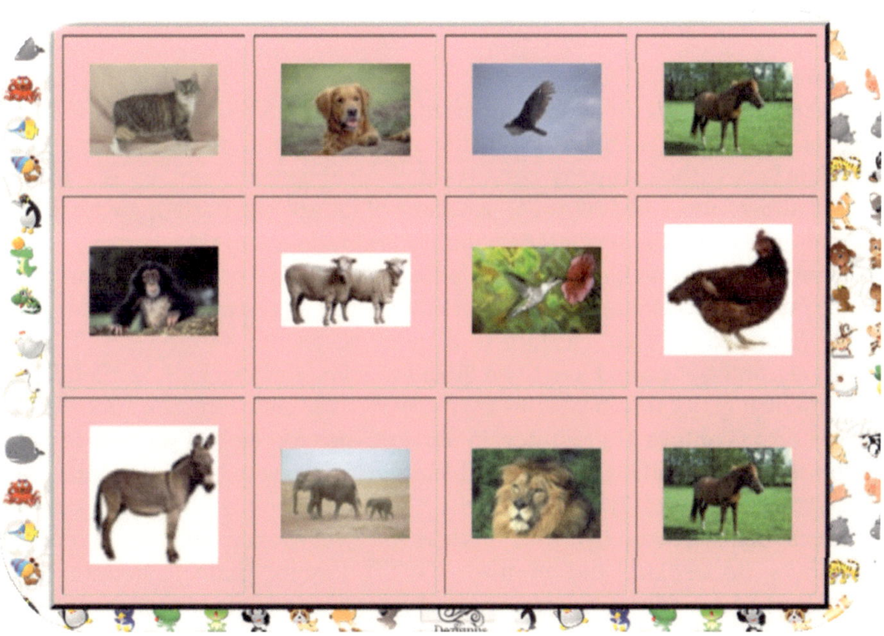

Fig. 14. Matching animals and voices game.

4.6 Assessments

ATB has been tested by some young students and teachers. The initial feedback is positive. We are in the process of getting permission to deploy the system in real schools for autistic children to have concrete surveys and statistics regarding how ATB affected their education experience. In general, autistic children in Kuwait are exempted from using computers in their early years.

Some of the main challenges include the lighting of the class room. Since the application depends mainly on capturing markers using a web-camera, the lighting, background of the markers could affect the accuracy in some cases. The results of the initial testing on 10 students is shown on Figure 15. The students were asked to solve some exercises and the ease of use was estimated based on the time they took to solve the assigned exercises.

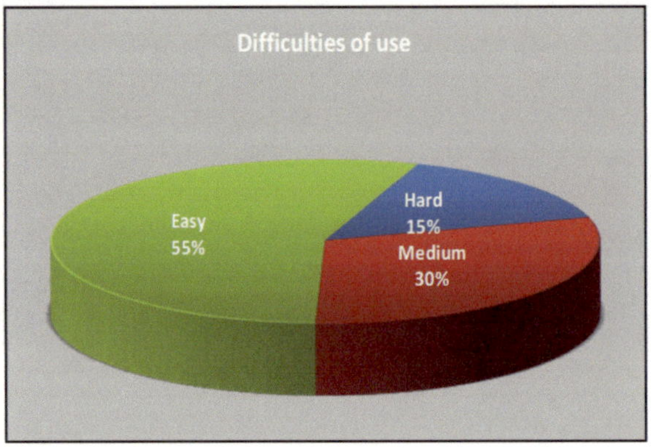

Fig. 15. Assessments for ATB.

4.7 Similar work

There are many technologies that are similar and related to ATB. CamSpace is software that enables users to interact with the PC using a webcam and without using a mouse or keyboard. CamTrax's [the company behind CamSpace] core technology is a pure software solution that allows most ordinary PC webcam (95% are supported) to track up to four objects in real-time and with reasonable accuracy and reliability [12].

Sixth Sense project was developed at the Media lab at MIT to provide a complete wearable gestural interface to mobile devices. Users of Sixth Sense use a camera, portable projects and their mobile phone to turn any surface to a smart projection surface [13]. The solution is economically feasible yet users have to be linked to some devices like the mobile phone and the projector which may cause problems in case of autistic children.

Gondy Leroy and Gianluca De Leo developed software for mobile devices to help autistic children communicate, make friends and blend in the society. The software mainly uses images for communication [15].

TWTD is educational software that uses markers and web-camera as a method of interacting with computers (to replace the mouse). TWTD targets mainly students with hand disabilities. Users of TWTD attach markers to that available parts of their hands (if any) and control the computer and educational applications accordingly. The markers are defined according to the level of disability. The users then get educated using computers in different subjects. The aim of this solution is to help physically challenged students who were not able to use computers to get educated in a creative way. Also the solution is economically feasible since it only requires a web-cam and a layer of software for interactions. There are several products that target the same problem. TWTD (since it used touchless SDK) remains by far more economically feasible [9].

5. Conclusion

In this chapter, we presented two solutions to help physically challenged students who suffer from different disabilities. We adopted the touchless SDK [2] to provide economical solutions for students with hand disabilities and autism. Both applications were tested in local schools in Kuwait. The intial results are promising and both projects are going through enhancements pahse now.

Future enhancements for TWTD

We are planning to add the following features to TWTD:

- Completing the intelligent tutoring subsystem that will customize the lessons based on the responses of the students.
- Tools to help tutors to design curriculum will be added to make it more friendly for tutors.
- A web-site to host tests and different subjects to be downloaded and uploaded by tutors.

Future enhancements for ATB

In the future we would like to add more features for the ATB system such as adding a virtual keyboard to let the child typing using his fingers only. Also we hope to create a full desktop for the autistic children where they can find different educational applications and other interesting applications such as painting and drawing applications and some music and entertainment applications. In addition, we are planning to use PLITS (Pattern Language for Intelligent Tutoring Systems) [3] to add intelligent tutoring features to ATB.

Recently, we started planning to port applications to use Microsoft Kinect sensor for better performance. The next generation of both applications will adopt Kinect sensor to utilize its powerful cameras and sensors.

6. References

[1] World Health Organization (WHO) main website about disabilities. http://www.who.int/topics/disabilities/en/ (Accessed October 28th, 2009)

[2] Neil McAllister, "Microsoft's Touchless SDK pulls a mouse out of thin air" InfoWorld, October 2008. http://www.codeplex.com/touchless (Accessed October 28th, 2009.

[3] Dina Salah, Amir Zeid, PLITS:A Pattern Language for Intelligent Tutoring Systems" at 14th European Conference on Pattern Languages of Programs, July 2009, Munich, Germany.

[4] Gamma, Helm, Johnson & Vlissides (1994). HYPERLINK "http://en.wikipedia.org/wiki/Design_Patterns_(book)" \o "Design Patterns (book)" Design Patterns (the Gang of Four book). Addison-Wesley.

[5] http://en.wikipedia.org/wiki/Multi-touch (Accessed October 28th, 2009)

[6] http://www.enablemart.com/Catalog/Head-Eye-Controlled-Input/Headmouse-Extreme (Accessed November 29th, 2009)

[7] http://www.eyetechds.com/assistivetech/products/qg2.htm (Accessed November 29th, 2009)

[8] http://www.disabledonline.com/products/direct-products/keyboardsmice/ergonomic-mice/jouse-2/ (Accessed November 29th, 2009)

[9] Amir Zeid, Abrar Amin, Mariam Al-Najdi, Aisha Al-Rowaished, 'TWTD: A MULTI-TOUCH TUTORING SYSTEM FOR THE PHYSICALLY CHALLENGED', Ninth IASTED International Conference on Web-based Education, March 2010.

[10] Autism", Wikipedia http://en.wikipedia.org/wiki/Autism Accessed May 15th 2011. http://www.searo.who.int/LinkFiles/Mental_Health_and_Substance_Abuse_autism.pdf

[11] Jon Hamilton, "Writing Study Ties Autism To Motor-Skill Problems", http://www.npr.org/templates/story/story.php?storyId=120275194 Accessed May 29th, 2011

[12] Roi Carthy, "CamSpace Creates a Wii For Everyone (Minus the Nintendo Console)" http://techcrunch.com/2008/06/11/camspace-creates-a-wii-for-everyone-minus-the-nintendo-console/ Accessed May 29th, 2011.

[13] P. Mistry, P. Maes. SixthSense – A Wearable Gestural Interface. In the Proceedings of SIGGRAPH Asia 2009, Sketch. Yokohama, Japan. 2009

[14] "HeadMouse Extreme" Prodcuts Details on InforGrip. http://www.infogrip.com/product_view.asp?RecordNumber=116 (Accessed May 29th, 2011)

[15] Gianluca De Leo, Gondy Leroy, "Smartphones to Facilitate Communication and Improve Social Skills of Children with Severe Autism Spectrum Disorder: Special Education Teachers as Proxies" , Proceeding IDC '08 Proceedings of the 7th international conference on Interaction design and children , 2008.

3

Advanced Pedagogical Approaches at Slovak Universities

Pavol Molnár and Ildikó Némethová
University of Economics in Bratislava, Slovak Republic

1. Introduction

This chapter aims to provide a specific insight into the latest forms of modern teaching implemented at designated universities in the Slovak Republic. The main concern is to highlight the greatest benefits of modern educational approaches and then to present their pragmatic and practical applications in tertiary education. Furthermore, this chapter focuses on the provision of reliable data based upon authentic results generated through research projects which are closely linked both to e-learning and complementary web-based teaching practices. The overall scope of this chapter revolves around the following subjects: (1) latest achievements in advanced tertiary educational approaches at Slovak universities; (2) dissemination of gained results in the Leonardo da Vinci Project REDILEM; (3) practical utilisation of e-learning outcomes based upon applied research; (4) benefits of feedback provision in e-learning education; (5) knowledge management as a tool of assessing students' cognitive understanding and holistic comprehension; (6) major advantages and key obstacles in e-learning education; (7) complementary advanced teaching practices.

2. Advanced pedagogical approaches in tertiary education

Advanced pedagogical approaches in tertiary education represent innovative efforts in the realm of human activities in the 21st century. Various approaches such as interactive online learning, web-based courses, hyperlinks to websites on the Internet, collaborative learning, online discussion forums, "guided didactic conversations," or "tutorials in print," and blended learning have become significant constituents of innovative learning and teaching techniques and methods.

A plethora of pedagogical activities both in their classical and contemporary forms have been provided by many Slovak higher educational institutions. One of the reasons, except for a unique support of information and communication technology and Internet media, is goodwill (for the universities) and demand (from learners) for this more convenient form of teaching and learning model.

At the outset, it is necessary to stress that in accordance with all these modern pedagogical and didactical approaches the winners are the learners. It has been noticed that such an innovative process of education receives less interest from the teachers, although various lengthy articles, papers and/or books dedicated to this particular matter emphasise the importance of web-based education, e-learning and blended learning pedagogical activities. Some of the former and recent results in connection with tertiary (university) education at Slovak universities will be presented throughout this chapter.

A research project KEGA (3/3078/05) entitled "Web-Based Training for Business English and German" has been implemented at the University of Economics in Bratislava, Slovakia. The project has been designed to foster work-related language skills. This particular course has been designed as a blended form of study. It has benefited from the combination of face-to-face classroom learning and an instructor driven presentation and social interaction, which is delivered, online. Throughout the elaboration of this web-based teaching material the authors have accommodated different learning styles (visual, aural, verbal, and social), made the course accessible to learners with special needs, provided a variety of opportunities to accurately assess progress, applied a blend of learning theories (the cognitive learning theory, which promotes learners to control their own learning; and the constructivist learning theory, which challenges learners with tasks that refer to skills and knowledge just beyond their current level of mastery), and so they have set the course apart from the norm.

They have clearly defined the learning objectives, identified the skill gaps of the potential learners, selected the right content, built in a good instructional design including assessment and utilised subject matter experts when creating content. They have also established a support for an effective blended programme, communicated the importance and urgency of the learning programme to their learners, instructed them how to learn online, ensured learners' success by providing them with appropriate technical support, and tried to keep all the learners motivated by facilitating and supporting the entire programme.

As a courseware package and learning management system, they have chosen Moodle that enables the instructor to create powerful, flexible and engaging learning experiences. All the resource materials involve texts, which are intended to convey specific details, and facts that learners can marshal in support of an argument, they are also used for vocabulary enhancement and are supported by JavaScript.

In order to increase the interactivity within Moodle, they have applied the Hotpotatoes Suite. It has allowed teachers to use various evaluation tools to check the quality and accuracy of the acquired knowledge and skills.

Moodle has been suitable for the creation of adequate patterns for the rehearsal of failed answers. When a learner is unable to complete a language problem correctly, it is demonstrated repeatedly until he/she can manage to resolve the problem without mistakes. This technique functions to keep learners revisiting problem areas until their performance improves. Rehearsal is then delivered more widely over time until problems no longer require practice. Rehearsal is more broadly applied for learning new business-related vocabulary. The course uses online newspapers as large collections of authentic texts, which can contribute to rendering learning a foreign language more effective since students will be faced with real language. Throughout the rehearsal task the main emphasis has been to assist learners in getting started in building up a technical English vocabulary. The authors have used the lexical approach which argues that language consists of meaningful chunks that, when combined, produce a continuous coherent text. Activities used to develop learners' knowledge of lexical chains include intensive and extensive online reading in the target language, repetition and recycling of online activities, noticing and practicing language patterns and collocations, working with dictionaries and other e-reference tools. Furthermore, they have taken advantage of the eclectic approach based on language performance, as they believe that most learning is preparation for actual performance. Particular negative observations, based on generally acknowledged experience, have been connected with instructors' (teachers') involvements. Both during synchronous and/or asynchronous learning there have been numerous complaints concerning the enormous burden of establishing the necessary contacts between learners and teachers (instructors). In most cases, learners did not have access to the Internet during the week, therefore they could devote their attention to the required resource materials only at the weekends or they were constantly forced to visit some public facilities, e.g. an Internet Café.

The second experience results from the implementations of the Leonardo da Vinci Project, REDILEM, involving nine partners from six European countries (Austria, the Czech Republic, France, Germany, the Slovak Republic, and Sweden) to create a new type of education for SME managers, managed and organised both by representatives of the Slovak Technical University in Bratislava and the University of Economics in Bratislava. The purpose of the project was to combine the theoretical interdisciplinary education with practical training within a learning network. It was intended to support managers of newly established SMEs.

The starting motivation of the project was the intention that products and experiences from the project gained should help various groups of inhabitants to ensure their continual education, and life-long reception of proper knowledge and skills, the improvement of skills and competence, the improvement of quality and the strengthening of relations between professional education and innovations, as well as the creation of new work-places and the improvement of conditions for employment and to improve entrepreneurial abilities and increase competitiveness, especially in regions with high rates of unemployment and restricted possibilities of learning, by the creation of a system of interdisciplinary distance learning for current and prospective managers of Small and Medium-sized Enterprises.

One of the particular aims was to provide learners with interdisciplinary education, since their present education was considered to be excessively one-sided (their orientation was overly technological), in order to increase their flexibility and adaptability to the changing labour market needs, to raise their competitiveness as well as their abilities to co-operate with domestic and foreign partners, mainly their customers and other SME managers. Another important goal was to support the socio-economical development in regions with high rate of unemployment and with a limited access to learning opportunities.

Syllabi, curricula and teaching materials have been designed as a new type of educational material, which requires a form and content of modern e-based learning materials providing an effective and low cost opportunity to gain target-oriented information and knowledge. Therefore, specific study materials have been produced. Reference materials for these courses need specific texts and materials, where reasoning is inevitable; some experts refer to them as "guided didactic conversations" or "tutorials in print." The teacher shall guide learners through the course material via the study guide, ask questions, give instructions and explanations, and communicate in a "language", which learners can easily understand. The design of such teaching materials should resemble the atmosphere and situation characteristic for traditional classroom learning and teaching.

In order to ensure the quality of the teaching process a manual in the field of "Pedagogy and Methodology" was accomplished. University professors and teachers were trained how to use "multimedia applications" within the framework of the teachers training. The aim of the teacher-training course was to support the teaching staff in course design, particularly in specific methodology and pedagogy, e.g. in distance communication, dialogues, tasks, and other learning activities. On the other hand, the course was designed to support the teachers of web-based learning in developing their paper-based study guides in compliance with the study materials. Furthermore, these study materials were accessible on specific websites and allowed learners to access more detailed information packages. These hyperlinks were selected and provided for learners by experts in the related fields.

Two types of online courses have been applied, namely synchronous and asynchronous. The synchronous online course (analogical with the team discussion) connected professors and learners within the system and they interacted as a classical (face-to-face) discussion group. Learners could "raise their hands" (electronically), and professors answered their questions, etc. Situations were made similar to face-to-face classroom applications.

The asynchronous online course enabled learners to familiarise themselves with particular topics containing aims, glossaries, explanatory notes, case studies, tests, assignments and exercises, questions for discussion, and further reference materials. The verification of their knowledge was accomplished via tests and case studies, as participants uploaded their solutions into the e-learning system. Each case study ended with a set of questions for discussion. The participants could discuss possible solutions with other colleagues using the discussion forum.

Learners were fully responsible for establishing mutual contact with their peers via particular online systems, but in a shifted time frame. Questions were answered some days later. This kind of learning application seemed to be very popular among learners as they highly appreciated the possibility of having access anytime they wanted. Many of them had limited access to computers, even during their business trips, etc. Professors were forced to control and react to learners on a daily basis in order to serve their needs, which, however, put teachers under pressure and, eventually, was in conflict with their other duties, e.g. research and development activities at their universities, elaboration of textbooks and/or conference papers, study materials, etc.

The next relevant experience is related to activities which greatly focused on the implementation of web-based learning within the educational process at a private Bratislava college in the Slovak Republic. The main aim and motivation was to increase the influence and activity of this private university throughout Slovakia. E-learning was one of the instruments to achieve this goal. Maybe, this was one of the reasons why the stimulation of future players (mainly lecturers) did not meet the right response, and the project was finished after the first trial of its introduction.

Most activities have entailed the elaboration of curricula, study materials, negotiations and supporting resources. Frankly speaking, the "state of the piece of art created" did not satisfy the expectations of the founders of the idea. The end result resembled the experience seen in the above-mentioned two cases - an enormous interest from the learners, but a limited enthusiasm demonstrated by the professors.

Effective experience is crucially associated with feedback in e-learning education. At the University of Economics in Bratislava, some of the subjects are constantly delivered and supported via e-learning applications. A reliable experience was provided by one of our colleagues.

3. Explanation of the motivation of the authors

Feedback plays a crucial role in the provision of incessant inducement and motivation for students. A teacher should not only explain new knowledge but also motivate students to continuous preparations. Some students are satisfied with the number of lectures attended which allow them to pass the exams successfully, others would need more time for being dealt with. Such students highly evaluate the presence of e-based learning materials which to a certain extent provide frequent contact with the teaching materials and help them reach the required levels of attainment.

The implementation of ongoing feedback through classical questionnaires could also be realised by using different test-systems, assignments or other applications. Realistic feedback is possible to be achieved by checking a variety of students' assignments, too. The number and quality of assignments received from students renders answers to many questions, which include solutions that enable teachers to understand how well they execute their work. It should also be pointed out that a continuous control of students' work acts as a prerequisite for achieving better results. Selected findings will be later presented here using Moodle in connection with the implementation of feedback.

A teaching experiment was carried out to detect the impact of Moodle utilisation on feedback frequency increase in education during a semester. Full-time students engaged in the field of Database systems and data warehouses were selected for the realisation of the experiment. They were third year students with sufficient experience in the utilisation of IT, and therefore the application of the given system was not a novelty for them. The total number of students, and other participants in the experiment was two hundred. They were divided into six groups. All the results of students' work were continuously evaluated. The obtained results were later compared with the results of the Automated Information System of the university. The results of the experiment are described below.

The author of the experiment tested the hypothesis which assumed that there had been a direct correlation between the number of solutions and the average number of points scored on the test. Contingency tables were generated based on these results, which reflected the relation between the number of solutions and the average number of points scored, and also the dependence of the overall assessment upon the average number and regularity of the assignments faced.

These results indicate the necessity of introducing various forms of feedback between teachers and students. At universities, feedback should occur mainly in the realisation of various tasks, forums, discussions, project implementations, and the like. It is assumed that these assignments must be continuously evaluated and this form of evaluation can act as a stimulus to students' activities. The LMS Moodle seems to be a very appropriate means for the implementation of the abovementioned.

The e-learning application of knowledge management as a tool of assessing students' performance was accomplished at the University of Technology in Kosice (eastern Slovakia).

Knowledge assessment has been an inseparable part of current e-learning technologies. Grading is a process, which should answer students' abilities, knowledge, skills etc. In such a way it could be used as important information in the decision making process of external bodies. However, grading is very often required to be relative. It means it does not answer questions about student's knowledge (abilities, skills etc.) but only answers her/his position in a selected (often later unidentified) group of students.

For external bodies (next level educational institutions, employers) it is important to gain assessment of applicant personal abilities, knowledge, skills. In this case relative grading according to selected groups (class, school) is inappropriate. That is why external bodies very often do not take into account the grades acquired at the educational institutions.

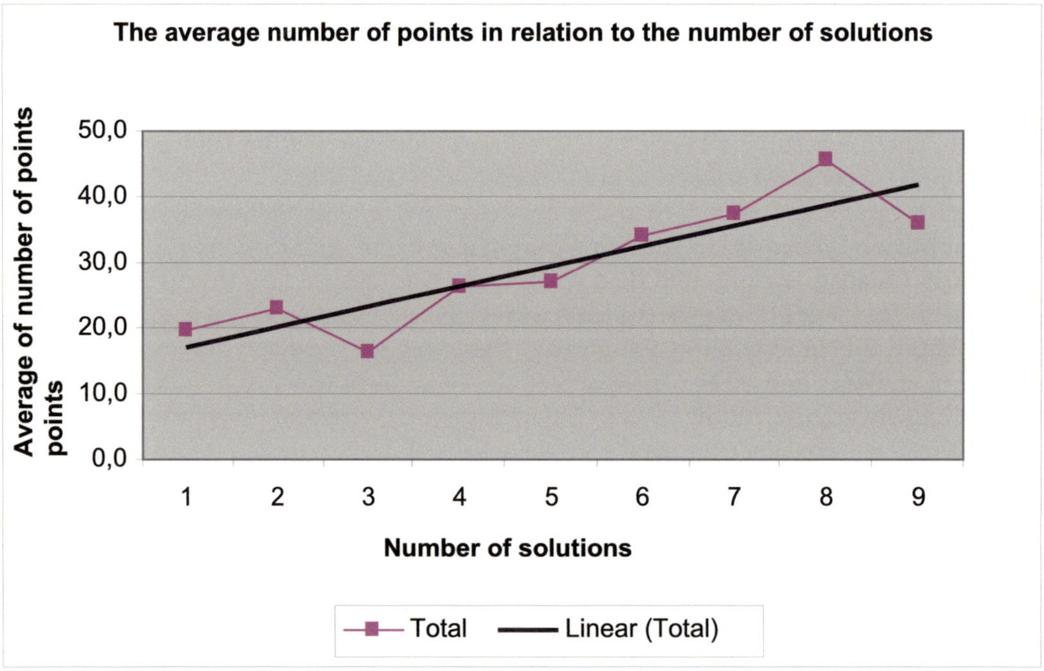

Fig. 1. The relationship between the number of solutions and the average number of points scored during a semester (max. 50).

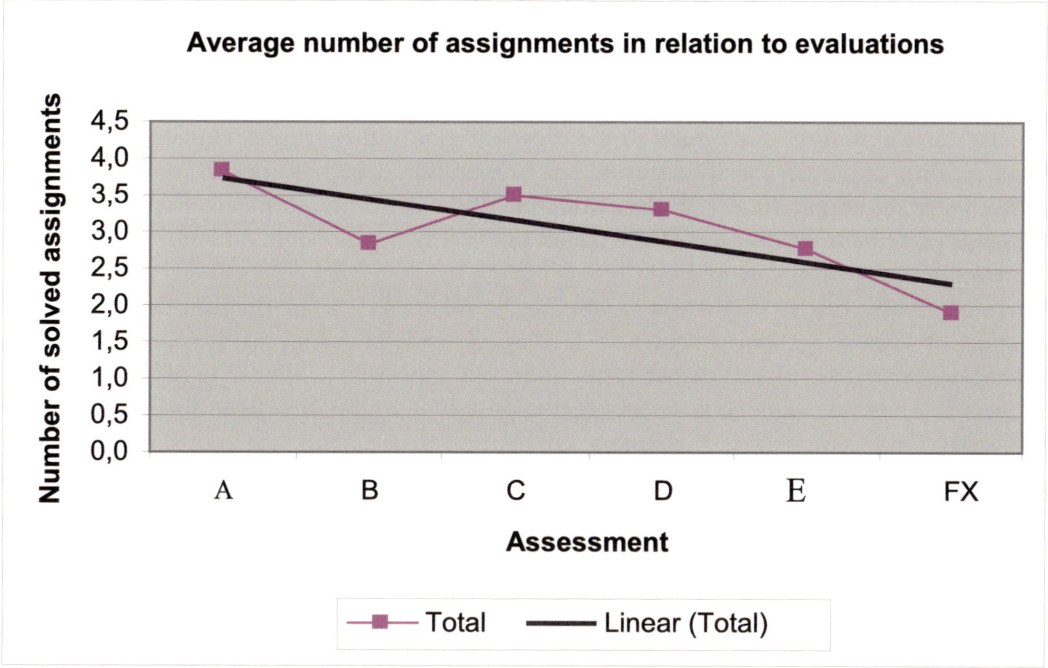

Fig. 2. Dependence of the total assessment of students' tests and the regularity of the assignments faced (the number of solved tasks).

It can be used for students' self-assessment to give them feedback about their progress during their studies or (on the other hand) for intermediate or final grading. However, knowledge tests are not developed with adequate care. Unfortunately, they are not designed to reveal the attained level of knowledge. Moreover, testing suites are very seldom reviewed with regard to their validity and items correlation. Experts at the University of Technology in Kosice examined the LMS Moodle with the aim to develop plug-in modules for the implementation of the ideas described below.

The term "didactic test" is often used in the Slovak and Czech pedagogical communities. It usually denotes the examination process designed for the fair evaluation of the attained level of mastering the given study material. The English speaking communities prefer the term "achievement test."

Regardless of the term preferred, this type of examination is considered as a tool for systematically measuring the teaching outcomes. It has been widely accepted that a didactic/achievement test has to be prepared in accordance to specified rules by a team of specialists.

However, basic principles are not followed in practice during test design and its implementation. Tests are usually developed ad-hoc, without a clear specification of aims, using only basic sets of question items (true-false, one from many choices, sometimes many from many choices). Moreover, testing items are usually not linked with the appropriate level of taxonomy of cognitive aims (if any taxonomy is chosen at all) and they are usually developed for specific curriculum sets.

As a result, questions are very often targeted to lower levels of taxonomy (knowledge/ remembering and comprehension/understanding) and in such a way they do not evaluate the participants' knowledge.

The next problem directs attention to the processing of testing results. In every test there is some grading approach specified during test preparation, which is applied to the evaluation of the tested items and, finally, to the evaluation of the entire test. It means that there should be some permanent evaluation of the tested items (finding possible ambiguities, revealing correlations between items, etc.).

There are many causes of the above specified problems. One of them is the inadequate support of knowledge assessment test development methodology in the current learning management systems (LMS). Most systems do not support a wide range of question-item types, these systems have no support of taxonomy of learning objectives and test items are required to be linked to specific chapters, not to appropriate composite knowledge.

Nowadays, assessment test are performed by computer systems. Most computer systems are connected to the Internet without any limitations during testing. Due to increasing computer literacy there is a great chance for participants to "steal" testing items and publish them online in a very short period of time. But even in the case of certain restrictions (fire walled computer classes, restrictions to using computer keyboards for closed type only testing suites), students overcome them by using new technological achievements (i.e. they take a photo of computer screen by mobile phone digital cameras to publish items on-line; use mobile phones for on-line consultancy). In such a way students prove their competence in using technological achievements, but their test results do not reflect their knowledge (skills, abilities).

Learning Management Systems (LMS) have evolved to matured systems in the area of course development during the last ten years. However, it is hard to find any methodology applied to LMS with regard to knowledge assessment. Therefore, the recommended fundamental requirements for knowledge assessment modules of learning management systems with regard to the implementation of assessment methodology are as follows: defining the taxonomy of cognitive aims; defining the cognitive structure of curricula in addition to the basic structure of the curriculum; linking each testing item to an appropriate level of taxonomy and an appropriate mode of cognitive curriculum structure; providing a rich set of question-item types, including open items; supporting item and test life-cycle support; supporting the functionality for teamwork development of tests; providing well-developed approaches for items and test statistics".

Application of the so called "functional model" can provide an "added" value for knowledge assessment test development. Linking testing items to specific level of cognitive taxonomy may give possibility to a better selection of the corresponding items. It gives the possibility to test the "knowledge" of participants after lectures and prior to seminars. Newly designed tests can be targeted to checking the comprehension (or higher) level. Moreover, different levels can be combined with the different parts of curriculum. This model seems to be suitable for building an adaptive test. We can start from any level and based upon the correctness or incorrectness of participants' answers we can adjust the level of subsequent items presented to the tested persons.

4. Conclusion

Web-based learning is understood as one of the most important innovations in education. Moreover, this form of learning has many benefits, both social and economic, and belongs to the most flexible types of learning, which suits the target groups of all presented projects - learners, current and perspective entrepreneurs, managers and other similar beneficiaries. Moreover, web-based learning is one of the most important possibilities of improving access to continuous vocational training, and lifelong acquisition of the necessary skills and competencies of inhabitants in the regions.

The web-based learning systems, applied in the projects, consist of separate techniques, such as e-learning, self-learning and regular meetings of self-learning groups of learners - three main parts of a blended learning approach.

Teachers' participation in the preparatory phase of these e-learning and blended learning materials and activities was satisfactory and efficient. On the other hand, teachers were less enthusiastic about the day-to-day online contact with their learners. Even very active and zealous colleagues complained about this new approach in tertiary education. Some of them explained that constant participation in online courses, and/or ex-post educational participation represented a significant burden on their mental and physical well-being.

As our present paper suggests, various pros and cons are the real experience outcomes of the presented advanced teaching approaches. The success of any educational change largely depends on how instructors perceive it and what they do to implement change, since it is the instructors who reflect on change, absorb and realise new ideas and improvements.

It goes without saying that these approaches will be realised in a broad extent in the near future. The reasons are as follows: (1) very convenient, rational, effective and time saving ways for learners; (2) support for knowledge-based social environment for regions; (3) engagement in "home working" educational activities in a pleasant ambiance; (4) contribution to the lessening of the burden on the environment in general (e.g. "classroom-less" universities, transport-less" commuting/communication, etc.)

This current "pioneer" era requires some inevitable steps to be taken in order to develop and accelerate positive approaches, and to find solutions for diminishing the obstacles within the process. One of the possible ways to eliminate the presence of relevant problems is to involve young teachers in the process, who are much keener on using these innovative means of information and communication technologies.

5. References

Brokeš, P. (2005). *E-learning – The Most Effective Technique in SME Manager's Distance Education.* In.: Proceedings of the Final conference of REDILEM, Bratislava, Slovakia. ISBN 80-89085-37-7

Genči, J. (2007). *Some Consideration about Knowledge Assessment.* 8th International Conference Virtual University VU'07. E-ACADEMIA SLOVACA, Bratislava, Slovakia. ISBN 978-80-89316-09-0

Kultan, J. (2010) *Realizácia spätnej väzby v elektronickom vzdelávaní.* In.: Proceeding of International Conference on Innovation process in e-learning. University of Economics in Bratislave, Slovakia. ISBN 978-80-225-2724-8

Molnár, P. (2006). *Experience with the Implementation of Leonardo da Vinci Pilot Project REDILEM.* In.: Proceeding of International ACEE Conference on Engineering Education. Puerto Rico, USA. ISBN 1-58874-648-8

Molnár, P. (2008). *Experiences with Advanced Pedagogical Approaches at Slovak Universities.* In: Proceedings of the 9th Biennial ASME Conference on Engineering Systems Design and Analysis, ESDA2008. Haifa, Israel. ISBN 0_7918-3827-7

Némethová, I. (2007). *Web-Based Business English.* In: Proceeding of International Conference on ProfiLingua. Plzeň, Czech Republic. ISBN 978-80-7043-610-3

Némethová, I. (2009). *Controversies in Teaching English for Specific Business Purposes.* In: FORLANG 2009: International Conference, Košice. ISBN 978-80-553-0325-3

Sterner, R. (2005). *REDILEM and Net-based Learning.* In.: Proceedings of the Final Conference of REDILEM, Bratislava, Slovakia. ISBN 80-89085-37-7

4

Digital Faces on the Cloud

S. L. Jones
Texas A&M University
Qatar

1. Introduction

Videos of practice problem solutions have been used extensively at Texas A&M University in College Station for a number of years. When counters have been inserted in the website where these videos reside, thousands of hits by students have been recorded. Students have given positive feedback to instructors about the videos. They particularly like the ability to pause and rewind the video, a feature not available in a live lecture. Students who are reluctant to speak up in a lecture class appreciate the opportunity to review the video over and over, pausing at points that are critical to their own understanding.

The Second Life environment has been growing over the last four years(Harris &Rea, 2009). As was shown in the background research, it is being used more for mathematics instructions in the last two or three years, with positive results. Students enjoy the virtual world and the anonymity it provides to open the door to more interaction and to decrease the anxiety about asking questions about mathematics problems. The Second Life environment is ideal for solving the problems that need to be addressed for increased participation in Science, Technology, Engineering, and Mathematics (STEM) majors by

1. stimulating the interest of more students.
2. providing support to ensure that they have the required mathematics background knowledge for STEM majors.
3. providing social interaction and collaborative learning opportunities for students.

Second Life seems to be the most appropriate environment in which to develop the maximum success.

Moreover, mathematics anxiety can be extreme; often caused by having a negative attitude due to a previous bad experience. Studies show that one-half of all students in a developmental mathematics class suffer forms of this type of anxiety. The good news is that a student can manage this behavior but they must learn to manage both the stress as well as improve the basic mathematic skills.

The goal of this project is to increase interest and enjoyment in mathematics to entice more students to excel in mathematics. In particular, success in college calculus is very important to the goal of engineering majors in Qatar. As the background research indicates, there is a dire need for strategies to increase success in college calculus in order to reach the goal of a highly skilled technological workforce with knowledge in science, engineering, and the underlying mathematics necessary for these fields as well as to prepare the undergraduate engineering students to work on meaningful, real-world problems in the short time while they are studying at college and to contribute to research after they graduate without spending valuable time learning on the job.

Data mining tools predict future trends and behaviors, allowing researchers and organizations to make proactive decisions. Data mining predicts the hidden information in the database unlike typical statistics. Therefore the clustering algorithm that will be used in this project should detect characteristics of students studying mathematics. Moreover the cluster analysis can be generalized to other grouping and would be capable of detecting other similarities as well [Jones, & Gupta, 2006; Jones, 2009). Flow chart and stages as seen below in figure 1.

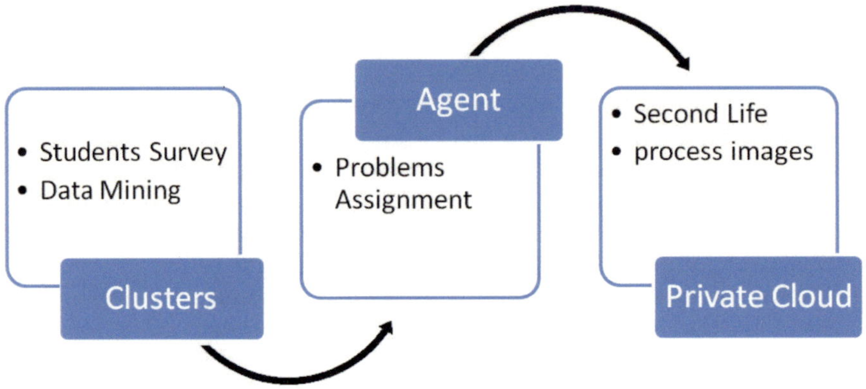

Fig. 1. Flow chart of stages of project

Clustering Techniques

Clustering is a division of data into groups of similar objects. Each group consists of objects that are similar between themselves and dissimilar to other groups. Most commonly techniques are the following:

Data clustering: is the process of dividing data elements into classes or clusters so that items in the same class are as similar as possible, and items in different classes are as dissimilar as possible,

Hard clustering: where data is divided into distinct clusters, where each data element belongs to exactly one cluster, and

Fuzzy clustering: where data elements can belong to more than one cluster, and associated with each element is a set of membership levels. These indicate the strength of the association between that data element and a particular cluster.

In this project we will be using the clustering technique (K-Means) where the main idea is to place each point/ student in the cluster whose current centroid it is nearest. It works with numeric data only as follows:

1. Pick a number "k" of cluster centers (randomly).
2. Assign every item to its nearest cluster center (using Euclidean distance)
3. Move each cluster center to the mean of its assigned items
4. Repeat the steps until convergence.

Therefore, given a set of observations ($\mathbf{x}_1$, $\mathbf{x}_2$, …, $\mathbf{x}_n$), where each observation is a ***d***-dimensional real vector, the ***k*-means** clustering aims to partition the ***n*** observations into ***k*** sets ($k < n$) $\mathbf{S} = \{S_1, S_2, \ldots, S_k\}$ so as to minimize the within- cluster sum of squares:

$$\underset{\mathrm{S}}{\arg\min} \sum_{i=1}^{k} \sum_{x_j \in S_i} \left\| x_j - \mu_i \right\|^2$$

where $\boldsymbol{\mu}_i$ is the mean of points in S_i.
and the Euclidean distance equation is:

$$d(i,j) = \sqrt{(\mathrm{I}x_{i_1} - x_{j_1}\mathrm{I}^2 + \mathrm{I}x_{i_2} - x_{j_2}\mathrm{I}^2 \cdots + \mathrm{I}x_{i_p} - x_{j_p}\mathrm{I}^2)}$$

Where:

$$d(i,j) \geq 0$$
$$d(i,i) = 0$$
$$d(i,j) = d(i,j)$$
$$d(i,j) \leq d(i,k) + d(k,j)$$

This chapter sections are organized as follows: section 3 will contain the Review of literature and 3.1 Mathematics Achievement Using Interactive Games; 3.2 Second Life Environment; 3.3 Cultural difference in coeducational school. The rest of the chapter sections are organized as follows: 4. Proposed Research; 5. Engineering Calculus Successes at TAMU Qatar, 6. The Approach, 6.1 Step1, describes the model applied and developed to new data based on distances using the Euclidean distance, 6.2 Step 2 describes the results of the cluster analysis modules developed for Second Life, 6.3 Sep3 talks about the typical uses of cloud and its activities, 7. Grid Computing, is the large-scale cluster computing to be used for public collaboration which is known as peer-to-peer computing which is computers acting together to perform very large tasks, 8. Grid and Cloud Computing is the Grid and Cloud Computing concentrates on high performance computing, Web services and grid services, 9. Results and Summary contains the output of the project which showed that the students are learning a great deal from the rewards and they finished the tasks within 52% less time which is about half time, 10. Conclusions explains that the global social networks are changing and transforming, the old ways of education which is a challenge to some of us. This study has already demonstrated some benefits to students using collaboration tools, video, and mobile technology to minimize the Math anxiety in the classroom, 11. Future Work expects that this may include remote mentoring between multicultural teams and systems monitoring as well as writing an iPhone application, and section 12. Benefits and Concerns discuses Second Life and the applications that can be developed and deployed in a 3D.

2. Background

Texas A&M University at Qatar (TAMUQ) is a branch campus of the main campus in College Station. Students at Qatar get their degree from the main campus and are allowed to spend time taking classes in either campus. Most faculty members in Qatar have been relocated from the main campus to teach the same classes they teach at the main campus.

Since the fall of 2003, Texas A&M University at Qatar has offered Bachelor of Science degrees in chemical, electrical, mechanical and petroleum engineering. In addition to engineering courses, Texas A&M University at Qatar provides instruction in science, mathematics, liberal arts and the humanities. The curriculum offered at Texas A&M at Qatar are identical to the ones offered at the main campus in College Station, Texas. Courses are taught in English and in a coeducational setting. The goal of TAMUQ is: to strengthen the University's presence nationally and internationally through teaching and learning and develop student participation and leadership in relevant technical fields.

3. Review of literature

Important factors predicting success in calculus among freshmen engineering students included a student's ability to regulate his own learning in areas of classroom engagement and time on task (Mwavita, 2005). Certain personality variables such as persistent, responsibility, and patience contributed considerably to the prediction of success in college calculus classes (Shaughnessy, 1994).

For many students calculus has become a stumbling block in the path to careers in science, technology, engineering and mathematics. In a 2010 study, 30% of students who took calculus in high school were placed into pre-calculus in college. Students believed they already knew the material when they entered college calculus, but were stunned to find that they did poorly in the first half of the course. Few actually managed to successfully complete the course. It is necessary to find a way to smooth the transition into college calculus and be sure students are ready for the challenges they face (Bressoud, 2010).

The University of Nebraska at Omaha developed a procedure to implement calculus placement. A calculus readiness test was given initially, with reliability and validity measures computed. At the end of the semester, a comprehensive final was given, with reliability and validity measures computed. Then the correlation coefficient between calculus readiness test scores and final exam scores was calculated and found to be statistically significant, with r = .42 and r = .55 for the two forms of the readiness test (Stephens & Buchalter, 1987).

Many colleges are facing difficulties with success rates in engineering and other majors that require proficiency in calculus. In a study of actuarial students at Bryant College success in calculus was an important predictor of success in the major (Smith, & Schumacher, 2005).

A study on retention of underrepresented minorities revealed that only 35% of all students who begin college as science, engineering, or mathematics majors graduate in one of those fields (Smith, 1995).

King Fahd University of Petroleum and Minerals (KFUPM), in a study on the preparatory mathematics and English courses, also examined the effect of lowering the level of prerequisite knowledge, based on grades in the preparatory courses in mathematics. Results showed that the students who entered calculus with lower grades in prerequisite courses were generally not successful (Yushau, & Omar, 2007).

Several factors are important in designing a successful intervention for student success in engineering calculus. Educators must consider mathematics deficiencies as well as placement into the appropriate college course. One college pre-calculus revision to increase mathematics learning included

1. smaller class size
2. student collaboration in small groups

3. problem based learning. Three classrooms, each using one of these nontraditional approaches were compared to a traditional classroom.

Students who needed to improve skills for success in calculus were randomly assigned to one of the four sections. Student test scores on four common exams revealed that students in the problem based learning class performed better than students in the other three classes, one that used a traditional approach, and two that used other nontraditional approaches (Olson, Knott, & Currie, 2009).

A discussion-based seminar format was deemed a successful strategy for teaching various levels of college mathematics. Students were required to read textbook materials, work relatively simple exercises, and submit a short reaction piece to the professor before attending class so that they were prepared for the discussion. More difficult homework exercises were completed after the class meeting. The professor believes the primary benefits of the seminar type instruction in his classes of size twenty or less were that students become more independent and more successful life-long learners of mathematics (King, 2001).

The Rochester Institute of Technology implemented a process by which a calculus project was designed and piloted, resulting in increased calculus success rates. A placement exam was used to place students who were considered at risk for failing calculus into a course that integrated Precalculus review as needed throughout the calculus (Maggelakis, & Lutzer, 2007).

The Emerging Scholars Program developed by the University of Texas Austin was used to add workshops of class size about 25 with collaborative learning to all calculus classes, in addition to the regular four lecture hours. The change was expensive but resulted in a 16.3% increase in student success in Calculus I. California State University Los Angeles also added workshops to several calculus courses, and found that it increased success rates. Students have asked that the workshops be added to some other courses. The university planned to implement the model in Precalculus and remedial math courses (Subramanian, Cates, & Gutarts, 2009).

Similar results were reported in the McNeill Program at the University of Colorado at Boulder with at risk students in college mathematics courses involving workshops and collaborative learning (Mendez, 2006).

3.1 Mathematics achievement using interactive games

Using technology in the mathematics classroom supports different teaching and learning strategies and objectives (Ozel, Yetkiner, & Capraro, 2008). The use of games fosters mathematical learning and encourages students' mathematical processes (Su, Marinas, & Furner, 2010). In particular, students typically apply mathematical skills and processes such as reasoning, deduction, and pattern-finding when playing computer games. A study showed that students also tended to stay on task longer when playing games requiring computations and problem solving (Hui, 2009). Role-playing games provide a motivating strategy for students to practice skills already learned (Ahmad, Shafie, Latif, 2010).

Fewer studies have been done on mathematics games at the secondary or college level. However, one such study asserted that results of mathematics computer games showed a statistically significant improvement in mathematics achievement on students in an urban high school (Kebritchi, Hirumi, & Bai, 2010).

A study on reviewing calculus skills, finding derivatives and evaluating integrals, showed that using an interactive game was successful (Forman, & Forman, 2008). In general, interactive games have had positive effects on interest and motivation in mathematics (Su, Marinas, & Furner, 2010; Ahmad, Shafie, Latif, 2010; Kebritchi, Hirumi, & Bai, 2010; Jones, 2009).

3.2 Second Life environment

Second Life is an online 3D virtual environment that

1. allows participants to engage directly and interactively,
2. provides an opportunity for rich social networking, and
3. provides opportunities for collaborative work (Jones, 2009; Bourke, 2009; Cheong, 2010; Lucia, Rancese, Passero, & Tortora, 2009). Second Life information is generally freely available to all residents (Jones, 2009), although the client uploading content for a virtual classroom pays a fee for upload access. Second Life has the capability to support not only asynchronous distance learning products but can also support synchronous lectures and increase interaction and communication opportunities between teachers and students [Lucia, Rancese, Passero, & Tortora, 2009).

3.3 Cultural difference in coeducational school

After conducting interviews at a variety of public and private co-ed schools, all-girls schools and all boys schools it was noticed that "the real variables affecting a girl's performance seems to have more to do with class size, and the expectations of society and the family. The size of the group, affects their ability to speak out and to feel comfortable in expressing themselves. Adding to that the problems of discipline that may arise in the class and it's easy to understand why quieter students, or those who lack confidence, might be intimidated.

Moreover more studies in the literature cited that the popular belief that girls will do better academically at single-sex schools is not sustained by the data. School type does not appear to be an important factor in attempts to improve the performance levels of girls in mathematics and science however the Mathematics anxiety and lack confidence does.

Finally, it is already established in the literature the need of graduates to have skills working with the digital communications tools as well as having long life learning skills in the real and the virtual environment. Moreover, accreditation criteria include the problem solving and team shearing particularly in Engineering is required by utilizing a variety of technologies.

4. Research

This research uses learning tools with collaborative opportunities with the main campus of Texas A&M in Second Life using private cloud to improve student success in engineering calculus.

It will bridge the gap in knowledge, using interactive games and social networking in the context of success in mathematics conceptual knowledge and skills necessary to be successful in Engineering, and Mathematics.

The purpose is to investigate different online e-technology methods used in Mathematics classes at Texas A&M University at Qatar to accelerate learning and detecting the best practice in using them in education. Five different software applications and class management systems used in Calculus I and Calculus II for Engineers which are: Turning Point System for students' attendance, 3D online system (Second life) for conducting help sessions and student meetings, WebCT for posting class notes, grads and notices, WebAssign for online quizzes and practice, and Pod casting for posting solved homework problems and using iTunesU.

The general idea is to produce an intelligent program, called agent, through a process of learning using Reinforcement Learning (RL) which is a Machine Learning technique that has become very popular in recent days. The technique has been applied to a variety of artificial domains, such as game playing, as well as real-world problems. In principle, a Reinforcement Learning agent learns from its experience by interacting with the environment. The agent is not told how to behave and is allowed to explore the environment freely. However once it has taken its actions, the agent is rewarded if its actions were good and punished if they were bad. This system of rewards and punishments teaches the agent which actions to take in the future, and guides it towards a better outcome. The basic idea is the visual perception of the ability to be familiar with the environment visually. Computer simulation used as follows: Users will sign on their second life virtual space with their virtual names and join a study session whereas a simulation by computer images is mainly focused on their images processing machine vision digital input/output that will be fed to computer networks to observe the behavior in a computer grid format.

Data mining tools used to predict future trends (Neel, 2011). It predicts the future and the hidden information in the database. Data mining tools can answer questions that traditionally were very time consuming to resolve and experts may miss because it lies outside their expectations. The most commonly techniques used in data mining are artificial neural networks, decision trees, and clustering which used in this research.

5. Engineering calculus successes at TAMU Qatar

Since Qatari students are approximately the same age as United States students and are exposed to very similar mathematics curriculum, it is expected that similar interventions are needed to address the needs of students who wish to major in STEM fields at Texas A&M University at Qatar.

A pilot study conducted by the author at Texas A&M University at Qatar revealed that students were very productive and engaged in the learning experience and the average student's attendance during any session is 98% of the time. Moreover a subculture difference has no appearance in the virtual world for exploring cultural alternatives. Jones (Jones, 2009; Jones, S. L. 2009) also noted that the collaborative aspect available in Second Life does not exist in any other online platforms.

As was seen in the literature background, this is an important feature. Jones also found that the average of student group project grades was seven percentage points higher than that of students who did not use Second Life (from 72% to 79%). A snapshot of a class in Second Life at TAMU Qatar is shown (see figure 2).

6. The Approach

6.1 Step1

A model created by evaluating training data using domain experts' knowledge. Then the model applied and developed to new data based on distances using the Euclidean distance (see figure 3).

Then based on the distances we create the classes (see figure 4).

Fig. 2. Second Life at TAMU Qatar

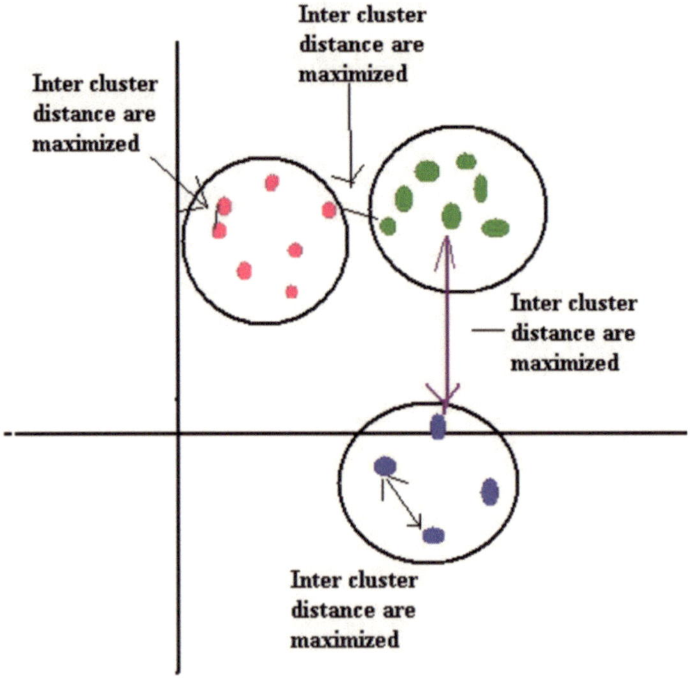

Fig. 3. Euclidean distance

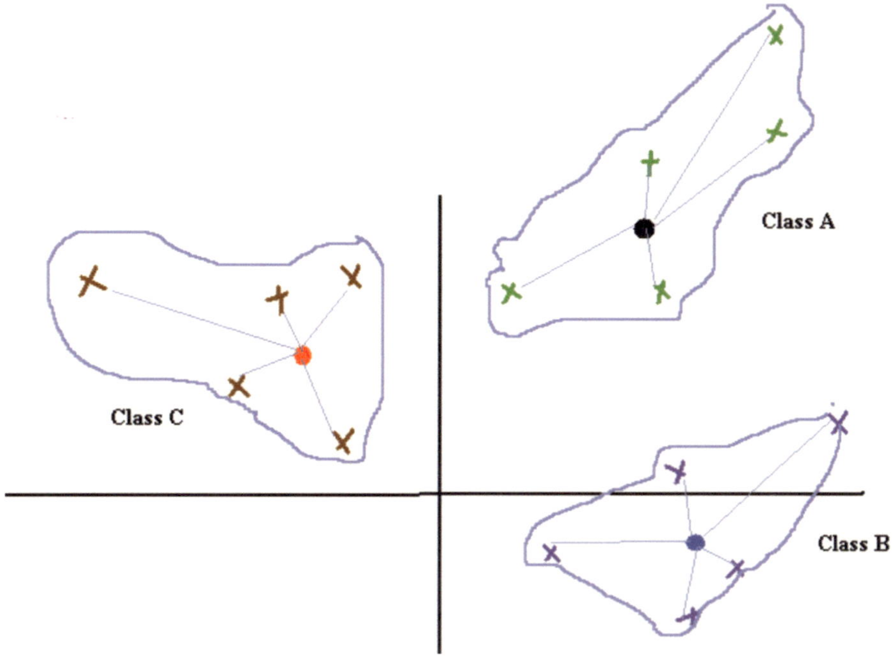

Fig. 4. New classes

This algorithm will minimizes the intra-cluster variance however the results will depend on the initial choice of weights. Thus we will repeat the algorithm with different weights until it converges (that is when the coefficients fail to change between two iterations) and each time we will compute the centroid for each cluster. Based on the learning preference choices after an assessment test we will choose the number of classes based on the outcome. We will assign membership to each student based on their preference of learning. For example, if a student has a membership value of 0.0, thus he/she is not a member of this class. However if a student likes to learn using more than one method the he/she could have a memberships in more than one class (partial member to more than one group) and lastly if the student has a membership value of 1.0 that means he/she belongs only to this group.
By assigning memberships we will know our population better and we will design the learning and teaching modules based on that outcome. For example, see figure 5.

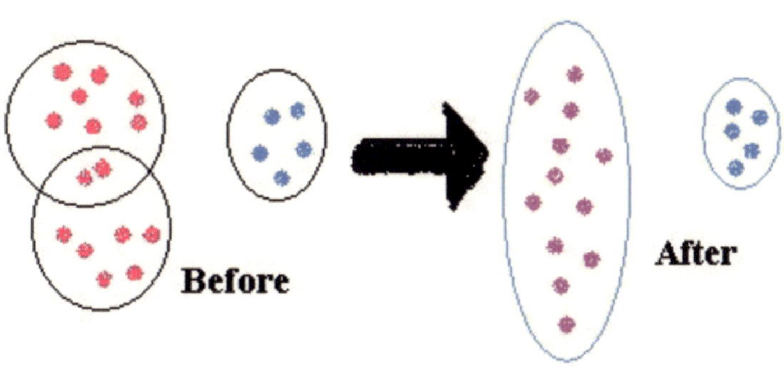

Fig. 5. Memberships assignment

6.2 Step 2

Based on the results of the cluster analysis modules developed for Second Life. The modules designed to address the issues revealed in the analysis and to benefit of all future Qatari college students desiring to pursue STEM careers.

For each topic, lessons developed around student weakness and materials provided in a format that is downloadable to computers, iPad, iPod, or G3 phones as well.

These modules are tailored to students here in Qatar based on the clustering and classes model that been developed and that will differentiate them from one method fits all which is on the market place. Moreover these modules can be modified very easy.

Lessons include the following:

- Instructional videos. These are less than 10 minutes each so that students may focus on very specific instruction to meet their individual needs. *Camtasia* software used to create the streaming videos. Instructional videos may be focused on concepts, definitions, and theorems, but will usually include an example.
- Problem Videos. Additional videos showing how to work additional problems will be provided for many topics. *Matlab* is used by students for more complex problems.
- Games. For many topics, simple interactive games to practice skills developed using flash animations.
- Assessments. Each module will have an assessment so that students will know when they have mastered the skills necessary to apply knowledge of the topic to the college calculus course (see figure 6).

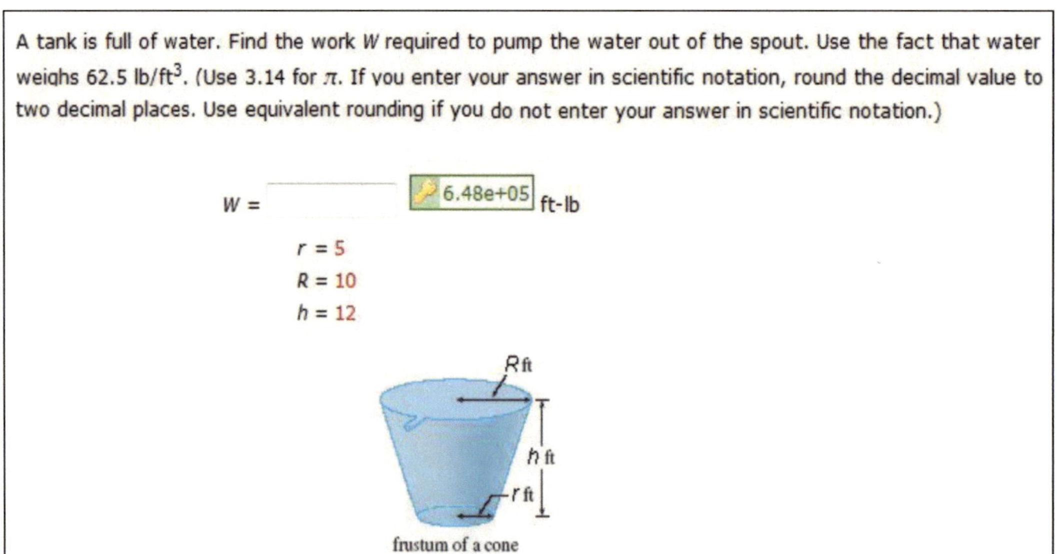

Fig. 6. Class activity sample

Internal reliability on student scores for this project is expected to be acceptable as well. The instrument using a Likert scale to measure attitudes about mathematics learning in a face-to-face regular class and a virtual classroom is developed as follows with these questions:

1. How comfortable are you in asking questions in a regular face-to-face classroom?
2. How comfortable are you in asking questions in a virtual classroom?

3. How comfortable are you working on problems in a face-to-face classroom?
4. How comfortable are you working on problems in a virtual classroom?
5. How often do you have opportunities for collaborative learning in a face-to-face classroom?
6. How often do you have opportunities for collaborative learning in a virtual classroom?

Learning Model using cloud-based strategy

We use to think that having our documents and financial statements on our computers is the only safe place for them. Now, cloud computing has changed our way of thinking.

A cloud is basically a giant server that we access remotely; typically with a mobile device or a computer since with cloud computing we only need a mobile device or a monitor and keyboard to access the information. If we are using hotmail, yahoo mail or facebook then we are using the cloud since the e-mail in not on our own device but it is somewhere on a server and we just have access to it with a login id.

Clouds exist all over the world and are mostly operated by giant corporations such as Google, Yahoo, and Amazon. Now Texas A&M University at Qatar has teamed up with IBM, Carnegie Mellon at Qatar, and Qatar University to create a consortium called Qatar Cloud Computing to the Middle East (Qloud). The Qloud is developing courses on cloud computing and have an environment for industry experts and researchers.

Students at Texas A&M University at Qatar (TAMUQ) are no longer having to travel miles to experience life at the main campus in Texas. Students could interact virtually with students at the main campus and enjoy the interaction with the students on the other side.

Here at TAMUQ students take as many courses as they can in the first few years in the Qatar campus and then relocate to university's main campus in Texas-USA during their senior year working on the rest of their courses if they wish.

The cloud is on-demand computing, for anyone with a network connection accessing applications and data anywhere, anytime, from any device these are similar to Facebook or e-mail which are repositories for data and we can access this data from any internet-enabled device, from our iPhones to our desktop computers. From the consumer point of view, the storage of digital images or e-mail messages is stored somewhere in the cloud. We don't need to know where specifically, we just can to use it with a valid id and web connection. No doubt that cloud computing is the next big wave in computing. It is changing what we are using on our desks and schools and how we access and share documents.

6.3 Sep3

Typical uses of cloud

1. For usage as a personal workspace that can be accessed anywhere, anytime (see figure 7).
2. For Personal Learning Environments, students can have personalized tools to meet their own personal needs and preferences (see figure 8).
3. To minimizes the need to back up all files or transfer files from one device to another
4. To use large amounts of processing power for solving big problems
5. For teaching and learning so instructors can use YouTube, iTunes, e-mail, or mic on the cloud (see figure 8).

Fig. 7. Cloud activities

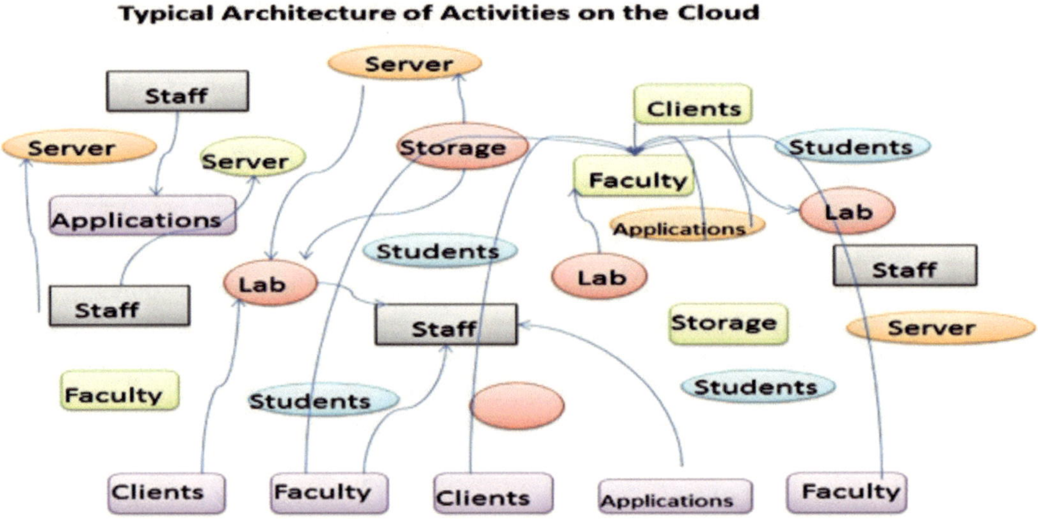

Fig. 8. Architecture of activities on cloud

7. Grid computing

Grid computing - the use of a *computational grid* -- is applying the resources of many computers in a network to a single problem at the same time using large amounts of data (SAS, 2010). It also could be referred at the combination of computer resources from multiple domains to reach a common goal. It can divide a program to as many as several thousand computers and can be thought of as large-scale cluster computing and can be confined to the network of computer workstation or it can be a public collaboration which is known as peer-to-peer computing.

Grid computing are distinguished from conventional high performance computing systems such as cluster computing because grids tend to be more loosely coupled -- computers acting together to perform very large tasks -- and geographically dispersed. However, it is more common that a single grid can be used for a variety of different purposes (Liang, Gang, & Yifei, 2011).
Therefore, grid computing appears to be a promising because it suggests that the resources of many computers can be cooperatively and perhaps can be connected together and managed as collaboration toward a common objective and with our awareness.

8. Grid and cloud computing

This is the power of all time computing; creating a single universal source of computing power by making computational and data resources available to users and applications programmers on a scale never before possible. The Grid and Cloud Computing concentrates on high performance computing, Web services and grid services.
The *Dedicated server* is slowly starting to vanish and being replaced by *Cloud Computing*, however people are still afraid of security issues and letting go of their data on the cloud.
It is predicted that as they start getting on the cloud bandwagons, they would be using *Virtual Private Server* (VPS) which is fairly common among hosting solutions on the cloud where people share resources with the other clients on a particular server.
A set of characteristics that helps distinguish cluster, Grid and Cloud computing systems is listed in Table 1. The resources in clusters are located in a single administrative domain and managed by a single entity whereas, in Grid systems, resources are geographically distributed across multiple administrative domains with their own management policies and goals. Another key difference between cluster and Grid systems arises from the way application scheduling is performed. The schedulers in cluster systems focus on enhancing the overall system performance and utility as they are responsible for the whole system. However, the schedulers in Grid systems called resource brokers, focusing on enhancing the performance of a specific application in such a way that its end-users requirements are met. Cloud computing platforms possess characteristics of both clusters and Grids, with its own special attributes and capabilities such strong support for virtualization, dynamically composable services with Web Service interfaces, and strong support for creating 3rd party, value added services by building on Cloud compute, storage, and application services. Thus, Clouds are promising to provide services to users without reference to the infrastructure on which these are hosted (see table 1).

9. Results and summary

Students were positive with the help and the feedback given by the system agent they are using and they are learning from the rewards given by the engine.
This experiment was sufficient enough for generalization however, by adding more subjects and sample problems that will be solicited to allow for reliability and testing of the model. As well as testing the mechanism against empirical data.
Students finished the tasks within 52% of the normal assigned time which is about half time. They were delighted by the end of the task and had a positive experience.

Key characteristics of clusters, Grids, and Cloud systems.

Characteristics	Systems		
	Clusters	Grids	Clouds
Population	Commodity computers	High-end computers (servers, clusters)	Commodity computers and high-end servers and network attached storage
Size/scalability	100s	1000s	100s to 1000s
Node Operating System (OS)	One of the standard OSs (Linux, Windows)	Any standard OS (dominated by Unix)	A hypervisor (VM) on which multiple OSs run
Ownership	Single	Multiple	Single
Interconnection network|speed	Dedicated, high-end with low latency and high bandwidth	Mostly Internet with high latency and low bandwidth	Dedicated, high-end with low latency and high bandwidth
Security/privacy	Traditional login/password-based. Medium level of privacy – depends on user privileges.	Public/private key pair based authentication and mapping a user to an account. Limited support for privacy.	Each user/application is provided with a virtual machine. High security/privacy is guaranteed. Support for setting per-file access control list (ACL).
Discovery	Membership services	Centralised indexing and decentralised info services	Membership services
Service negotiation	Limited	Yes, SLA based	Yes, SLA based
User management	Centralised	Decentralised and also virtual organization (VO)-based	Centralised or can be delegated to third party
Resource management	Centralized	Distributed	Centralized/Distributed
Allocation/scheduling	Centralised	Decentralised	Both centralised/decentralised
Standards/inter-operability	Virtual Interface Architecture (VIA)-based	Some Open Grid Forum standards	Web Services (SOAP and REST)
Single system image	Yes	No	Yes, but optional
Capacity	Stable and guaranteed	Varies, but high	Provisioned on demand
Failure management (Self-healing)	Limited (often failed tasks/applications are restarted).	Limited (often failed tasks/applications are restarted).	Strong support for failover and content replication. VMs can be easily migrated from one node to other.
Pricing of services	Limited, not open market	Dominated by public good or privately assigned	Utility pricing, discounted for larger customers
Internetworking	Multi-clustering within an Organization	Limited adoption, but being explored through research efforts such as Gridbus InterGrid	High potential, third party solution providers can loosely tie together services of different Clouds
Application drivers	Science, business, enterprise computing, data centers	Collaborative scientific and high throughput computing applications	Dynamically provisioned legacy and web applications, Content delivery
Potential for building 3rd party or value-added solutions	Limited due to rigid architecture	Limited due to strong orientation for scientific computing	High potential – can create new services by dynamically provisioning of compute, storage, and application services and offer as their own isolated or composite Cloud services to users

Table 1. Courtesy of (Future Generation Computer Systems 25 (2009) 599_616)

10. Conclusions

The goal of this project is to increase interest and enjoyment in mathematics to entice more students to excel in mathematics. In particular, success in college calculus is very important to the goal of engineering majors in Qatar.

Learning from each other as well as using new technologies for collaborating is an important aspect of education. Therefore, transforming this basic idea into the classroom will promote interactive learning and enhance communication between students and teachers. The modules suggested here been developed based on students' need to encourage them to actively read and practice their subject matter like they do on the social networks sites –i.e. facebook and e-mail. This type of social learning is great for Qatari students because it helps them with the technical reading and practices more English as well as the understanding of the technical content. Moreover, these activities help students to work together in an anonymous way so they are not having any culture discomfort in a co-ed sitting and enable collaborative problem-solving using grid computing on the cloud through the usage of second life (see Figure 9). Moreover, although this model offers fairly good accuracy/efficiency tradeoff, it is believed that further research should explore different ways to try to improve the computational efficiency and the memory usage, by introducing modifications specifically to improve learning.

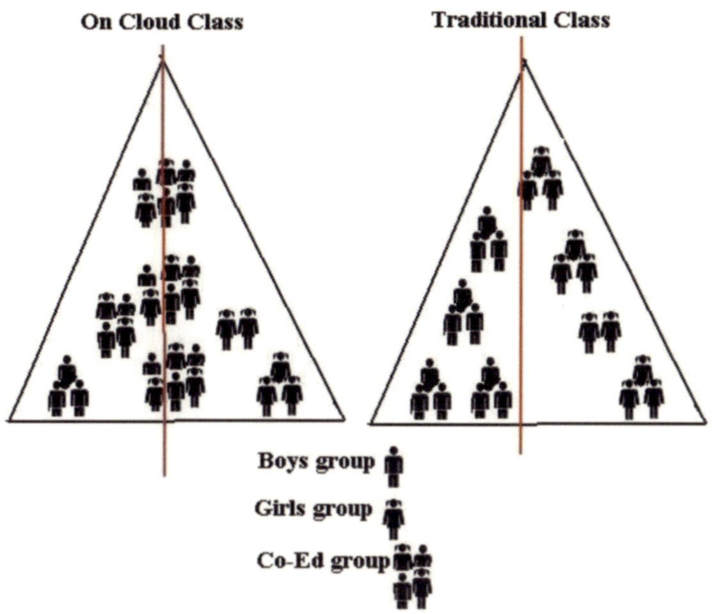

Fig. 9. Coeducational Traditional and on cloud

The global social networks are changing and transforming, the old ways of education. It is a challenge to some of us. This study has already demonstrated some benefits to students using collaboration tools, video, and mobile technology to minimize the Math anxiety in the classroom.

In Second Life environment students are completely focused on the task at hand because if they drift to other activities, their avatar would quickly slump over and fall asleep, which is an embarrassing seen conveying to everyone that his/her mind has wandered off.

Most students had a pleasant experience using the games to learn mathematics and believed that it made learning fun and social. Moreover, the author also believes that second life and other virtual worlds represent a perfect convergence of social media, simulations and gaming which hold promise for a new generation of learners.

11. Future work

Future research will include remote mentoring between multicultural teams, white-board brainstorming, integration of social networking tools, and systems monitoring. As well as writing an iPhone application that aggregates information from several places, including Google cloud and others and make this application available to all via a single intuitive interface on the mobile device--an interface that many of our students are already using. Moreover it is believed to have been a huge success with students; for example, they can get real-time information about new assignment or chat with others students or faculty on their iPhones. Mobile apps are a big part of what is coming. Also, several professors have committed to add social network activities to their courses and in the classroom after learning about this successful study.

12. Benefits and concerns

Cloud computing is web-based computing where our information is no longer stored on our computer but rather on a larger server that we can access with a mobile device. Scalability and flexibility are some of the benefits of cloud computing where we can get 10 computers today and 1000 computers tomorrow. We rent them on the cloud instead of buying them. Therefore, by integrating our new cloud-based applications with our internal systems, we have benefited our IT team as well as our users. Cloud computing has freed us to change the rules in a way that gives IT as much free time. However, some of the concerns are the privacy and security by having our data on a cloud server and not stored on our own machine and of course that required the use of the internet too.

Second Life provides a platform where collaborative applications can be developed and deployed. The advantage of creating an application in a 3D social environment such as Second Life is that it's automatically presence-enabled. You can see who is using it and interact with them at the same time. It supports text chat, voice functions, and avatar customization. Yet there are more reasons to use virtual spaces because students learn more about social aspects, technologies used, architecture, subject matter, and education games

13. Acknowledgment

It is a pleasure to thank those who made this project possible. In particular I would like to thank Mr. Brian J. Weekes who gave me the moral support I required and helped me with the research suggestions. I also would like to thank Ms. Sandra Nite and the students at Texas A&M University for participating in the project.

14. References

Ahmad, W. F., Shafie, A. B., Latif, M. H. (2010). Role-playing game-based learning in mathematics. *The Electronic Journal of Mathematics and Technology, 4*(2), 185-196.

Bressoud, D. (2010). The rocky transition from high-school calculus. *Chronicle of Higher Education, 56*(19), A80.

Bourke, P. (2009). Evaluating Second Life for the collaborative exploration of 3D fractals. *Computer & Graphics, 33*, 113-117.

Cheong, D. (2010). The effects of practice teaching session in Second Life on the change in pre-service teachers' teaching efficacy. *Computers & Education, 55*, 868-880.

Forman, S. & Forman, S. (2008). Mathingo: Reviewing calculus with Bingo games. *PRIMUS: Problems, Resources, and Issues in Mathematics Undergraduate Studies, 18*(3), 304-308.

Harris, A, Rea A. (2009). Web 2.0 and Virtual World Technologies: A Growing Impact on IS Education. *Journal of Information Systems Education,* Vol. 20(2).

Hui, C. S. (2009). Learning mathematics through computer games. In *Proceedings of 14th Annual Asian Technology Conference in Mathematics, China,* Retrieved from http://atcm.mathandtech.org/EP2009/pages/regular.html on December 4, 2010.

Jones, S. L. (2009). Avatar-based learning in Second Life. *China-USA Business Review, 8*(10), 58-64.

Jones, S. L. & Gupta, O. K. (2006). Web-data mining: A case study. *Communications of the IIMA, 6*(4), 59-64.

Jones, S. L.(2009). Intelligent grid of computations. In J. Kacprzyk (Ed.), *Advances in Soft and Intelligent Computing* Vol. 56: Sixth International Symposium on Neural Networks. H. Wang, Y. Shen, T. Huang, Z. Zeng (Eds.) (pp. 131-136). New York: Springer.

Jones, S. L. (2009). Pattern recognition in a virtual world. *Integrated Learning and Management Journal, 13*(1), 1-13.

Kebritchi, M., Hirumi, A., & Bai, H. (2010). The effects of modern mathematics computer games on mathematics achievement and class motivation. *Computers & Education, 55*, 427-443.

King, D. L. (2001). From calculus to topology: Teaching lecture-free seminar courses at all levels of the undergraduate mathematics curriculum. *Primus: Problems, Resources, and Issues in Mathematics Undergraduate Studies, 11*(3), 209.

Liang Yu, Gang Zhou, Yifei Pu (2011). An Improved Task Scheduling Algorithm in Grid Computing Environment. *Intarnational Journal of Communications, Network and System Sciences.* Vol. 4. No. 4 .

Lucia, A. D., Rancese, R., Passero, I., & Tortora, G. (2009). Development and evaluation of a virtual campus on Second Life: The case of SecondDMI. *Computers & Education, 52*, 220-233.

Maggelakis, S., & Lutzer, C. (2007). Optimizing student success in calculus. *Primus: Problems, Resources, and Issues in Mathematics Undergraduate Studies, 17*(3), 284-291.

Mwavita, M. (2005). *Factors influencing calculus course success among freshmen engineering students.* (Doctoral dissertation). Available from Dissertations and Theses database. (UMI No. 3167614)

Mendez, C. G. (2006). Teaching calculus and other challenging courses to nontraditional and at-risk students at a research university. *College Teaching, 54*(4), 291-297.

Neel, Mehta (2011). Predictive Data Mining and discovering hidden values of data warehouse. *ARPN Journal of Systems and Software. Vol. 1. No.1.*

Olson, J. C., Knott, L., & Currie, G. (2009). Discursive practices in college pre-calculus classes. In L. Knott (Ed.), *The Role of Mathematics Discourse in Producing Leaders of Discourse* (pp. 41-59). Charlotte, NC :Information Age Publishing.

Ozel, S., Yetkiner, E. Z., & Capraro, R.M. (2008). Technology in K-12 mathematics classrooms. *School Science and Mathematics, 108*(2), 80-85.

SAS (2010). Best Practices for Data Sharing in Grid Distributed SAS Environment. *SAS white paper, July 2010*

Shaughnessy, M. (1994). Scores on the 16 personality factor questionnaire and success in college calculus. *Psychological Reports, 75*(1), 348-350.

Stephens, L., & Buchalter, B. (1987). Implementing a calculus placement procedure. *International Journal of Mathematical education in Science and Technology, 18*, 621-623.

Smith, R. M., & Schumacher, P. A. (2005). Predicting success for actuarial students in undergraduate mathematics courses. *College Student Journal, 39*(1), 165-177.

Smith, T. Y. (1995). *The retention status of underrepresented minority students: An analysis of survey results from sixty-seven U. S. colleges and universities*. Paper presented at the Association for Institutional Research Annual Forum, Boston, MA.

Subramanian, P. I., Cates, M., & Gutarts, B. (2009). Improving calculus success rates at California State University Los Angeles. *Mathematics and Computer Education, 43*(3), 259-269.

Su, H. F., Marinas, C., & Furner, J. M. (2010). Connecting the numbers in the primary grades using an interactive tool. *Australian Primary Mathematics Classroom, 15*(1), 25-28.

Yushau, B., & Omar, M. H. (2007). Preparatory year program courses as predictors of first calculus course grade. *Mathematics and Computer Education, 41*(2), 92-108.

Part 2

E-Learning Tools

5

Lego Based Computer Communication for Business and Learning

Rapelang Marumo
Department of Mechanical Engineering, University of Botswana, Gaborone, Botswana

1. Introduction

First launched in 1998, LEGO® MINDSTORMS® for Schools (LMfS) and ROBOLAB™, each year have helped countless students grasp science, technology, engineering, and mathematics concepts with hands-on, naturally motivating building sets, programming software, and curriculum relevant activity materials. Hands-on experiences are vital to stimulate the interest of students. One of the key challenges of undergraduate engineering education is providing students with this experience that includes solid theoretical underpinnings and a clear connection to industrial practice. Nowhere is it truer than in engineering, process control, mechatronics and robotics. Just about a decade ago, LEGO introduced a new line of kits called MindStorms that focused on robotics. LEGO MindStorm education is the next generation in educational robotics, enabling students to discover science, technology, engineering and mathematics in a fun, encouraging hands – on way. At the heart of these kits is the microcomputer called the RCX brick. It is a completely programmable LEGO brick with three power outputs and three sensor inputs. Students want to know what awaits them when have completed their mathematics, computer studies and science courses. By combining the power of the LEGO building system with the LEGO MindStorm education technology, teams of students can design, build, program and test robots. Showing students interesting future possibilities will help motivate them and encourage them to continue, where many students might otherwise drop or change fields. LEGO MindStorm is the ideal equipment to do the trick. This unit accomplishes three goals; it creates interest in robotics, engineering and science and it also encourages creativity and team work among students. Working together on guided and open ended engineering projects, the team members develop creativity and problem solving skills along with other important mathematics and science knowledge. Students also become more skilled in communication, organization and research, which help prepare them for future success in higher levels of schooling and in the work place. Although the MindStorms kit is a wonderful way to teach students about robotics, it is limited to a dry environment, such as class room floor. For the past decade, the MindStorms have been used in computer science resources to teach concepts from object-oriented programming (Barnes D., 2002) to artificial intelligence (Klassner F., 2002). They have been used to introduce students to the exciting world of computers (Weisheit F., 2004). The LEGO robots are often said to increase the interest of students in computing courses and they make class work more fun and exciting.

1.1 Problem statement

Technology has advanced a great deal since the beginning of the 20th century. The workplace and especially the industry have had evident and visible use of modern technology in handling operations and conducting other works. Today, the main work a human being does is manufacturing or designing and programming a device to perform certain tasks.

From another point, if students have to make projects in the machine shop, they cannot make very complicated parts. With Lego bricks, they can prototype far more quickly, and the complexity of the part correspondingly increases. The same is true with the software such as LabVIEW that allows rapid software prototyping and students can develop much more complicated software without many of the difficulties associated with a syntactical language. By letting students create the experiment themselves, rather than giving them a canned experiment, one can get them more excited about and more involved in what they are learning.

1.2 Objective of the research work

Objective of the project are:

- To learn the basic interfacing of different software; LabVIEW and Mindstorm NXT in modeling a simple industrial tool to carry out and execute assigned duties.
- To apply the virtual instruments and the Lego mind storm in the workplace.
- To advance technology, especially in the developing countries, in making it known to the people that a human operated task can be performed by programmed equipment.
- To take the engineering technology to the people i.e. promoting engineering for the society.

In this work, the problem of developing a laboratory kit that allows students to go through all steps of synthesizing a control system, a dynamic system and a process plant is addressed. Students assembled the process they were controlling, including placing sensors and control valves, using a collection of process units, pipes and fittings that have simple quick release connectors. It must be noted that to accomplish these student learning goals, the laboratory kits should be an inexpensive flexible system that:

- Can easily be used for open ended projects
- Are inexpensive enough that multiple steps can be easily purchased
- Are portable
- Require only standard power and water so setups can be used outside traditional laboratory facility
- Can be used as a lecture demonstration or active learning exercise in a regular class session
- Are simple and safe enough to be used by unsupervised students for out of class assignments
- Allow for application to various other engineering classes in future

1.3 Scope and summary of the research work

With e-learning emerging from the shadow of its post-dot.com readjustments, an entire generation of new practitioners is being drawn to e-learning for the first time (Sehurutshi et., al 2009). The virtual instrument and Lego Mindstorm is a laboratory set up which is done to teach various people on how complicated projects can be made easier with the use of toys called Lego bricks. The NXT is actually a little computer and interface unit that you can

program to take sensor input from up to three inputs and react to that input by controlling the direction and speed of up to three motors. Combined with the technical parts, you can quickly build and program sophisticated, mobile, autonomous robots.
In this project, Lego bricks are built to perform different tasks. The NXT robot was programmed manually with different configurations. Each sensor was tested with a short program and it worked very well. Upon testing all sensors, (sound, light, ultrasonic and touch sensors) the software was used to develop exercises comprising of a combination of different sensors. The results of testing the brick manually and with the NXT software were the same.
The main components of the project are LabVIEW and Mindstorm NXT softwares. It is with these softwares that our focus is on. The NXT is actually a little computer and interface unit that that can be programmed to take sensor input from up to three inputs and react to that input by controlling the direction and speed of up to three motors. Combined with the technical parts, sophisticated program can be built quickly to control mobile, autonomous robots. It is an autonomous Lego microcomputer that can be programmed using a PC. The NXT serves as the brain of Lego Mindstorms inventions. It uses sensors to take input from its environment, process data, and signals output motors to turn on and off. Users first build their robot using the NXT and Lego elements. They then create a program for their invention using NXT code, a simple yet powerful programming language. Next, the program can be downloaded to the NXT using a special infrared transmitter. The creations can now interact with the environment, and fully independent.

1.4 Related work

In 1989 Martin created the MIT Robot Design course following from Flowers' Introduction to Design course that was offered in the Mechanical Engineering department. The work on this project culminated into a textbook (Martin F., 1989). Students learn about the basics of building robots from kits and the course ends with a contest. Yanco in 2001 has adopted this course using the Bot-ball game as the tournament at the end of the term (Martin F., 2000). Mataric in 1998 has developed an award winning course called Introduction to Robotics (Yanco H., 2001) which takes a hands-on approach to the field of robotics. Students use both Handy board microcontroller and Lego MindStorms system. Another introductory course on robotics that uses Lego MindStorms is the Building Intelligent Robots course taught by Dean at Brown in 2001 (Martaric M., 1998). A few people have developed courses using hands-on robotics that do not focus on teaching robotics as the main subject. Littman's course on Programming Under Uncertainty (Dean T., 2001) teaches about a variety of methods for programming as its title says, under uncertainty, including Markov Decision Process and POMDP's and variety of machine learning techniques like reinforcement learning and genetic algorithms. Students in this course used Lego robots to demonstrate their knowledge to the methodologies studied. The course ended in a project, where some of the students developed their own application for their robots, from line-following task to making breakfast. One of these, described in (Littman M., 1999), carried out on-line reinforcement learning to complete a task analogous to the pole-balancing-an indication of what is possible at the upper limit of the MindStorms capabilities. Since 2001, Klassner has been teaching introductory artificial intelligence using Lego MindStorms and Russel & Norvig followed in 2003 (Baum D., 2000b and Klassner F., 2001) . Klassner's students make extensive use of the robots and are supported by tools developed by Klassner and his colleagues (Klassner F., and Anderson S 2003). These extend the capabilities of the RCX, making use of the infra-red communication built into the unit (normally used for downloading programs) to allow off-board control. The description of the robot blocks maybe as shown in Table 1.

First Block	Introduction the basics of MindStorms, such as the RCX, RCX code, motors and sensors. Construction of a robot that uses a single touch sensor to avoid objects
Second Block	Introduction to the NQC (Not Quite C) and the RCX command center (RCXCC) Program first robot using the RCXCC and modification to use two touch sensors to go around obstacles
Third Block	Construction of robot that is capable of following a black line on a white paper using RCXCC
Fourth Block	Introduction to the datalog on the RCX Introduction to the first major project, students must map the reflectivity of the bottom of a prepared box
Fifth Block	Completion of remote sensing project
Sixth Block	Introduction to the final project; the creation of a robot animal, an environment, and a non-Lego component of the robot
Seventh Block	Presentation of the results

Table 1. Description of robot blocks.

1.5 The heart of Lego Mindstorm

The RCX is capable of outputting a maximum of 700mA and 9V through each of its power outputs. This translates into 6.3 Watts, which is very small amount of power. Because of this limited supply, LEGO manufactured motors are the most efficient to use for the ROV because they are already rated for such a low power level. LEGO MINDSTORMS for school is a modular concept for teaching groups of children from pre-University level in a classroom or after-school club environment. It is made up of core construction and add-on resource sets, a software program, and curriculum relevant activity packs.

1.6 The next technology now

LEGO MindStorms education features an advanced 32-bit computer controlled NXT brick, interactive servo motors, sound, ultrasonic and other sensors, Bluetooth communication and multiple downloading capabilities. The icon-based LEGO MindStorm education NXT software is built on the Lab View software from National Instruments, an industry standard with applications in many engineering and research fields. The LEGO MINDSTORMS for school software, called ROBOLAB, is developed specifically for teachers or adults working with groups of children. The program is icon-based, which means that youngsters can visualize the instructions they are stringing together for their robot. It provides basic, intermediate, and advance programming techniques including data logging.

1.7 Introduction to LEGO Mindstorms for schools & ROBOLAB overview

ROBOLAB is a powerful programming language that can be used by students at all levels. It was developed by the partnership between Tufts University, LEGO Education and National

Instruments. The ROBOLAB software is based on Lab VIEW, the software that was used to control the Sojourner rover on Mars in 1997. In Lab VIEW, programs are called virtual instruments (VI). In the professional edition of Lab VIEW, the software uses a computer as a virtual instrument. The Lab VIEW program is then used to acquire and analyze data. ROBOLAB programs are saved as .vi files. There are different programming levels within ROBOLAB. The Pilot and Inventor sections of ROBOLAB are based on the Lab VIEW programming language. It is an icon-driven language based on a logical sequencing if images and is basically independent of written language.

The Pilot section of ROBOLAB is made up of a series of templates that have a format associated with them. It is an easy way to introduce the logical sequence to students. The user can not modify the templates and therefore the program will always work. The program will always run each time and do the commands as listed in the sequence presented. The Inventor section of ROBOLAB uses the same command icons as in Pilot. There are more command icons as the user moves into higher levels of the program. Inventor is less structured allowing for greater potential for the software. The Investigator section allows users to collect and analyze data and create projects. It includes all the features of the ROBOLAB Programmer. Project management features are built into ROBOLAB Investigator. They include all the components needed to investigate questions with the RCX inventions. This includes writing programs, uploading data, viewing data, computing with data and documentation of that data. This software runs on either PC or Mac. The PC version requires Windows 98. There are several new features in this version:

USB support
Piano Player - updated musical support
Extended help features
Digital camera interface
New RCX firmware
Web support
Auto wiring of icons
Pilot - level capability for uploading a program from RCX to computer

The RCX Brick (Robotic Command Explorer)

As already mentioned, the heart of the system is the RCX, i.e. an autonomous LEGO microcomputer that can be programmed with either a PC or Mac computer. The RCX can be considered the "brain" of the system. It uses sensors to take input from its environment, to process data and to signal output motors and lamps to turn on and off. Students build their device using the RCX and the LEGO pieces in the building sets. They then create a program for their device using the ROBOLAB programming language. They then download their program to the RCX using the infrared transmitter. Their device can now interact with the environment, totally autonomous of the computer. There are 3 output ports - A, B, and C. These are connection points for LEGO motors, lights and other sensors. There are 3 input ports - 1, 2 and 3. These are connection points for sensors such as: touch sensor that turns the motors on and off when activated. Light sensor that allows RCX to differentiate between light and dark. Temperature sensor that distinguishes between varying degrees of temperature. Additional sensors are available for data logging.

The RCX brick has an infrared eye that allows the brick to communicate with the computer via the infrared transmitter (IR). It must be aimed towards the IR transmitter to function. Firmware is the RCX operating system level software. It must be downloaded to the RCX before the RCX can receive and execute a program from the computer. The firmware remains in the RCX memory until the batteries are removed. If batteries are changed quickly, this will not affect the memory. An external power supply can also be used to save on batteries.

Fig. 1. LECO MindStorm.

The Lego MindStorms can yell & spin, catch & run, record & play.

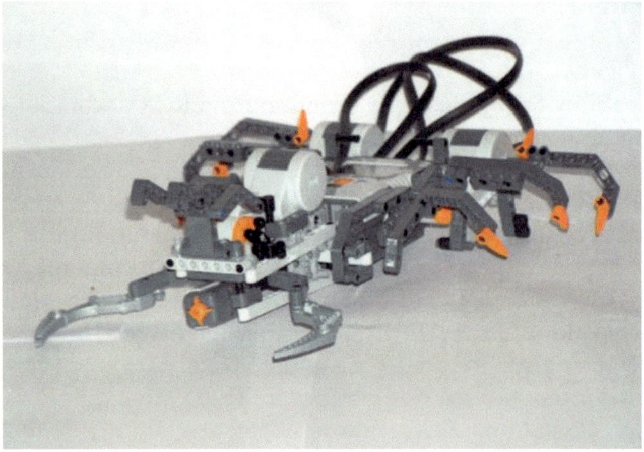

Fig. 2. MindStorm NXT.

What it comes down to is that, with the combination of the mechanical flexibility of the Legos and the connectivity and ease of programming of the brick, students are no longer limited by execution and even those without masters in mechatronics can take crazy ideas and make them into a reality. These applications can all be downloaded from the MINDSTORMS website, and they represent just a small sampling of the crazy inventions that these Lego users are devising when they are limited only by their imagination.

2. Research procedures

The MINDSTORMS® equipment is located in the Instrumentation and Control laboratory room 2069/2 of Mechanical engineering Department. This project reflects the results of a review of literature about engineering classes taught at other Universities and proposed courses for the University of Botswana, Faculty of Engineering & Technology in the Department of Mechanical Engineering. Many Universities have incorporated MindStorms into introductory engineering classes because of their ease of use, relative cost effectiveness and ability to give hands - on experience with engineering projects while encouraging creative processes.

2.1 Control paradigm

In manual operation, the RCX delivers a constant 9V to each of its power outputs, and the remote operated vehicle (ROV)'s motors are controlled by switching the current flow with Double Pole Double Throw (DPDT) rockers switches. When the rocker switch is in the neutral position, no current flows. When it is switched forward, the current flows and the motor turns forward. When the DPDT is switched backward, the poles are reversed, resulting in the current flowing backwards, making the motor to turn backwards. Additionally, in each motor's control circuit is a manual override Double Poles single Throw (DPST) switch to give RCX direct control of the motor. With this switch, autonomous control can be turned on and off for motor individually, so the operator has the option of the RCX is controlling one function while another function controlled manually. One application of this ability would be the (ROV) hovering. The RCX would monitor the pressure and adjust the vertical thrusters while the operator could still manually drive in the horizontal plane.

The general control box design is a container for the RCX that is held with two hands on either side. The top has two horizontal motor control switch sets in reach of the thumbs in addition to the three switches. Each subroutine switch hooks directly into one of the sensor inputs and so when it is tripped it shorts out that input. In the ROBOLAB program a shorted input will return the maximum value of the sensor programmed to be hooked up to that input. When the maximum value is reached, the program can be triggered to do the task. This makes it possible for a manual switch to run a subroutine. The front of the box has the connection to the tether as a well as the vertical motor control switch set which is in reach of the index fingers. Additionally, the box has an AC adaptor input on its left side.

2.1.1 Control algorithm

As mentioned earlier, the LEGO RCX brick provides the computer interface. Control systems were constructed using ROBOLAB investigator software which is an adaptation of the National Instrument's LabVIEW software. The sensor is read and its raw reading is converted to 0 to 100% range. This signal is sent to a discrete (Proportional Integral Derivative) PID velocity algorithm (Riggs, James B, 2001), which outputs a change in valve position. The signal from the controller can be positive or negative depending on which way the motor should go. The programs integrate both LabVIEW and ROBOLAB languages.

2.1.2 Data logging program

This program's function is to collect data from a sensor connected to the RCX and to display that data in real time. Once the data collection is completed, the user may save it to a text file

in order for it to be used for analysis. Typical examples that students performed include step test (sudden increase in control valve position) and height of the liquid in the tank recorded by he data logging program of the Siemens programmable controllers (PLC). The program also allows for user control of a flow control valve so that, a change in valve position can be logged along with the resulting sensor reading. The data could be transferred to control station (Cooper, Doug, 2002) or a spreadsheet and a First Order Plus Dead Time model for the system can be obtained.
Another feature of this program is its calibration element. The user may enter a maximum and minimum calibration value to coincide with the raw value of 0 and 1023. Raw numbers are the values recorded by the RCX when receiving a signal from a sensor. The user can get the computer to output the actual raw values by altering calibration values in a range of 0 to 100% of a given attribute (i.e. full scale defection, span or reading) or the actual height of a liquid in a vessel.

2.1.3 Control program

The program collects data from a sensor, enters the value into a PID equation, which outputs a value to represent necessary valve position change. Like the data logging program, all of this occurs within a while loop which runs until the user presses the stop button. The front panel consists of a chart, which displays the calibrated sensor value and another chart, which displays the motor outputs. The front panel also has fields which enable the user to control setpoint as well as the tuning parameters of the controller.

2.2 LEGO education resources (eLab example)

The LEGO Education eLAB series introduces students to concepts of energy; allowing them to take the next natural step in the development of their scientific and technological knowledge and experience.
With a unique combination of LEGO® System sets, a motor, solar panel and capacitor, students can investigate how to generate, store and use sources of energy. The eLAB Renewable Energy Set allows students to build and test realistic models of wind and water mills, and a solar-powered Ferris wheel.
LEGO Education offers a scheme of work to use with the Renewable Energy Set, consisting of 49 activities designed to help students explore, investigate and solve problems.
Find out how to use the eLAB series together with the intelligent LEGO brick, the RCX, which features in the LEGO® MINDSTORMS® for Schools series.

2.2.1 Science & technology

Science and Technology solutions from LEGO Education help teachers to capitalize on students' natural curiosity and enthusiasm about the world around them. Tools and design tasks for exploration and experimentation are provided, so that teachers can introduce the basics and let students try out their own ideas. Students build structures and simple machines and mechanisms, and test forces and motion. They experiment with the functions of wheels and axles, gears, levers and pulleys. They investigate the effects of friction and gravity on speed, and explore sources of energy. The series starts with a range of LEGO® DUPLO® construction sets for year 2 dynamics (MMB 222 course) students and continues with LEGO® System and eLAB sets that introduce motorized power and other forms of energy such as wind and solar power, for students in subsequent years.

3. Lego MindStorm as teaching tool for mechatronics, measurement & instrumentation courses

Information and Automation Technology will be part of the future careers of virtually all students in Mechanical Engineering, Faculty of Engineering & Technology (FET of the university of Botswana (Marumo., 2007). Traditionally students are exposed to a course in a higher order computer language, which is perceived by many students as unexciting and tedious. To introduce students to automation in a far more challenging and exciting manner, LEGO Mindstorms will be used in the following courses: measurement and instrumentation and mechatronic, robotics, process control and systems & control. The LEGO Mindstorms kits contain a programmable brick which essentially is a micro controller built in a plastic LEGO package with three connectors for actuators (motors) and three sensor inputs such as switches, optical analog sensors, angle encoders etc. The micro controller has an infrared serial link through which programs can be uploaded and executed. The brick also has buttons to start, stop, and select programs and to check the status of actuators and sensors in real time. The Mindstorms brick can be programmed in a variety of languages. LEGO supplies its proprietary pictorial ladder-style language, there is NQC (Not Quite C), which is a C-derivative, and advanced users can even use C/C++ that runs on a dedicated operating system called BrickOS. Robolab is a pictorial programming environment, where actuators, sensors and control structures are joined together has shown to be very suitable for students with no procedural language background. The reason for selecting this language was the widespread use of Lab View in industry and the basic philosophy behind it. Users select components and attach modifiers to change their properties. Components are linked using a wiring tool very similar to building electrical circuits.

3.1 Mechatronics, measurements & instrumentation courses

The objectives of the LEGO Mindstorms projects are:

- To introduce the concepts of Automation to undergraduate students in B Eng Degree programmes
- Develop communication skills among students
- Exercise critical thinking and engineering design principles
- Promote enthusiasm for studying engineering
- Develop skills of graphical programming
- Enforce precision automation concepts
- Promote creativity and engaged learning
- Experience the feeling of accomplishment by completing a group design

The mechatronic design projects assigned in mechatronics course involve students' teams designing and developing mobile robotic platforms using Lego components. The activities will not only inspire students' creativity but also enhance their strength in engineering design course

3.2 Pilot programming

The RCX programming software has two options or phases. These are Pilot and Inventor. Pilot is the introductory section of the ROBOLAB software. A "click and choose" interface is utilized within a template. There are four levels of Pilot and these serve as an introduction to

ROBOLAB programming. Level 1 is the easiest and Level 4 has more flexibility. Each level builds on the previous one. There are limitations within this section but it is a simple way for users to become familiar with the software. The Pilot Level 1 template is a simple task that introduces students to the programming features of ROBOLAB. Each level of Pilot provides additional flexibility and options. Students will always be successful in their programming within Pilot.

4. Dynamics course

The design of a low-cost balancing robot is accomplished by using a popular development platform plint pack for the components and Lego for the construction material. The balancing robot is intended to improve the learning experience of students or hobbyists who are interested in control of mechanical components by presenting hands-on experiments and controller design examples that anyone would be able to follow easily and cost effectively.

4.1 System description

The system consists of motors, wheels, and two pairs of spur gears that connect the motors and the wheels. The spur gear was added because the motor shaft was not long enough to support the distance required by the optical encoder. The optical encoder requires some space between the striped disk and the optical sensors to read black and white. The top stage consists of a microcontroller and an H-bridge. The microcontroller is the brain of the robot and is responsible for sampling and processing all the data collected by the sensors. The H-bridge is used with the microcontroller to control the directions of the motors. There is one more sensor attached to a vertical strut between the two stages. In general it is called an Inertial Measurement Unit, (IMU), and this one contains two accelerometers and one gyro to determine the robot's attitude in one angular direction.

4.2 System modeling

To make the project simple and manageable, only a two-dimensional movement in which the system moves in one plane will be considered. The two motors are assumed to move together symmetrically when an identical input is given. Although this is unlikely the case, it is a good approximation for motors which are manufactured as the same product. A control voltage is applied to the motors, which results in displacement of the wheels and change in angular attitude of the body. A mathematical model for the system is obtained by observing the free body diagram.

4.3 Actuator assembly dynamics

There are two fundamental equations describing the characteristics of a DC motor. The first one relates torque (τ) on the shaft proportional to the armature current (I) and the second expresses the back emf voltage (e) proportional to the shaft's rotational velocity (ω_{enc}), where ω_{enc} represent the velocity measured by the encoder mounted on the same frame as the DC motor. This velocity represents the shaft velocity with respect to the DC motor itself.

$$\tau = Ki \tag{1}$$

$$e = K_e \omega_{enc} \tag{2}$$

4.4 Body dynamics

The rotational motion of the pendulum body about its center of gravity can be described by

$$I\ddot{\theta} = -2\tau + -2Hl\cos\theta + 2Vl\sin\theta \tag{3}$$

where I is the moment of inertia of the pendulum body about its center of gravity. The horizontal force, vertical force and torque are applied as pairs on both sides and each pair is assumed to be equal because only two-dimensional motion was considered.
The horizontal motion is given by:

$$2H = M\frac{d^2}{dt^2}(x + l\sin\theta) \tag{4}$$

The linearised equations are:

$$I\ddot{\theta} = -2\tau - 2Hl + 2Vl\theta \tag{5}$$

$$2H = M\left(\ddot{x} + l\ddot{\theta}\right) \tag{6}$$

$$2V = Mg \tag{7}$$

4.5 System dynamics

The objective here is to find suitable ordinary differential equations that fully describe the system in terms of input v, the states x, θ and their derivatives $\dot{x}, \dot{\theta}$. The following formulae describes how to characterize the essence of the system in two differential equations.

$$\tau = \left(\frac{J}{r} + rm + \frac{rM}{2}\right)\ddot{x} + \frac{rMl}{2}\ddot{\theta} \tag{8}$$

$$\frac{R}{K}\left(\frac{J}{r} + rm + \frac{rM}{2}\right)\ddot{x} + \frac{R\tau Ml}{2K}\ddot{\theta} + \frac{K}{r}\dot{x} - K\dot{\theta} = \upsilon \tag{9}$$

$$\left(I + rMl + ml^2\right)\ddot{\theta} + 2\left(\frac{J}{r} + rm + \frac{rM + lM}{2}\right)\ddot{x} - Mgl\theta = 0 \tag{10}$$

Finally the overall equation yields:

$$\left(I + rMl + Ml^2\right)\ddot{\theta} + 2\left(\frac{J}{r} + rm + \frac{rM + lM}{2}\right)\ddot{x} - Mgl\theta = 0 \tag{11}$$

These equations describe the motion of the system and constitute the two-dimensional linearized mathematical model of the system. Finally this set of equations can be expressed in a more convenient state space form:

$$\begin{bmatrix} \dot{x} \\ \dot{\theta} \\ \ddot{x} \\ \ddot{\theta} \end{bmatrix} = \begin{bmatrix} 0 & 0 & 1 & 0 \\ 0 & 0 & 0 & 1 \\ 0 & A_{32} & A_{33} & A_{34} \\ 0 & A_{42} & A_{43} & A_{44} \end{bmatrix} \begin{bmatrix} x \\ \theta \\ \dot{x} \\ \dot{\theta} \end{bmatrix} + \begin{bmatrix} 0 \\ 0 \\ B3 \\ B4 \end{bmatrix} \upsilon \tag{12}$$

The unknown properties, J, M, m, r, K and R should be obtained by direct or experimental measurements.

4.6 Sensors

In here, inertia measurement unit (IMU) is developed by an open source approach from the Kalman filter. The graphs below illustrate how the Kalman filter can be useful in fusing single-axis angular attitudes collected separately. Ideally a jig would be required to provide an absolute reference angle at any given moment, but since the data will only be used as an observational reference and not in the core algorithm itself, it is reasonable to do without a costly jig and roughly compare data from the two sources, accelerometer unit and gyro unit and ultimately with the Kalman filtering results

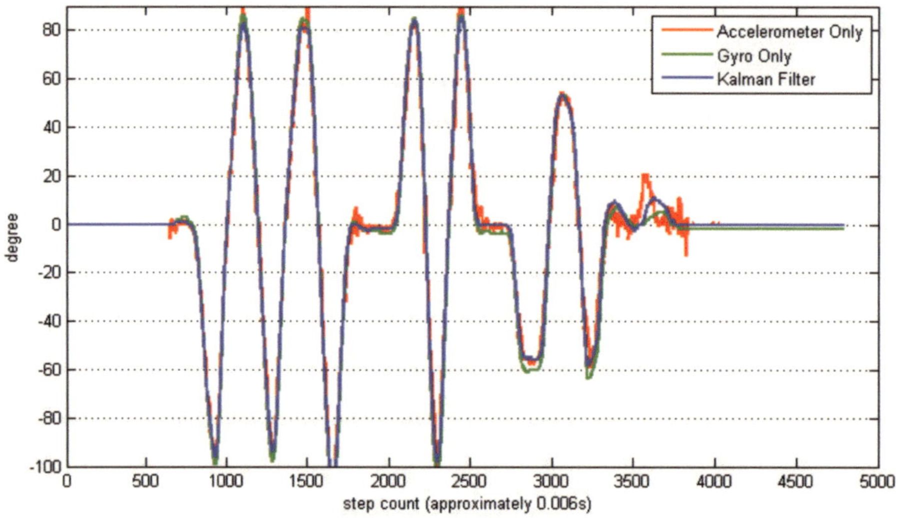

Fig. 3. Steady motion using Kalman filter.

Figure 3 represents a response to a steady movement. The Y-axis indicates the angle in degrees and the X-axis is the step count or sampling count from the microcontroller. Usually when implementing a microcontroller a task is programmed to be executed in a routine basis, but the experiment may also be operated in an endless loop without any delay time allowing the Euler Integration to produce higher quality results. It can be observed that both units reflect the angle quite similarly. The experiment was not long enough to catch the drift of the gyro but overall all data seemed to be reliable. So it was necessary to provide a harsh environment to intentionally invoke degradation in data. The next experiment was performed in a hard shaking circumstance.

Figure 4 shows interesting results. The IMU board was not only rotated radically but also shaken in order to generate lateral acceleration. The lateral acceleration introduces noise to the system so that by using accelerometers alone one cannot measure where about the angular attitude is. At the end of the shaking process the gyro reveals an offset compared to the angle provided by the accelerometer. In this case the accelerometer is more reliable and the offset can be considered as an integration propagation error or a continuous drift angle.

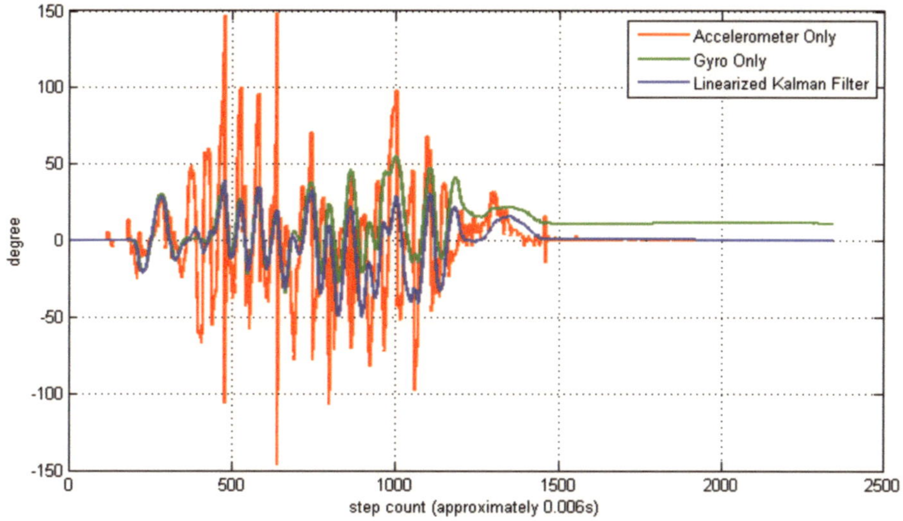

Fig. 4. Unsteady motion measurement using Kalman filter.

It is very interesting to observe that the Kalman filter is following well the patterns of the gyro in a very noisy environment, whereas, at the end of the shaking process the sensor is stable; it pertains to the more accurate accelerometer data.

5. Digital control for the motor position

One of the easiest ways may be through implementing a controller for the DC Motor. A digital controller for position reference will transform the DC motor to behave like a servo. The code for the controller was generated using the MATLAB Real time Toolbox Embedded encoder. To confirm the DC motor model, a simple proportional control was designed and implemented.

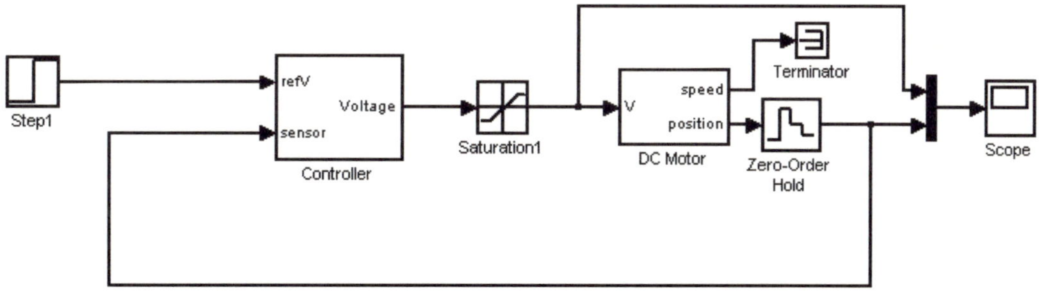

Fig. 5. Block diagram for motor position control.

Figures 6 and 7 illustrate the simulation result versus the real data. The rise time is shorter in reality. This is probably because of the sensor dynamics that was not considered in simulation. In reality the encoder has large quantization error. When conducting this experiment 64 lines were used by the encoder. This means 5.6 degrees was the maximum precision the sensors could have which is quite poor. After this experiment the sensitivity was increased by a factor of 2 to achieve greater accuracy in position and velocity values. The gain value used in this experiment was 2, and the step input was 90 degrees.

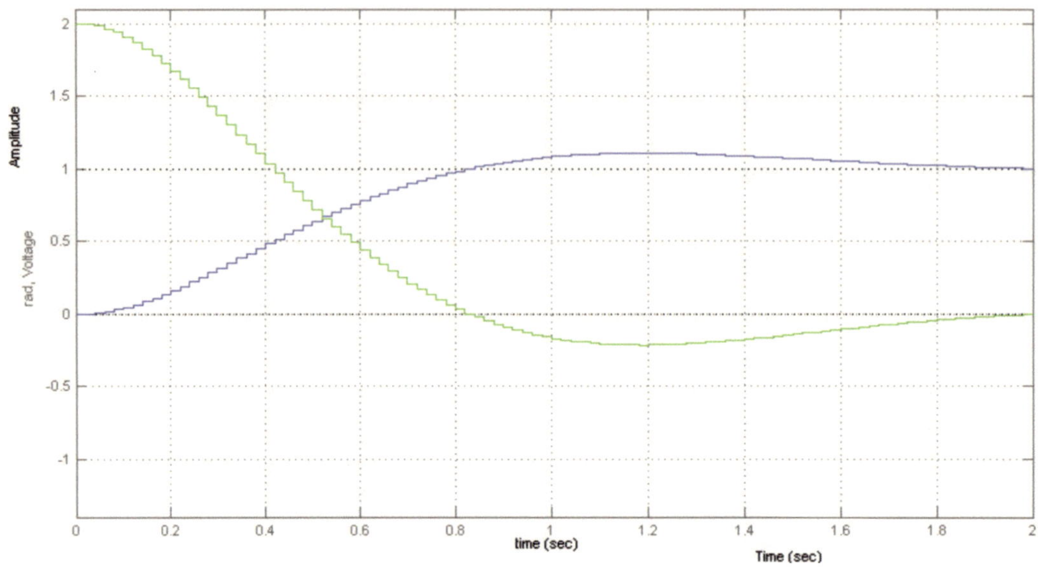

Fig. 6. Simulated results versus real data - continous.

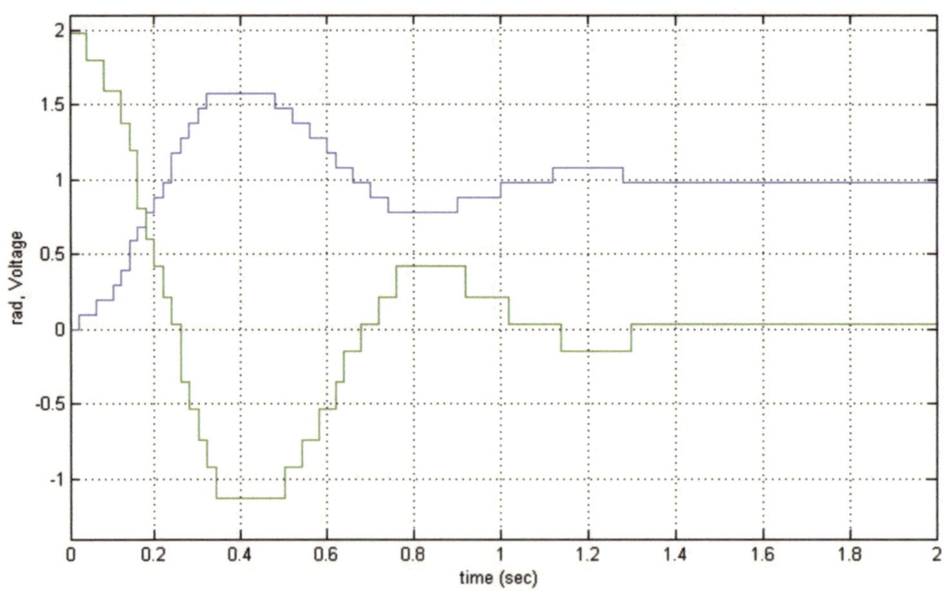

Fig. 7. Simulated results versu real data - digital.

6. Digital control root locus

In this experiment Control System Toolbox in Matlab, more especially 'sisotool' was used to design a Root Locus Controller by applying a gain and placing poles and zeros. Several designs were devised that looked robust in theory, but performed not as well. The difference of theory and practice became prominent as the solution required greater control effort. While the control design technique was intended for linear systems, the effect of saturation was becoming more outstanding in the real world.

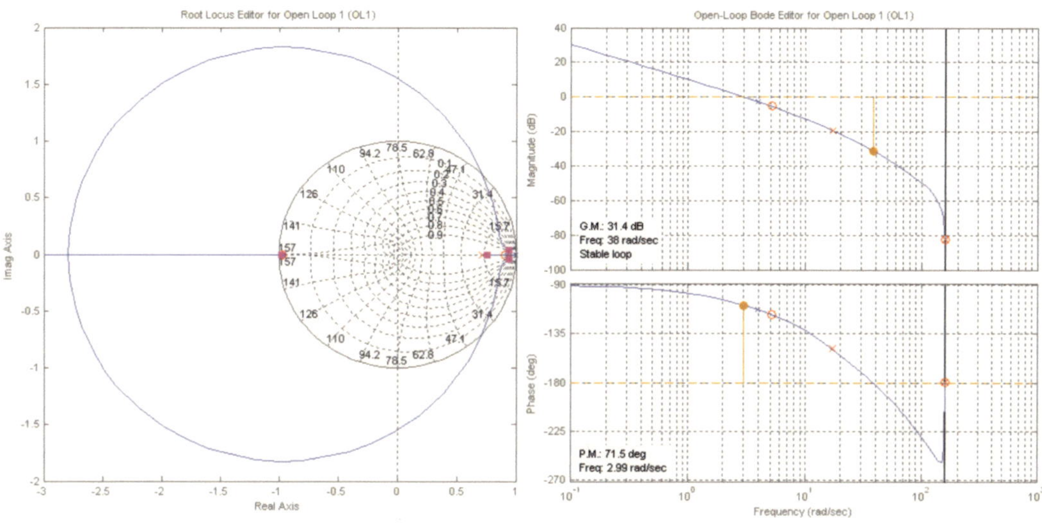

Fig. 8. Root locus plot of motor position control.

One of the working designs is presented. The control effort was designed to be kept below the saturation point; however the same quantization error that occurred in Proportional Control experiment was also observable here as well.

7. Hands-on artificial intelligence education

Educational researchers have long suggested that instruction utilizing a variety of delivery modes helps students with differing learning styles to better understand the studied material. Few, if any of us, would think about teaching our introductory programming courses solely via textbook readings and lecture. It is firmly believed that, to learn, students must "do." Thus, a variety of assignments and "labs" are provided that allow students to participate in both reflective practice in the classroom, and active practice in the computer lab. Thomas et al. (Thomas L., Ratclife M., Wodobury J., and Jarman E.,) have studied the success rate in traditional computer science courses by students exhibiting each of the different learning styles described in the work of (Richard Felder) and suggested that instruction targeted across styles greatly improves the performance of students from all styles, but in particular from those styles less prominent in the domain of computer science.

8. Conclusion

Lego Mindstorms kits have been be used as a tool to introduce automation concepts at the University of Botswana's undergraduate level courses in engineering. Robolab, which is a programming environment similar to Lab View, helped to enhance programming skills and strength for students in measurement & instrumentation course MMB 314. The acquired skill can then be used to programme very small components such as 8-pin PIC16F84 micro controller used by mechatronic students in course MMB 416. It is therefore evident to conclude that by tapping into the competitive human spirit and the fun of playing with Lego Minstorm robotic development will help to enrich the emphasis on the merit of using automation technology in precision instrumentation and mechatronics.

9. Acknowledgements

The results of this work are obtained within the University of Botswana's project research work No. R715 entitled "Control Education Survey & Machine Intelligence". The author thank the University of Botswana, office of research and development for financial support of this work.

It is recommended that the Department avails the necessary softwares in the rightful places to increase access to students when the need arises. There are currently four computers loaded with both NXT Mindstorm and LabVIEW softwares. The same computers are fully utilized when such softwares like Gambit, MATLAB, LabView and CAMaster are being used and when there are iterations going on, it is impossible use the computer for at least 24 hours. One thing which has puzzled us a lot is the fact that the PCs in the CAD/ cam center have loads of softwares and they usually will complain of low virtual memory. This really makes working difficult because amongst other things, the chances of these computers executing tasks successfully are very low.

It is further requested that the Department should avail all the items like; PLCs, DAQ plug in boards and transducers for signal conditioning- these will enable successful working environment with such VIs like LabVIEW.

10. References

Arai, T. & Kragic, D. (1999). Variability of Wind and Wind Power, In: *Wind Power,* S.M. Muyeen, (Ed.), 289-321, Scyio, ISBN 978-953-7619-81-7, Vukovar, Croatia

Barnes, D., Teaching Introductory Java through Lego Mindstorms Models. Proceedings of the 33rd SIGCSE technical Symposium on Computer Science education (SIGCSE 2002), Covington, Kentucky, 2002, pages 147-151

Baum, D., ed. 2000b. Extreme Mindstorms: An advanced guide to Lego Mindstorms: A press, New York

Cooper, Doug., 2002. Control Station Software for Process Control Analysis, Tuning and Training, Storrs, CT

Dean, T., 2001. CS148: Building intelligent without representation. Artificial intelligence 47:139-59.

Felder, R., Learning style strategies home page, http://www.ncsu.edu/felder~public/ILSdir/styles.htm http://sciyo.com/articles/show/title/wind-power-integrating-wind-turbine-generators-wtg-s-with-energy-storage

Klassner, F., 2001. Introduction to artificial intelligence. http://www.csc.vill.edu/`klassner/csc4500

Klassner, F., A case study of Lego Mindstorms Suitability for Artificial Intelligence and Robot Course at College the Level Proceedings of the 33rd SIGCSE technical Symposium on Computer Science education (SIGCSE 2002), Covington, Kentucky, 2002, pages 8-12

Klassner, F., and Anderson, S., 2003. Lego Mindstorms: Not just for K-12 anymore. IEEE robotics and automation (in press)

Lego mindstorms education NXT user guide manual

Li, B.; Xu, Y. & Choi, J. (1996). Applying Machine Learning Techniques, *Proceedings of ASME 2010 4th International Conference on Energy Sustainability*, pp. 14-17, ISBN 842-6508-23-3, Phoenix, Arizona, USA, May 17-22, 2010

Lima, P.; Bonarini, A. & Mataric, M. (2004). *Application of Machine Learning*, InTech, ISBN 978-953-7619-34-3, Vienna, Austria

Littman, M., 1999. CPS196: Programming under uncertainty. http://www.cs.duke.edu/`mlittman/courses/cps196

Martaric, M., 1998. CS 445 Introduction to robotics, a Lego-kit-based hands-on lab course. http://www-scf.usc.edu/-csci445/

Martin, F., 1989. 6.270: The MIT Lego robot design project competition. http://fredm.www.media.mit.edu/people/fredm/projects6270

Martin, F., 2000 Robotic explorations: A hands on introduction to engineering. Prentice Hall.

R. Marumo (2007), A proposal to Introduce LEGO® MindstormsTM Teaching Aids into University of Botswana's Engineering Programmes. Proceedings of the Botswana Institution of Engineers conference. Gaborone. Botswana, on CD, 17th - 19th October.

Riggs, James B., 2001. Chemical Process Control, Ferret Publishing, Lubbock TX, pp 221

Sehurutshi R, Marumo R and Wangombe K (2009), E-learning Platform for Education Innovation: A Case for Botswana. E-learning Journal. Volume 6 November (issue 4), pp. 351 - 362.

Siegwart, R. (2001). Indirect Manipulation of a Sphere on a Flat Disk Using Force Information. *International Journal of Advanced Robotic Systems*, Vol.6, No.4, (December 2009), pp. 12-16, ISSN 1729-8806

Thomas, L., Ratclife, M., Wodobury, J., and Jarman, E., learning styles and performance in introductory programming sequence. Proceedings on the 33rd SIGCS technical Symposium on Computer Science Education, pp 33-77.

Van der Linden, S. (June 2010). Integrating Wind Turbine Generators (WTG's) with Energy Storage, In: *Wind Power*, 17.06.2010, Available from

Weisheit, F., Using practical toys, modified for technical learning: A class aimed at increasing children's interest level in computer science. ACM Crossroads, Volume 10, Issue 6, 2004.

Yanco, H., 2001. 91.450: Robotics I. http://www.cs.uml.edu/`holly/91.450

6

Multimodal Intelligent Tutoring Systems

Xia Mao and Zheng Li
School of electronic and information engineering, Beihang University, Beijng
China

1. Introduction

Intelligent Tutoring Systems (ITS), also known as Intelligent E-learning Systems, is the task of providing individualized instruction, by being able to adapt to the knowledge, learning abilities and needs of each individual student. The offer of the ITS is increasing at an unrestrainable pace (Butz & Hua, 2006; Chen, 2008; Reategui & Boff, 2008; Roger, 2006). The "intelligence" in these systems is seen through the way they adapt themselves to the characteristics of the students, such as speed of learning, specific areas in which the student excels as well as falls behind, and rate of learning as more knowledge is learned. However, they are still not as effective as one-on-one human tutoring. We believe that an important factor in the success of human one-on-one tutoring is the tutor's ability to identify and respond to the student's attention information and affective state. In ITS, these two characteristics may give the student the sensation that there is someone behind the program who follows his learning development and cares about him as a human tutor would. In this paper, we propose the Multimodal Intelligent Tutoring Systems (MITS), which detects the attention information and affective state and uses the information to drive the agent tutor to individualize interaction with the learner.

2. Architecture for MITS

ITS is a computer-based educational system that provides individualized instruction like a human tutor. A traditional ITS decides how and what to teach based on the student pedagogical state. However, it has been demonstrated that an experienced human tutor can manage the attention information and affective state (besides the pedagogical state) of the student to motivate him and to improve the learning process. Therefore, the interface between the student and tutor in traditional ITS needs to be augmented to include attention information interface and affective information interface. ITS needs the ability of reasoning about the attention information and affective state to provide students with an adequate response from a pedagogical, attentive and affective point of view; in this sense, the module of attention information processing and affective information processing are required. The attention information processing module analyzes the gaze behavior of student in real-time and is capable of adapting the presentation flow according to the student's interest or non-interest. The affective information processing module analyzes the facial expression, speech and text input by the student to sense the underpinned affective qualities. Once the attention information and affective state have been obtained, the agent tutor has to respond accordingly. We must enable a mapping from the attention information and affective state to actions of the agent tutor. We refined our tutoring strategy module by means of questionnaires presented to teachers. In the questionnaires we presented several scenarios of tutoring and asked the teachers to give the appropriate pedagogical and affective action for each scenario. The affective action includes the facial expression, emotional speech synthesis and text that produced from the Artificial Intelligence Markup Language (AIML) Retrieval Mechanism. The Architecture of MITS can be seen in figure 1.

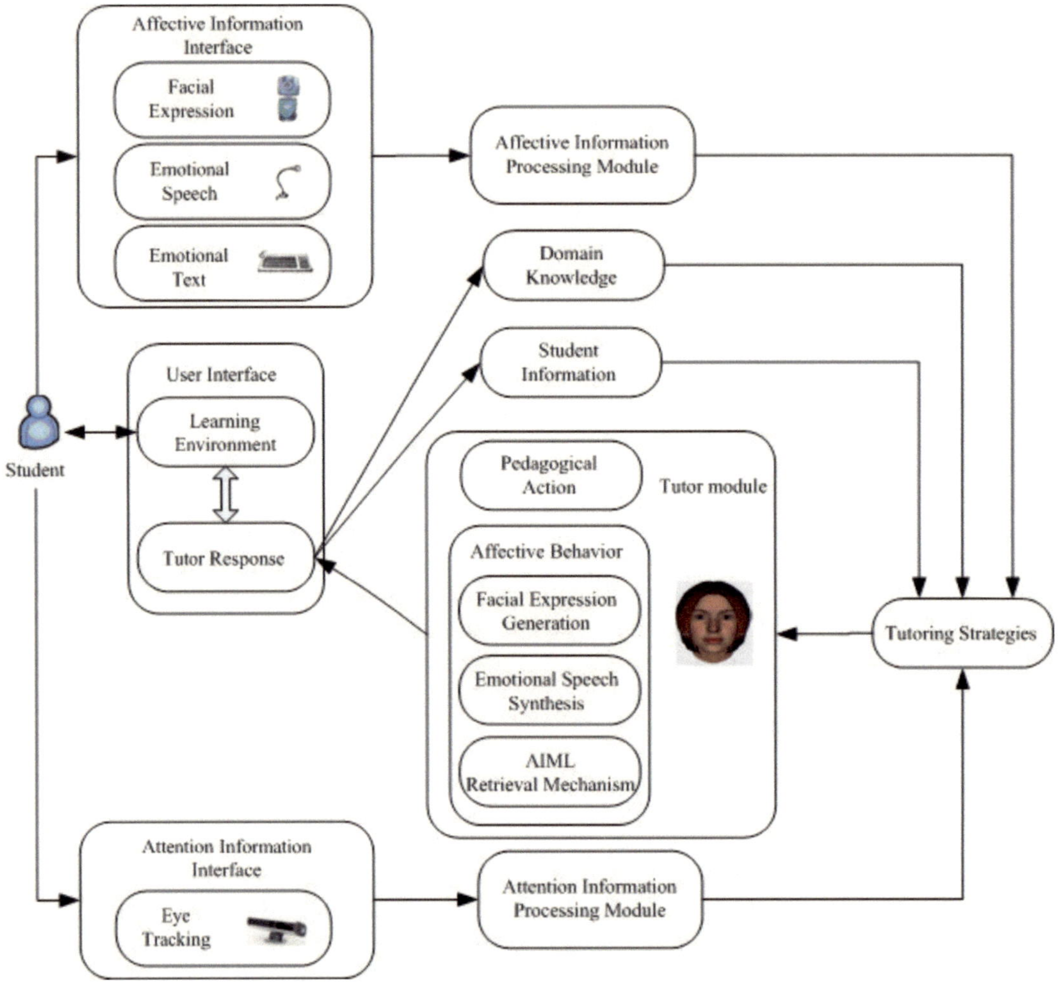

Fig. 1. Architecture of MITS.

3. Attention information

Being "a window to the mind", the eye and its movement are tightly coupled with human cognitive processes. In this paper, we use the eye tracker iView RED from SMI (IView RED. http://www.smivision.com/) to follow student's gaze. Eye movement provides an indication of student's interest and focus of attention. Screen areas that may trigger a system response when being looked at (or not looked at) are called "interest areas". Figure 2 illustrates one example of the interest areas. For each interest area, the interest score is calculated. When the score for an area exceeds a threshold, the agent will react if a reaction is defined.

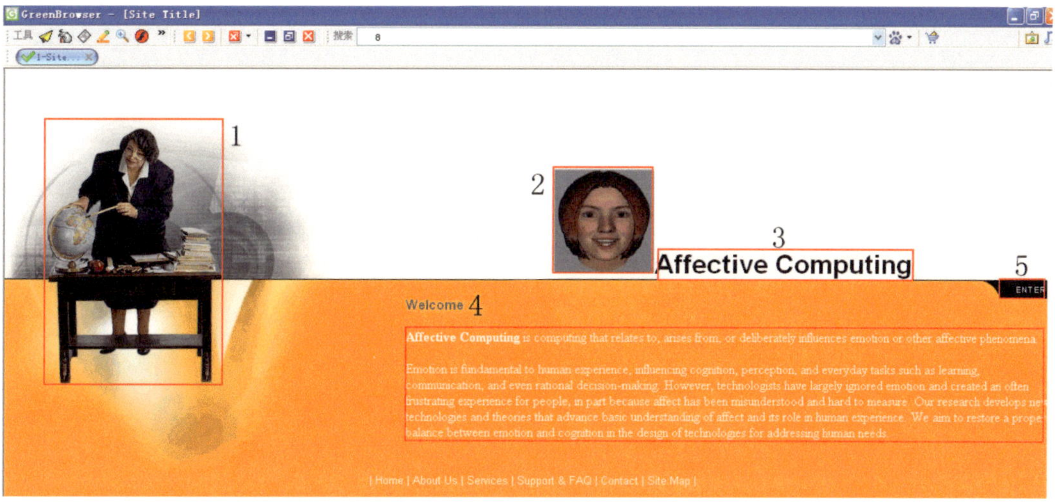

Fig. 2. Example of "interest areas".

The key functionality of the attention information processing module in our MITS is characterized by three main components:

- Monitor the grounding. In human face-to-face communication, grounding relates to the process of ensuring that what has been said is understood by the conversational partners, i.e. there is "common ground". During the learner-tutor interaction, grounding is considered successful if the following condition is met: the student's gaze shows a transition from the screen area of the speaking tutor to the screen area of the referent mentioned by the tutor. When positive evidence in grounding is observed, the course will continue. And a window of contextual content, i.e. the related contend, maybe popup according to the referent.
- Guarantee the attention. The agent will perform an interruption if the student attends to interest areas that are not considered as part of the current content the agent is talking about. An "alert" action will be performed if the student does not gaze at the display, for example, gaze out of the window.
- Note the history. This function records which area and how much of the area has been accessed by the student. If an important area that the student does not pay enough attention to, this area might be proposed again. While the area previously has been accessed for enough time, it is not very likely that the student intends to activate it again.

The components aforesaid are all based on the modified version of the algorithm described by Qvarfordt (Qvarfordt & Zhai, 2005), where it is used for an intelligent virtual tourist information environment (iTourist). Two interest metrics were developed: (1) the Interest Score (IScore) and (2) the Focus of Interest Score (FIScore). IScore is used to determine an area's "arousal" level, or the likelihood that the user is interested in it. When the IScore metric passes a certain threshold, the area is said to become "active". FIScore measures how the user keeps up his or her interest in an active area. If the FIScore for an active area falls below a certain threshold, it becomes deactivated and a new active area is selected based on the IScore. According to the key functionality of the attention information processing module in our system, a simplified version of the IScore metric is sufficient for our purpose. IScore basic component is eye-gaze intensity p:

$$p = \frac{T_{ISon}}{T_{IS}} \tag{1}$$

Where T_{ISon} refers to the accumulated gaze duration within a time window of size T_{IS} (in our system, 1000 ms) and T_{IS} is the size of the moving time window. In order to account for factors that may relate to user's interest, Qvarfordt characterized the IScore as $p_{is} = p(1+\alpha(1-p))$, where p_{is} is the arousal level of the area and α is the excitability modification defined as below in (Qvarfordt & Zhai, 2005).

$$\alpha = \frac{c_f\alpha_f + c_c\alpha_c + c_s\alpha_s + c_a\alpha_a}{c_f + c_c + c_s + c_a} \tag{2}$$

Where α_f, α_c, α_s, α_a are constants empirically adjusted, they are defined as:

- α_f is the frequency of the user's eye gaze entering and leaving the area
- α_c is the categorical relationship with the previous active area
- α_s is the relative size to a baseline area
- α_a records previous activation of the area

We modified the formula 2, only α_f, α_s, α_a were integrated into MITS. The factor α_f is represented as $\alpha_f = \frac{N_{sw}}{N_f}$, where N_{sw} denotes the number of times eye gaze enters and leaves the area and N_f denotes the maximum possible N_{sw} in the preset time window. α_f is identified as one indication of a user's interest in an area. Since some noise in the eye movement signal, larger areas could have a higher chance of being "hit" than smaller ones, α_s is defined to avoid this. α_s is represented by $\alpha_s = \frac{S_b - S}{S}$, where S_b is the area size of the common areas which are also the smallest, and S represents the size of the current area. As for the α_a, it is employed to indicate whether the area has been paid enough attention. $\alpha_a = -1$ when the area has been paid enough attention and 0 when it has not been paid enough attention.

4. Affective information

Our interest in the emotion integrated in tutoring systems is motivated by the social cognitive theory suggesting that learning takes place through a complex interplay between both cognitive and affective dimensions. Researches in cognitive sciences argue that emotion enables people to communicate efficiently by monitoring and regulating social interaction, by evaluating and modifying emotional experiences. ITS would be significantly enhanced if computers could adapt according to the affective state of the student. In order to get an idea about the effectiveness of machine-based emotion recognition compared to humans, a review of research has been done by Huang (Huang & Chen, 1998). They investigated the performance of machine based emotion employing both video and audio information. Their work was based on human performance results reported by DeSilva (DeSilva & Miyasato, 1997). Their research indicated that the machine performance was on average better than human performance with 75% accuracy. In addition, comparing detection of confusions indicated similarities between machine and human. These results are encouraging in the context of our research for integrating multimodal affective interaction into tutoring systems. Although the term "affective tutoring systems" can be traced back as far as Picard's book "Affective computing" in 1997, to date, only few projects have explicitly considered emotion for ITS. However, all the projects in existence are single-channel, and mainly concentrated on the facial expression recognition. In this paper, we detect the student's emotion through facial expression, speech and text which are main carriers of human emotion. The following subsection will give a brief description of our methods to capture the emotion through the three channels.

4.1 Facial expression

Facial expression recognition has attracted a significant interest in the scientific community due to its importance for human centered interfaces. Many researchers have integrated the facial expressions into ITS (Reategui & Boff, 2008; Roger, 2006; Sarrafzadeh & Alexander, 2008). However, the performance of facial expression recognition could be influenced by occlusion on the face caused by pose variation, glass wearing, and hair or hand covering etc. The ability to handle occluded facial features is most important for achieving robustness of facial expression recognition. In contrast to normal methods that do not deal with the occlusion regions separately, our approach detects and eliminates the facial occlusions for robust facial expression recognition. Thus, the procedure of facial occlusion removal is added to normal classification procedure. Here, we propose a novel method for partial occlusion removal by iterative operation of facial occlusion detection and reconstruction using RPCA and saliency detection until no occlusion is detected. Then, the reconstructed face after occlusion removal is put to AdaBoost classifier for robust facial expression recognition, as shown in Figure 3.

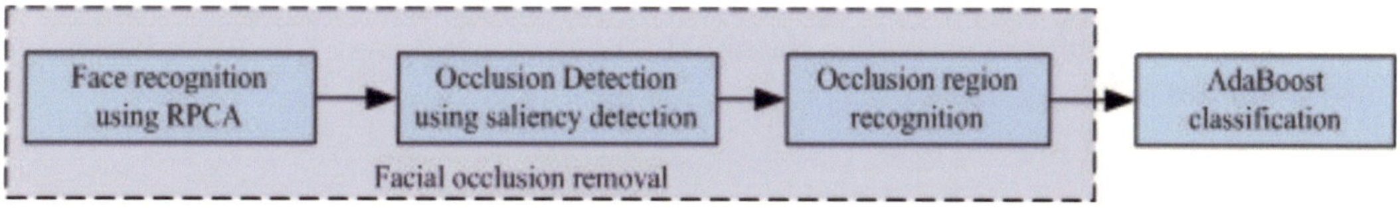

Fig. 3. Work flow of the robust facial expression recognition.

4.1.1 Face recognition using RPCA

Robust principal component analysis (RPCA) is robust to outliers (i.e. artifacts due to occlusion, illumination, image noise etc.) in training data and can be used to construct low-dimensional linear-subspace representations from noisy data. When the face contains a small fraction of the subjects with glasses, or forehead overlaid by hair, or chin surrounded by hands, the pixels corresponding to those coverings are likely to be treated as outliers by RPCA. Hence, the reconstructed image of the original face will possibly not contain the occlusions.

4.1.2 Occlusion detection using saliency detection

To find the occlusion regions on the face, we adopt the method of saliency detection. Firstly, the original face image is transformed into gray level and normalized to $I(x,y)$ using histogram equalization. Then, $I(x,y)$ is reconstructed to $R(x,y)$ using RPCA. We can obtain the residual image $D(x,y)$ between the reconstructed image $R(x,y)$ and $I(x,y)$ by:

$$D(x,y)=\left|R(x,y)-I(x,y)\right| \tag{3}$$

Then, the residual image $D(x,y)$ is put to a saliency detector to find the local places with high complexity, which is hypothesized to be the occlusion on the face. The measure of the local saliency is defined as:

$$H_{D,Rx}=-\sum_i P_{D,R_X}(d_i)\log_2 P_{D,R_X}(d_i) \tag{4}$$

Where $P_{D,R_X}(d_i)$ is the probability of descriptor (or difference image) D taking the value d_i in the local region R_x. We apply the saliency detection in the residual image over a wide range of scale, and set the threshold value of $H_{D,Rx}$. The region with biggest $H_{D,Rx}$ value over the threshold is set to the occlusion region. If all regions have $H_{D,Rx}$ less than the threshold, it is presumed that no occlusion exists. Note that we just choose one occlusion region in one operation of saliency detection even if there are multiple regions with saliency value over the threshold.

4.1.3 Occlusion region reconstruction

Detailed information is most important to facial expression recognition. To avoid the wrong information introduced by face reconstruction in non-occluded region, we adopt the mechanism of occlusion region reconstruction rather than the total face reconstruction. To obtain the new face image $P(x,y)$, pixel values of the detected occlusion region will be replaced by the reconstructed face using RPCA. Thus, the wrong information in the occlusion region may be shielded while the other regions of the face retain the same. To further decrease the impact of occlusion for facial expression reconstruction, we perform occlusion region reconstruction for several iterations until the difference of the reconstructed face between two iterations is below a threshold. The new face image $P_t(x,y)$ in iteration *t* can be obtained by:

$$P_t(x,y)=\begin{cases} I(x,y) & (x,y)\notin R_{occlusion} \\ R_t(x,y) & (x,y)\in R_{occlusion} \end{cases} \tag{5}$$

Where $I(x,y)$ is the normalized image, $R_t(x,y)$ is the reconstructed image using RPCA in iteration *t*, and $R_{occlusion}$ defines the occlusion region. Note that

$$R_t(x,y)=\begin{cases} RPCA(I) & t=1 \\ RPCA(P_{t-1}) & t>1 \end{cases} \tag{6}$$

Where *RPCA* designates the RPCA procedure, *t* is the iteration index.

4.1.4 AdaBoost classification

We employ harr-like features for feature extraction and implement multiple one-against-rest two-class AdaBoost classifiers for robust facial expression recognition. In the algorithm, multiple two-class classifiers are constructed from weak features which are selected to discriminate one class from the others. It can solve the problem that weak features to discriminate multiple classes are hard to be selected in traditional multi-class AdaBoost algorithm. The proposed algorithms were trained and tested on our Facial Expression Database. This database consists of 57 university students in age from 19 to 27 years old and includes videos with hand and glass occlusion when displaying kinds of facial expressions. We also randomly add occlusions on the face to generate occluded faces. The experiment results are listed in Table 1.

Emotion	anger	happiness	sadness
Accuracy	83.5	85.3	70.6
Emotion	disgust	surprise	average
Accuracy	75.0	73.3	77.5

Table 1. Facial Recognition Results.

4.2 Speech emotion

In the student-tutor interaction, human tutors respond to both what a student says and to how the student says it. However, most tutorial dialogue systems can not detect the student emotion and attitudes underlying an utterance. In this paper, we introduce the speech emotion recognition into the ITS.

4.2.1 Feature extraction and relative feature calculation

Study on emotion of speech indicates that pitch, energy, duration, formant, Mel prediction cepstrum coefficient (MPCC) and linear prediction cepstrum coefficient (LPCC) are effective absolute features to distinguish certain emotions. In the paper, for each frame, six basic features, including pitch, amplitude energy, box-dimension, zero cross ratio, energy-frequency-value, first formant frequency, as well as their first and second derivatives, are extracted. Besides, 10-order LPCC and 12-order MFCC are also be extracted. Though absolute features of speeches corresponding to same emotion have large differences among different speakers, the differences of feature change induced by emotion stimulation are small relatively. Hence, relative features which reflects feature change is more credible than absolute features for emotion recognition. Relative features used in the paper embody alterations of pitch, energy or other features. They are obtained by computing the change rate relative to natural speech. Features of the kind are robust to different speakers because its calculation is combined with normalization of the features of neutral speeches. For computing relative features, the reference features of neutral version of each text and each speaker should be obtained by calculating the statistics of some frame-based parameters. In this paper, the statistic features used are means of dynamic features, including pitch, amplitude energy, energy-frequency-value, box-dimension, zero cross ratio, and first formant frequency as well as their first and second derivatives. Then, the six statistic features are used to normalize the corresponding dynamic features for each emotion speech, including training samples and test samples. Assuming Mf_i, $i=1,2,\cdots,18$ are reference features of neutral version, $\vec{f_i}, i=1,2,\cdots 18$ are the corresponding dynamic feature vectors, the relative feature vectors $R\vec{f_i}$ can be obtained according to following formula:

$$R\vec{f}_i = (\vec{f}_i - Mf_i) / (Mf_i + 0.0000001) \quad (7)$$

where $\vec{f}_i = [f_{i1}, f_{i2}, ...f_{iL}]^T$, $R\vec{f}_i = [Rf_{i1}, Rf_{i2}, \cdots Rf_{iL}]^T$ and L indicates the length of feature vector.

4.2.2 Isolated HMMs

The HMMs are left-right discrete models. The most pervasive methods, Forward-Backward Procedure, Viterbi Algorithm and Baum Welch re-estimation are employed in this paper. Baum Welch re-estimation based on likelihood training criterion is used to train the HMMs, each HMM modeling one emotion; Forward-Backward Procedure exports the likelihood probability; Viterbi Algorithm, focusing on the best path through the model, evaluates the likelihood of the best match between the given speech observations and the given HMMs, then achieves the "optimal" state sequences. The recognizing process based on HMMs is shown as Figure 4. A speech sample is analyzed and then represented by a feature vector, according to which the likelihood between the speech sample and each HMM is computed. Then the emotion state corresponding to maximum likelihood is selected as the output of the classifier through comparison.

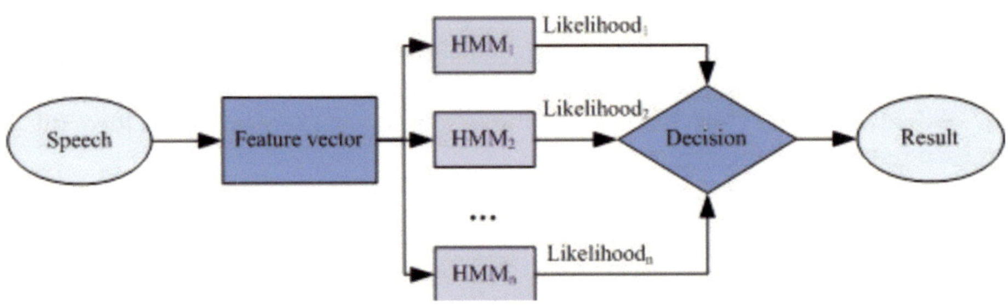

Fig. 4. Emotion Recognition by HMMs.

4.2.3 HMMs fusion system

For the complexity of speech emotion recognition, single classifier systems have limited performance. In recent years, classifier fusion proves to be effective and efficient. By taking advantage of complementary information provided by the constituent classifiers, classifier fusion offers improved performance. Classifier fusion can be done at two different levels, namely, score level and decision level. In score level fusion, raw outputs (scores or confidence levels) of the individual classifiers are combined in a certain way to reach a global decision. The combination can be performed either simply using the sum rule or averaged sum rule, or more sophisticatedly, using another classifier. Decision level fusion, on the other hand, arrives at the final classification decision by combining the decisions of individual classifiers. Voting is a well-known technique for decision-level fusion. It can mask errors from one or more classifiers and make the system more robust. Voting strategies include: majority, weighted voting, plurality, instance runoff voting, threshold voting, and the more general weighted k-out-of-n systems. In this paper, four HMMs classifiers, which have different feature vectors (see Table2), are used. HMMs classifier takes only the emotion which satisfies the model most as the recognition result. But the correct result often should be the emotion which satisfies the model secondly or thirdly. So a new algorithm named weighted ranked voting, which is a reformed version of ranked voting method provided by C De Borda, is proposed. Ranked voting method permits a voter to choose more than one candidate in proper order. Moreover, the improved algorithm also makes the voted emotions attached by different weights.

classifier	Feature vector
1	pitch, box- dimension, energy with their first and second derivatives; 10-order LPCC
2	energy-frequency-value, box- dimension, formant with their first and second derivatives; 12-order MFCC
3	pitch, zero cross ratio, formant with their first and second derivatives; 12-order MFCC
4	all features extracted in the paper

Table 2. Feature vector.

For a speech sample and a classifier, the voting weight of a certain emotion is determined according to the likelihood between the speech and the HMM model corresponding to the emotion. Firstly, the likelihood values between the speech sample and HMM models are calculated. Secondly, the emotion states are sorted according to likelihood. Then, the voting weights of the first three emotions are allocated according to the order. In the paper, the weight is determined as Table 3. Finally, the weights from four classifiers corresponding to each emotion are summed up and the emotion which has maximum value is selected as result.

	First	Second	Third
Weight	1	0.6	0.3

Table 3. Weight Allocation for Voting.

The steps are listed as follows for each speech sample.

- step1: Initialize weight value as 0 for each emotion.
- step2: Sort emotions according to likelihood for each classifier.
- step3: Vote the first three emotion attached by weight according to Table 3 for each classifier.
- step4: Sum up the weights from four classifiers for each emotion and choose the emotion which has the biggest weight sum as the recognition result.

To evaluate the performance of the proposed classifier in this paper, Database of Emotional Speech was set up to provide speech samples. This corpus contains utterances of five emotions, twenty texts and five actors, two males and three females. Each speaker repeats each text three times in each emotion, meaning that sixty utterances per emotion. For classifier evaluation, 1,140 samples of eight speakers, which have been assessed, are used. The evaluation was done in a "leave-one-speaker-out" manner. One feature vector, formed by six relative features combined with LPCC or MFCC, is used. The experiment results are listed in Table 4.

4.3 Text

Text is an important modality for learner-tutor interaction, many of the ITS have the function enabling the tutor to chat with the student or assist the student in theoretical questions. so studying the relationship between natural language and affective information as well as assessing the underpinned affective qualities of natural language is also

Emotion	Classifiers				
	1	2	3	4	fusion
anger	14.3	19.1	19.1	19.1	14.3
happiness	31.8	45.5	50.0	40.9	100
sadness	8.7	47.8	73.9	47.8	60.9
disgust	92.3	45.5	50.0	40.9	100
surprise	38.9	33.3	33.3	33.3	83.3
average	30.2	37.1	40.5	36.2	57.8

Table 4. Results Using Relative Feature Vector.

important. The Artificial Intelligence Markup Language (AIML) is used to represent the tutor's conversational knowledge, employing a mechanism of stimulus-response. The stimuli (sentences and fragments which may be used to question the tutor) are stored and used to search for pre-defined replies. When the learner poses a question, the tutor starts the AIML Retrieval Mechanism in order to build an appropriate reply using the information, patterns and templates from the AIML database. AIML is an Extensible Markup Language (XML) derivative, which power lies in three basic aspects: AIML syntax enables the semantic content of a question to be extracted easily so that the appropriate answer can be given quickly. The use of labels to combine answers lends greater variety to the answers and increases the number of questions to which an answer can be given. The use of recursivity enables answers to be provided to inputs for which, in theory, there is no direct answer.

Reategui have adopted the AIML in their ITS (Reategui & Boff, 2008), however, it can not sense the affective information conveyed by text automatically. In this paper, we integrate the textual affect sensing algorithm into the AIML Retrieval Mechanism. Figure 5 shows the work flow of the textual affect sensing. The approach for providing emotional estimations from the sentence input by the student is based on a keyword spotting technique and sentence-level processing technique.

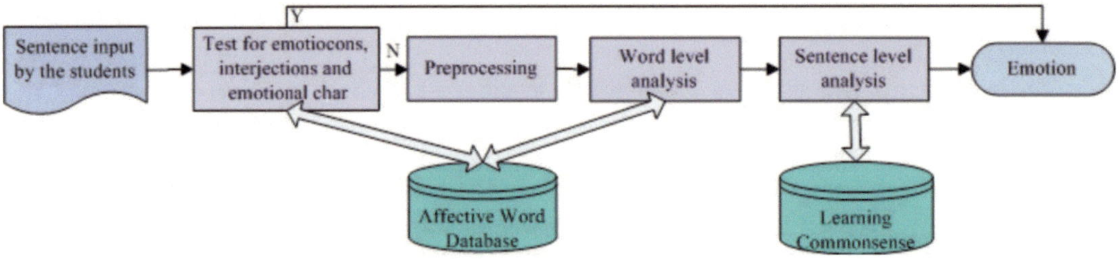

Fig. 5. Work flow of the textual affect sensing.

4.3.1 Affective database and learning commonsense database

In order to support the handling of abbreviated language and the interpretation of affective features of emoticons, abbreviations, interjections and words, an affective database was created using XML. We collected emoticons (such as, ":-)" for happiness and "QQ" for sadness), the most popular emotional acronyms and abbreviations (for instance, "LOL" (laughing out loud) for happiness) and emotional interjections (for example: "damn" for anger and "wow" for happiness). We also have taken emotional adjectives, nouns, verbs, and adverbs words into our database.

Besides the affective database, the learning commonsense database is also constructed. Our idea relies on having broad knowledge about student's common affective attitudes toward learning process. For instance, if the student input "The content is too difficult to understand", it implies that the student is not happy, as for the input "I got a high score in the test" indicates the student is happy. The structure of the learning commonsense database is based on the affect models generated from Open Mind Common Sense (OMCS) (Liu & Lieberman, 2003).

4.3.2 Textual emotion sensing

Firstly, the multiple-sentence input by the student is spited into single sentences. Each sentence is estimating the emotion separately. The sentence is tested for occurrences of emoticons, abbreviations, acronyms, interjections. If there is an emoticon, abbreviation, acronym or interjection related to an emotional state, no further analysis of affect in sentence is performed based on the assumption that the emoticon, abbreviation, acronym or abbreviation dominates the affective meaning of the entire sentence. If there are no emotion-relevant emoticons, abbreviations, acronym or interjection in a sentence, we prepare the sentence for the next processing: we use deep syntactical parser, Connexor Machinese Syntax, returns exhaustive information for analyzed sentences. From the parser output in XML style, we can read off the characteristics of each token and the relations between them in a sentence, such as subject, verb, object, and their attributes. Then, we use the word spotting technique to estimate emotion of word based on the affective database. However, the word spotting method is too simple to deal with sentences without any affective word. We hence perform the following steps on sentence-level processing. In this stage, we search the learning commonsense database to get the emotion effect of the verb. Finally, we detect "negation" in sentences. Since negatively prefixed words such as "unhappy" are already included in the emotion database, they do not have to be considered. On the other hand, negative verb forms such as "was not", "did not" are detected and flip the polarity of the emotion word.

When student inputs sentences, the function of textual affect sensing is called firstly. Then the AIML Retrieval Mechanism (www.alicebot.org/aiml.html) starts in order to generate an appropriate reply using the pattern and template from the AIML database. For instance, if the student input "What is Affective Computing? It sounds really interest!", the pattern with happy is mapped. While the question is "What is Affective Computing? It is really too abstract to understand! Can you help me?", the pattern with sad takes effect. Different answers are retrieved for the two patterns, as shown in the examples below:

*<pattern>*What is Affective Computing HAPPY *</pattern>*

<template> Affective Computing is a very interesting topic! It is computing that relates to, arises from, or deliberately influences emotion or other affective phenomena. *</template>*

<pattern> What is Affective Computing SAD *</pattern>*

<template> Oh, you seem a little unhappy. Be patient and it is easy to understand! Affective Computing is computing that relates to, arises from, or deliberately influences emotion or other affective phenomena. *</template>*

5. Agent tutor

In our MITS, an agent tutor "Alice" can adjust her behavior in response to learner's requests and inferred learner's needs. The agent is "eye-aware" and "affect-aware", and provides consistent empathy using facial expression and synthetic emotional speech. Its emotional response depends on the learner's action. For instance, an agent shows a happy emotion if the learner concentrates on the current study topic. In contrast, if the learner seems to lose concentration, the agent will show mild anger or alert the learner. The agent also shows empathy when the learner is sad. In general, the agent tutor interacts between the educational content and the learner. Other tasks of an agent tutor include explaining the study material and providing hints when necessary, moving around the screen to get or direct user attention, and to highlight information. The detailed tutoring strategies will be given latter. In this section, we focus on the facial expression generation and emotional speech synthesis of the agent. The famous agent "Alice" is employed as the tutor. Other agent systems can be used with appropriate diver programs.

5.1 Facial expression generation

Facial expression plays an important role in human's daily life, as indicated by Mehrabian, in face-to-face human communication 55% of the communicative message is transferred by facial expressions (Mehrabian, 1968). However, the limit in the existence researches is that facial expression generation is mostly monotone, or in the "Invariable View". They usually correlate one model of facial expression to one emotion, and generate facial animation based on that. Whereas, human tend to act more complicated to express one emotion. For example, human display kinds of facial expressions to express happiness, such as smile with mouth open or closed, symmetrically or asymmetrically, even with head wobbled. In this paper, we aim at generating humanoid and expressive facial expressions of agent to achieve natural, harmonious and believable student-agent interaction. Based on the cues of sources and characteristics of facial expression, we propose a novel model of fuzzy facial expression generation, as seen in figure 6.

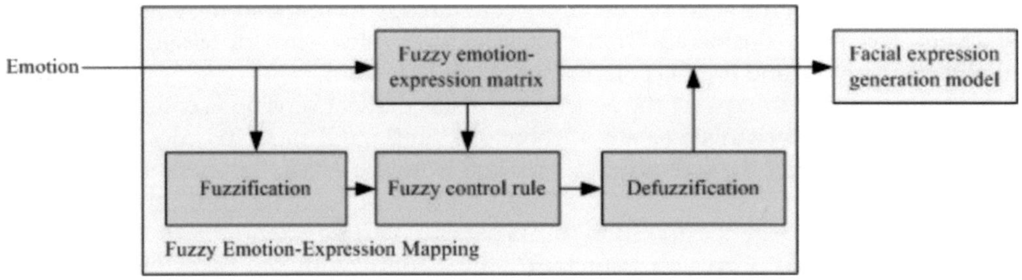

Fig. 6. Work flow of the textual affect sensing.

5.1.1 Fuzzy emotion-expression mapping

Fuzzy is one common characteristic of emotion and facial expression. There is also fuzzy relationship between emotion and facial expression. One emotion can be fuzzily expressed by multiple modes of facial expression. Here, we give the model of fuzzy emotion-expression mapping. The mapping of emotion to expression is one-to-many.

Based on the correlation of multiple facial expressions of emotion, fuzzy emotion-expression mapping is proposed, in which emotion and facial expression are supposed to be fuzzy vectors, and a fuzzy matrix consisting of degrees of membership maps the fuzzy motion vector to the fuzzy facial expression vector. Define the emotion space as $X = \{x_1, x_2 \cdots x_m\}$, where x_i is any emotion, such as surprise, disgust. Define the facial expression space as $Y = \{y_1, y_2 \cdots y_n\}$, where y_i indicates any mode of facial expression. The fuzzy relation $\tilde{R}$ from the emotion space X to the facial expression space Y is $R = (r_{ij})_{m \times n}$ where $r_{ij} = \tilde{R}(x_i, y_j) \in [0,1]$ indicates the correlation degree of (x_i, y_j) to $\tilde{R}$. Given the input emotional fuzzy vector E_S, the fuzzy facial vector E_X can be obtained via fuzzy mapping, as seen in $E_X = E_S \circ R(ex_1, ex_2 \cdots, ex_n)$,where ex_i is the membership of the mode of facial expression y_i to the fuzzy facial expression $\tilde{E}_X$, $\circ$ means the compositional operation of the fuzzy relations. Once the fuzzy facial expression $\tilde{E}_X$ is determined, its intensity will also be computed. The intensity of selected emotion x_i is fuzzified to the linguistic value, which is then mapped to the linguistic value of related facial expressions according to fuzzy control rule. The intensity of facial expression y_i is obtained by defuzzifying its linguistic value. The emotion intensity and facial expression intensity also have fuzzy characteristics. The fuzzy linguistic values of emotion and facial expression are listed as very low, low, middle, high and very high. According to the emotion-expression intensity mapping, the mapping from linguistic value of emotion intensity to linguistic value of facial expression intensity was realized through fuzzy control. An example of fuzzy control rule is shown in Table 5. Emotion x (surprise) can be fuzzily expressed by facial expression y_1 or y_2. The very low intensity of x can be expressed by small intensity of y_1 or very small intensity of y_2.

Emotion x(surprise)	facial expression y_1	facial expression y_2
Very low	small	Very small
low	middle	small
middle	large	middle
high	Very large	large
Very high	− −	Very large

Table 5. Fuzzy control rule of fuzzy emotion-expression intensity mapping.

5.1.2 Facial expression generation model

The facial expression generation model is the module that accepts input of the fuzzy facial expression $\tilde{E}_X$ with its intensity and output the agent's facial expression. In this paper, we adopted Xface, an MPEG-4 based open source toolkit for 3D facial animation, to generate multiple facial expressions of emotions mentioned above. Figure 7 are some keyframes of facial expressions.

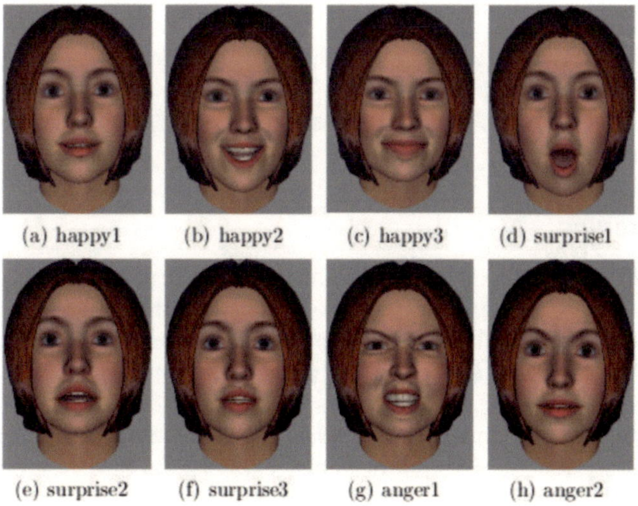

Fig. 7. Some keyframes of facial expressions.

5.2 Emotional speech synthesis

Speech is the easiest way to convey intention, and it is one of the fundamental methods of conveying emotion, on a par with facial expression. In this paper, the variety rule of prosodic features containing pitch frequency (F0), energy and velocity are concluded by analyzing emotional speech in our Emotional Speech Database. The autocorrelation function (ACF) method based on Linear Predictive Coding (LPC) and wavelet transform approach are employed to extract the F0 and tone respectively. Then prosodic features regulation is set up by utilization of Pitch Synchronous OverLap Add (PSOLA) and the original peace speeches are transformed into appointed emotional speech, including happy, anger, surprise and sad, based on the rules and regulation. Figure 8 illustrates the work flow of our approach.

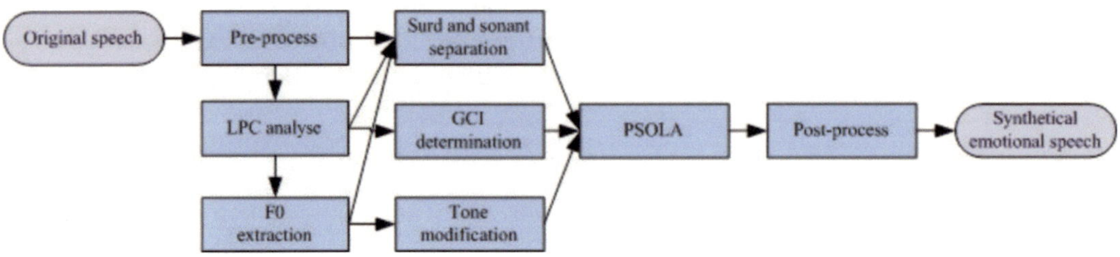

Fig. 8. Work flow of the emotional speech synthesis.

- **Pre-process.** Include noise elimination, pre-emphasis and amplitude normalization
- **LPC analyze.** Partition the original speech into frame, take LPC analysis of each frame, get the LPC residual function and first order reflection coefficient
- **F0 extraction.** Get the F0 through the autocorrelation analysis of the residual function and the F0 profile curve of the original speech
- **Surd and sonant separation.** Do the surd and sonant separation according to first order reflection coefficient, signal energy and frequency extraction result
- **Glottal Closure Instances (GCI).** determine the GCI according to the F0 extraction
- **Tone modification.** Extract the tone information using wavelet transform, modify the tone information according to the target-emotion; adopting inverse wavelet transform to get the F0 curve
- **PSOLA**. Using PSOLA technology to transform original speech into appointed emotional speech
- **Post-process.** De-emphasis, i.e. do the anti-operation of pre-emphasis in pre-process to restore speech effect

6. Tutoring strategies

Although our MITS can perfectly detect the attention information and affective state, it is also important to let the agent tutor know what to do with the information. As good human tutors can effectively adapt to the attention information and affective state of students, the most obvious way to learn about how to adapt the attention information and affective state of student is to learn from the human tutors. Sarrafzadeh videoed several tutors as they tutored students individually and a coding scheme was developed to extract data from each tutoring video to describe the behaviors, facial expressions and expression intensities of students and tutors. Tutoring actions are guided by a case-based method for adapting to student states that recommends a weighted set of tutor actions and expressions (Sarrafzadeh

& Alexander, 2008). However, this approach has two main shortcomings: firstly, the video only recorded three human tutors' behaviors and the students' reactions to these behaviors are not considered. What we want to get is the behaviors that can motivate the students, rather than arouse the students' averseness; and secondly, the coding scheme can not apply to the attention information and speech, text communication. In this paper, we use the traditional questionnaire to get the "optimal reaction" of the tutor towards the learner's attention information and affective state. The critical observation is that every excellent teacher has commonsense of the kind we want to give our agent tutor. If we can find good ways to extract commonsense from human tutor by prompting them, asking them questions, presenting them with lines of reasoning to confirm or repair, and so on, we may be able to accumulate many of the knowledge structures needed to give our agent tutor the capacity for commonsense reasoning for student's attention information and affective state. So we built a system called Human Tutor Commonsense make it easy for human tutors to collaborate to construct a database of commonsense knowledge. We invited more than 100 excellent teachers to log on our system to build the database. Then, a group of 50 students were asked to evaluate how much they satisfied with these commonsense, on a scale from 1 (strongly dissatisfied) to 5 (strongly satisfied). Then we chose two commonsense with highest mean score as the "optimal reaction" for each situation these questions described.

Based on the commonsense we obtained, MITS can be represented as a dynamic network as shown in Figure 9. Whenever the student's pedagogical state or attention information or affective state is changed, the following events are happen:

- Each time the dynamic network receives new evidence (the change of pedagogical state or attention information or affective state), a new time slice is added to the existing network
- The case-based method chose a tutorial action from the commonsense database
- The tutorial action is taken by the agent tutor "Alice"
- The history is updated
- "Alice" waits for the next student action

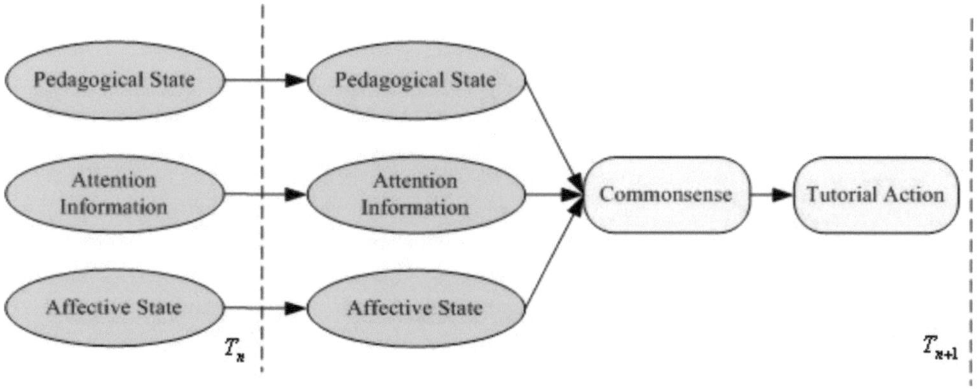

Fig. 9. Dynamic network for MITS.

7. Conclusion

This paper debuts a Multimodal Intelligent Tutoring Systems. Attention information detection and affective state detection are carried out. Meanwhile, the system adapts to the student via an emotionally expressive agent tutor "Alice" through facial expression and synthetic emotional speech. Tutoring actions are guided by a case-based method that recommends a set of tutor actions and expressions for adapting to student states. The data that this case-based program uses were generated from questionnaires presented to human teachers.

In future work, it is necessary that the accuracy of emotion recognition and classification algorithm should be improved. Meanwhile, the MITS will be extended to integrate information from other sources including posture recognition and physiological channels such as pressure. We hope to evaluate the effectiveness of our system in a range of learning situations including more both young and adult learners. The test will provide more important directions for improvements to be made in the next version of MITS.

8. Acknowledgment

This work is supported by the National Nature Science Foundation of China (No.60873269) and International Cooperation between China and Japan (No.2010DFA11990).

9. References

Butz, J. PC., Hua, S., Maguire B.R., A web-based bayesian intelligent tutoring system for computer programming. Web Intelligence and Agent System, 4, 1(2006), 77-97

Chen, C.M., Intelligent web-based learning system with personalized learning path guidance, Computers & Education, 51, 2 (2008) ,787—814

DeSilva, L.C., Miyasato, T., Nakatsu, R., Facial emotion recognition using multimodal information, In Proc. ICICS1997 (1997), 397--401

Huang, T.S., Chen, L.C., Tao, H., Bimodal emotion recognition by man and machine, ATR Workshop on Virtual Communication Environments (1998)

Liu, H., Lieberman, H., Selker, T., A model of textual affect sensing using real-world knowledge. In Proc. IUI 2003, ACM Press (2003).

Mehrabian, A., Communication without words. Psychology Today, 2, 4(1968), 53-56

Qvarfordt, P., Zhai, S., Conversing with the user based on eye-gaze patterns. In Proc. CHI 2005, ACM Press (2005), 221-230.

Reategui, E., Boff, E., Campbell, J.A., Personalization in an interactive learning environment through a virtual character, Computers & Education, 51, 2 (2008), 530-544

Roger, N., A framework for affective intelligent tutoring systems, In Proc. ITHET2006 (2006)

Sarrafzadeh, A., Alexander, S., Dadgostar, F., How do you know that I don't understand? A look at the future of intelligent tutoring systems. Computers in Human Behavior, 24, 4 (2008), 1342-1363

Siddappa, M., Manjunath, A.S., Knowledge representation using multilevel hierarchical model in intelligent tutoring system, In Proc. IASTED 2007 (2007), 323—329

Sun, P.C., Tsai, R.J., Finger, G., Chen, Y.Y., What drives a successful e-Learning? An empirical investigation of the critical factors influencing learner satisfaction, Computers & Education,50, 4,(2008), 1183-1202

7

Using the Smith Chart in an E-Learning Approach

José R. Pereira and Pedro Pinho
Universidade de Aveiro, Instituto de Telecomunicações
Instituto Superior de Engenharia de Lisboa, Instituto de Telecomunicações
Portugal

1. Introduction

Prior to the advent of digital computers and calculators, engineers developed all sorts of aids (tables, charts, graphs) to facilitate their calculations for design and analysis in different areas in particular for line transmission problems. To reduce the tedious manipulations involved in calculating the characteristics of transmission lines, graphical tools have been developed. The Smith chart is the most commonly used of these graphical techniques. It is basically a graphical indication of the impedance change along a transmission line as one moves along it. It becomes easy to use after a small amount of experience. We will first explain how the Smith chart is constructed and then how to use it to calculate transmission line characteristics such as: the reflection coefficient (ρ), the Voltage Standing Wave Ratio (VSWR), the impedance along the line ($Z(d)$), the maximum and minimum voltage localization and impedance matching. For the majority of these Smith chart applications lossless lines will be assumed, although this is not absolutely required.

Since the main topic of this book is concerned with e-learning, the aim of this chapter is to help the reader understand and learn how to use the Smith chart, following step by step procedure based on *MATLAB* scripts that will be available for download and should be used when reading this chapter. This approach should teach the students how to solve several kinds of transmission line problems by themselves, in a paper chart using a pencil, a ruler and a compass.

MATLAB scripts are a good tool to help students better understand the Smith chart and explain, step by step, several procedures related to transmission line problems, (Mak & Sundaram, 2008), (Pereira & Pinho, 2010).

The goals of the chapter are to explain the reasons why using and understanding the Smith chart is still important nowadays, despite the present generalization of personal computers and powerful calculators. It is easy to plug a few numbers into a program and have it spit out solutions. When the solutions are complex and multifaceted, having a computer to do the grunt work is especially handy. However, knowing the underlying theory and principles that have been ported to computer platforms, and where they came from, makes the engineer or designer a more well-rounded and confident professional, and makes the results more reliable. Moreover it is interesting to note that these kinds of graphical tools are still useful nowadays. For example some types of modern laboratory equipment, such as

network analyzers still have displays that imitate the Smith chart. Another example is the use of Smith charts in a lot of commercial software about antennas and microwave devices, to display the simulation results. The importance of the chart is enhanced by the global information that is possible to obtain simultaneously.
The authors believe that the use of the Smith chart by undergraduate students and engineers is an important pedagogical tool, since many aspects of the voltage, current, impedance, Voltage Standing Wave Ratio (VSWR), referred commonly as SWR, reflection coefficient and matching design problems can be easily interpreted and well visualized using the Smith chart.
The chapter will be organized as follows:

- History and use of the Smith chart and its importance in the resolution of classical transmission line problems. Justification of its current use despite the present generalization of personal computers and powerful calculators.
- Construction of this chart from basic equations and concepts. Explanation of the main parameters that can be obtained from the chart. All these aspects will be supported by *MATLAB* scripts that display, step by step, the graphical procedure involved in the process.
- How to use the Smith chart. How to mark a normalized impedance and from then on to get several related parameters such as, the corresponding admittance, the VSWR, the reflection coefficient, the concept of travelling toward the generator or toward the load, the impedance at a given distance etc. Again, all these transmission line concepts will be explained through step by step procedures based on *MATLAB* scripts.
- Presentation of some examples that integrates all these transmission line concepts. One example is the single stub matching. The authors developed a *MATLAB* script that display, step by step, the graphical procedure that must be used to solve this problem. Others examples will be presented, because we believe they are important so students can learn on their own.

Throughout the chapter, when explaining the step by step procedure, several displays will be shown to illustrate the use of the Smith chart.

2. History of the Smith chart

Phillip H. Smith, inventor of the well known Smith chart, was born in Lexington, Massachusetts, on April 29, 1905 and died in Berkeley Heights, New Jersey on August 29, 1987, at the age of 82. In 1928, after graduating from Tufts College (now Tufts University) at the top of his class with B.S. degree in electrical communications, he was offered a job at Bell Telephone Laboratories. After 42 years in this company, Phillip Smith retired in 1970 and started a small company –Analog Instruments Company in New Providence, New Jersey – which initially sold navigational instruments for light aircraft. In his lifetime Smith held 21 U.S. patents and published over 35 technical papers on antennas and transmission lines.
In 1931, by modifying J. A. Fleming's 1911 telephone equations in an effort to simplify the solution of the transmission line problem, Smith developed his first graphical solution in the form of a rectangular chart. Even though the rectangular chart was very useful, Smith knew it had some limitations, namely the amount of data that could be accommodated. In 1936, Smith constructed a new type of transmission line chart that eliminated most of the limitations in his first diagram. The new chart was a special polar coordinate diagram which

could show all values of impedance and is essentially the Smith chart used today. Smith approached a number of technical magazines for publications of his transmission line diagram, however acceptance was slow. Finally, after two years Smith's article describing his chart was published in January 1939 issue of Electronics magazine. In a second article, published in the January 1944 issue of Electronics, Smith incorporated further improvements into his chart, including its usage as an impedance chart or an admittance chart, (Inan, 2005).

An interesting historical and theoretical background of the Smith chart can be found in the article written by Aleksandar Marinčić, (Marinčić, 1997).

3. Construction of the Smith chart

The Smith chart is constructed based on the voltage reflection coefficient and can be considered as parameterized plot, on polar coordinates, of the generalized voltage reflection coefficient $\rho(|\rho|,\varphi)=|\rho|e^{j\varphi}$, within a circle of unit radius $(|\rho|\leq 1)$.

It is well known from transmission line theory, that the voltage reflection coefficient at the load is given by:

$$\rho_L = \frac{Z_L - Z_0}{Z_L + Z_0} \tag{1}$$

where Z_L is the load impedance and Z_0 is the characteristics impedance of the line. According to the transmission line theory, Z_0 is a real value but in general Z_L is a complex value. Equation 1 can be written as:

$$\rho_L = |\rho_L| \angle\varphi = \rho_r + j\rho_i \tag{2}$$

where ρ_r and ρ_i are respectively the real and imaginary parts of the reflection coefficient. Instead of having separate Smith chart for transmission lines with different characteristics impedances, it is preferable to have just one that can be used for any line. This is achieved using a normalized chart in which all impedances are normalized to the characteristic impedance Z_0 of the particular line under consideration. For example, for the load impedance Z_L, the normalized impedance z_L is given by,

$$z_L = \frac{Z_L}{Z_0} = r + jx \tag{3}$$

where r and x are respectively the real and imaginary parts of the normalized impedance. Substituting equations 2 and 3 into equation 1 gives,

$$\rho_r + j\rho_i = \frac{z_L - 1}{z_L + 1} \tag{4}$$

or

$$r + jx = \frac{(1+\rho_r) + j\rho_i}{(1-\rho_r) - j\rho_i} \tag{5}$$

Equating real and imaginary parts, we obtain

$$r = \frac{1-\rho_r^2-\rho_i^2}{(1-\rho_r)^2+\rho_i^2} \tag{6}$$

$$x = \frac{2\rho_i}{(1-\rho_r)^2+\rho_i^2} \tag{7}$$

rearranging the terms in equation 6 leads to:

$$\left(\rho_r - \frac{r}{1+r}\right)^2 + \rho_i^2 = \left(\frac{1}{1+r}\right)^2 \tag{8}$$

rearranging the terms in equation 7 leads to:

$$(\rho_r - 1)^2 + \left(\rho_i - \frac{1}{x}\right)^2 = \left(\frac{1}{x}\right)^2 \tag{9}$$

Each of equations 8 and 9 is similar to the circle equation. Equation 8 is a r-circle (resistance circle) with center at $\left(\frac{r}{1+r},0\right)$ and radius equal to $\frac{1}{1+r}$. Several of these circles for various values of normalized resistance *r*, are plotted in Figure 1a). From the Figure 1a), we see that all circles pass the point (1,0).

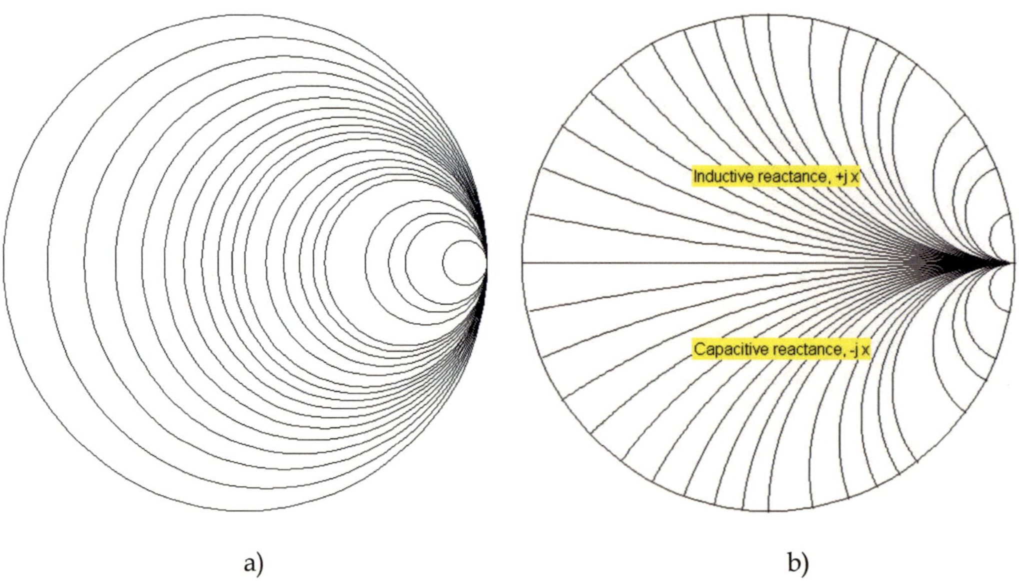

Fig. 1. Basic Smith chart. a)- normalized resistance circles. b)- normalized reactance curves.

Similarly, equation 9 is an *x* circle (reactance circle) with center at $\left(1,\frac{1}{x}\right)$ and radius equal to $\frac{1}{x}$. Several of these circles are plotted in Figure 1b), this time for positive and negative values of the normalized reactance x. Notice that while r is always positive, x can be positive (inductive impedance) or negative (capacitive impedance). From this figure we see that there are symmetry about the horizontal central axis of the chart. Only the portion of the circles inside the central circle of radius one is shown, since the maximum value of $|\rho|$ for any passive loaded line is one. The circles given by equations 8 and 9 are orthogonal circles that make a conform mapping chart.

If the r circles and the x circles are superimposed, the result is the Smith chart shown in the Figure 2.

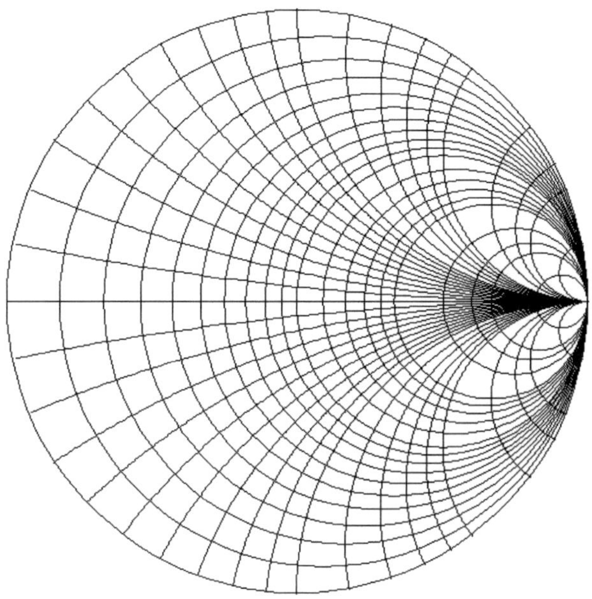

Fig. 2. Basic Smith chart.

3.1 Important features on a Smith chart

On a Smith chart there are some important points, lines and contours that should be mentioned. In Figure 3 some of these important features are indicated. The outer circle is the locus of the pure reactive impedances, that is, those with zero resistance. The horizontal axis is the locus of the real impedances. The left radius is the locus of the resistances less than Z_0 for which the reflection coefficient has a phase of 180º. The left extreme of this radius is the zero resistance and zero reactance point, that is, the short circuit point (SC). The right radius is the locus of the resistances greater than Z_0 for which the reflection coefficient has a phase of 0º. The right extreme of this radius is the infinite resistance and infinite reactance point, that is, the open circuit point (OC).

For a lossless transmission line terminated in a load with a reflection coefficient ρ_L, the circle with radius $|\rho_L|$ (known as the ρ circle or S circle), is the locus of all impedances appearing along the line, normalized to the characteristic impedance Z_0 of the line. These impedances can be obtained moving along the line either toward the load (counter

clockwise) or toward the generator (clockwise). When moving along the ρ circle, every crossing of the left horizontal radius corresponds to a voltage minimum (therefore a current maximum) in the line and to a real impedance less than Z_0 . Similarly, every crossing of the right horizontal radius corresponds to a voltage maximum (therefore a current minimum) in the line and to a real impedance greater than Z_0 .
In Figure 3a) some important features of when the Smith chart is used as an impedance chart are pointed out.
In the resolution of some problems, it is more convenient to work with admittances than with impedances. In these cases the Smith chart can be effectively used as an admittance chart. In this case the *r* circles and the *x* curves should be seen as *g* circles and *b* curves respectively. Also the upper half of the chart now corresponds to capacitive susceptances given by positive values of *b* and, the lower half of the chart corresponds to inductive susceptances given by negative values of *b*. In Figure 3b) some important features are indicated when the Smith chart is used as an admittance chart.
It is easy to transform a normalized impedance *z* in the corresponding admittance *y*. It will be located on the ρ circle in the opposite side of the diameter that passes through *z*.

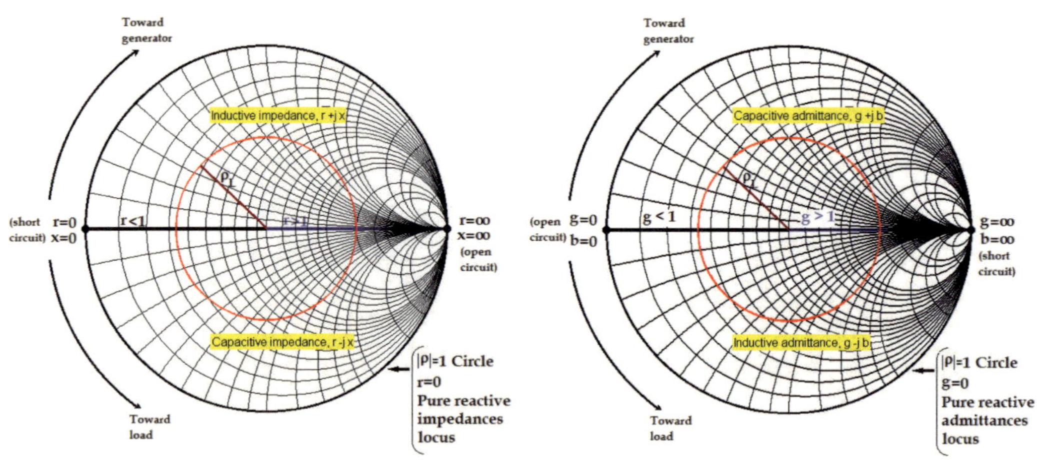

a) b)

Fig. 3. Some important features of a Smith chart. a)- When used as an impedance chart. b)- When used as an admittance chart.

Nowadays, the Smith chart appears in several different types. One of them is shown in Figure 4. The main difference between this chart and the basic Smith chart shown in figure 2 is the existence of three scales around the periphery.
The outermost scale is used to determine distances in wavelengths toward the generator and the next scale is used to determine distances in wavelengths toward the load. The innermost scale is a protractor (in degrees) and is primarily used to determine the phase of the reflection coefficient and the phase of the transmission coefficient. It can also be used to determine distances, toward the load or toward the generator, expressed in degrees bearing in mind that a distance of $\lambda/2$ corresponds to 360°.
The Smith chart illustrated in figure 4 has also other auxiliary scales useful for the determination of some parameters like for example, the VSWR, the amplitudes of the reflection and transmission coefficients, the return loss in dB etc.

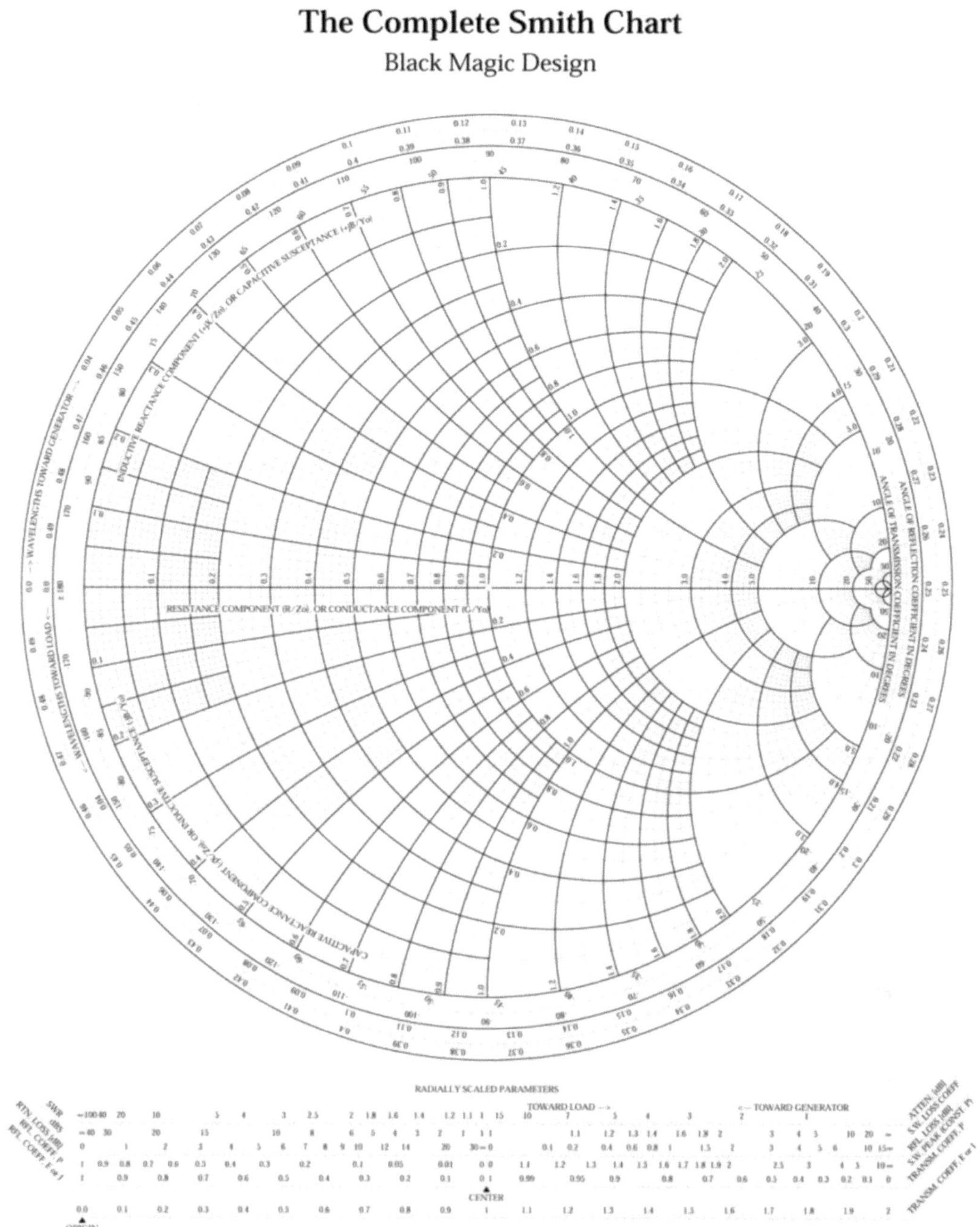

Fig. 4. Typical Smith chart. With permission of Spread Spectrum Scene, http://www.sss-mag.com/pdf/smithchart.pdf.

The Smith chart simplifies transmission line analysis, and is still used today in most modern textbooks and courses in electrical engineering. It promotes a better understanding of the problem being solved. And such an understanding might be relevant for the interpretation of the simulation results given by commercial software about antennas and microwave devices. Most modern computer based automatic network analyzers rely on the Smith chart for data display.

This chart is a unique diagram which has been used nearly for ninety years and we believe that it will be in use for many years to come not only as a pedagogically perfect analogue display, but also as an aid to professionals in obtaining quick answers to many line problems which they meet.

4. Getting started

As pointed out above, the aim of this chapter is to help the reader understand and learn how to use the Smith chart describing step by step procedures based in *MATLAB* scripts that should teach the students to solve different kinds of transmission line problems by themselves in a paper chart using a pencil, a ruler and a compass. One of the first things they should know how to do, is how to mark a given reflection coefficient in a chart and read related data associated to this reflection coefficient, such the transmission coefficient, the normalized impedance, the normalized admittance and the voltage standing wave ratio. The authors developed a *MATLAB* script called *SmithChart_InputRho_Eng_FV.m* that display, step by step, how to do this exercise.

The graphical solution given by this script, is shown in Figure 5, for a reflection coefficient $\rho = 0.6\angle 120^{\circ}$.

Figure 5a) shows the first 2 steps:

1. Marking ρ_L, from the amplitude and phase;
2. Drawing the ρ_L constant circle;

Figure 5b) shows the last 3 steps:

3. Getting the transmission coefficient $\rho_t = 1 + \rho_L = |\rho_t| e^{j\psi}$;
4. Getting the normalized impedance z_L;
5. Getting the normalized admittance, by inverting z_L to y_L;
6. Getting the associated SWR.

Another basic thing students should know how to do, is to mark a given normalized impedance in a chart and read related data associated to it, such as the reflection coefficient, the normalized admittance and the voltage standing wave ratio. The authors developed a *MATLAB* script called *SmithChart_InputZ_Eng_FV.m* that displays step by step, how to do this exercise.

The graphical solution given by this script, is shown in Figure 6, for a normalized impedance $z_L = 0.3 + j0.5$.

Figure 6a) shows the first 2 steps:

1. Highlighting the curves r_L and x_L;
2. Marking the normalized impedance z_L;

Figure 6b) shows the last 3 steps:

3. Getting the normalized admittance, by inverting z_L to y_L;
4. Getting the corresponding reflection coefficient $\rho_L = |\rho_L| e^{j\varphi}$;
5. Getting the corresponding transmission coefficient $\rho_t = 1 + \rho_L = |\rho_t| e^{j\psi}$;
6. Getting the associated SWR.

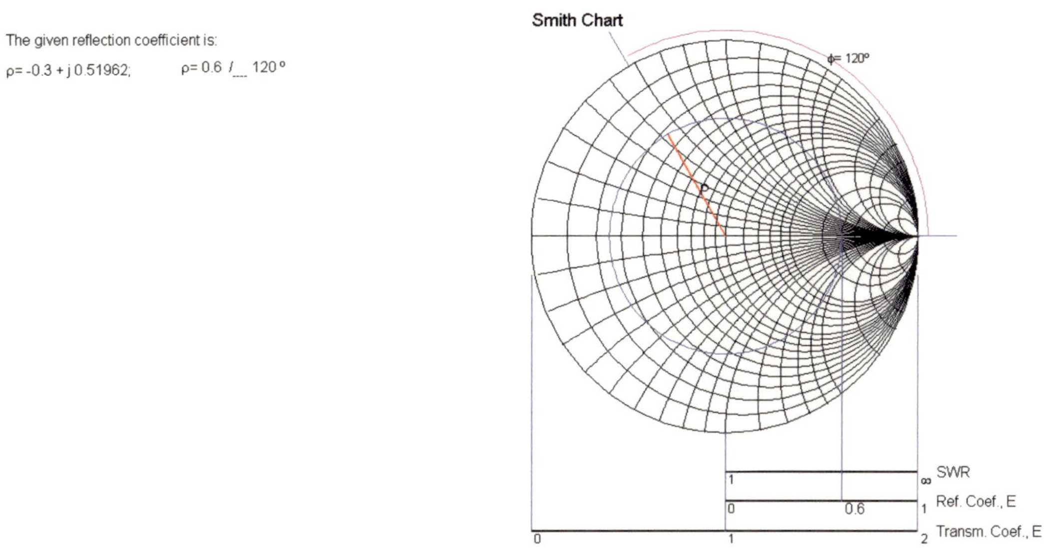

a)

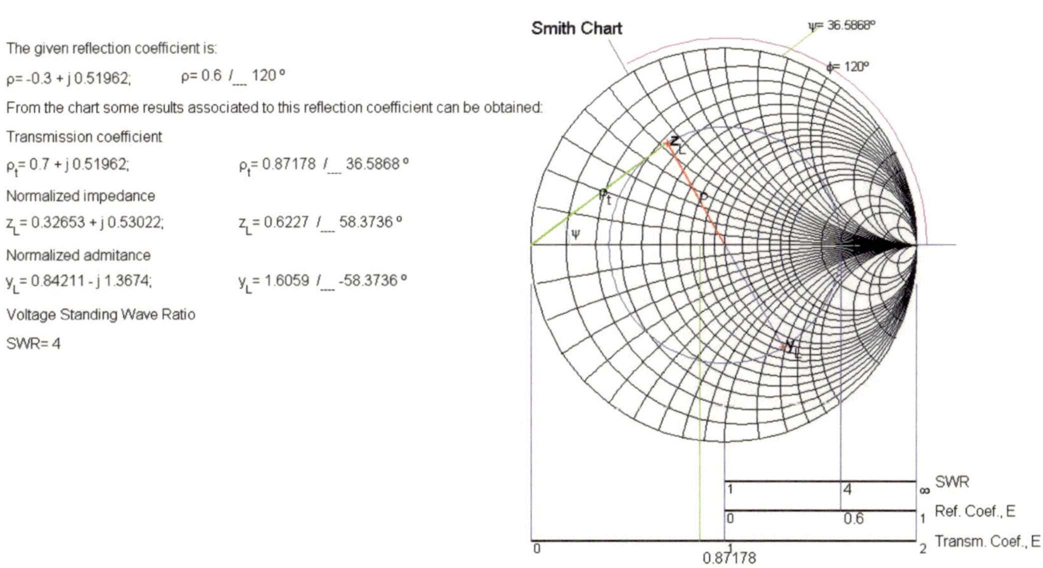

b)

Fig. 5. Inputting a reflection coefficient. Display given by *SmithChart_InputRho_Eng_FV.m*.

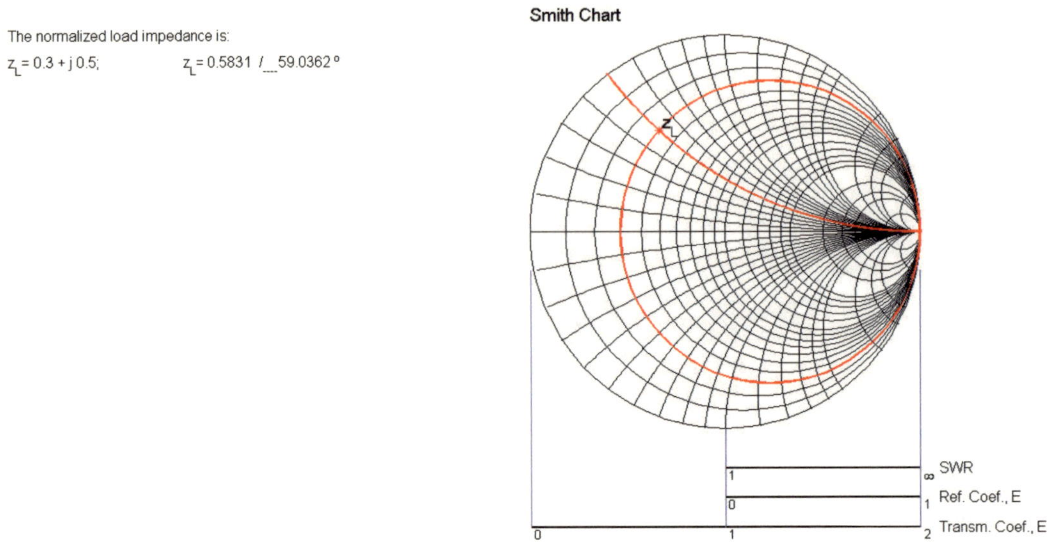

a)

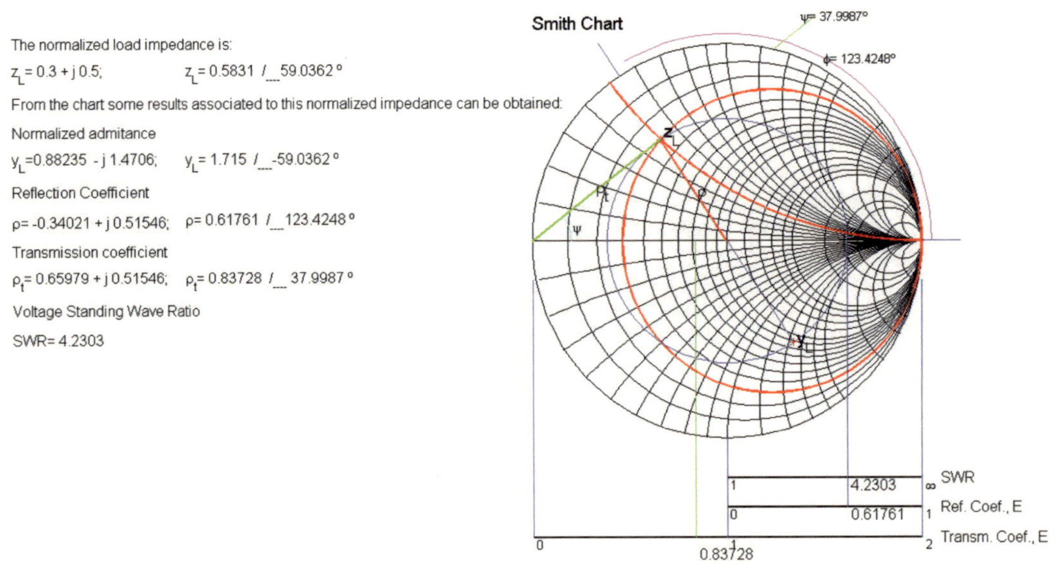

b)

Fig. 6. Inputting a normalized impedance. Display given by the script *SmithChart_InputZ_Eng_FV.m.*

It is also important to know how to locate the voltage maxima and minima along the line, given a normalized impedance using the chart. The *MATLAB* script called *SmithChart_InputZ_FindVmin_FindVmax_Eng_FV.m* displays, step by step, how to locate the first voltage maximum and minimum.

By definition, the reflection coefficient is the ratio of the phasors of the reverse and forward voltage waves. A voltage maximum occurs when these waves are in phase adding together constructively. If these waves are in opposite phase, a voltage minimum results. Therefore, travelling along the line, from the load toward the generator, if the right horizontal axis is reached first this corresponds to a reflection coefficient with a 0° phase, which means a voltage maximum. If, however the left horizontal axis is reached first, this corresponds to a reflection coefficient with a 180° phase, which means a voltage minimum.
The graphical solution given by this script, is shown in Figure 7, for the normalized impedance $z_L = 1.4 + j1.6$.

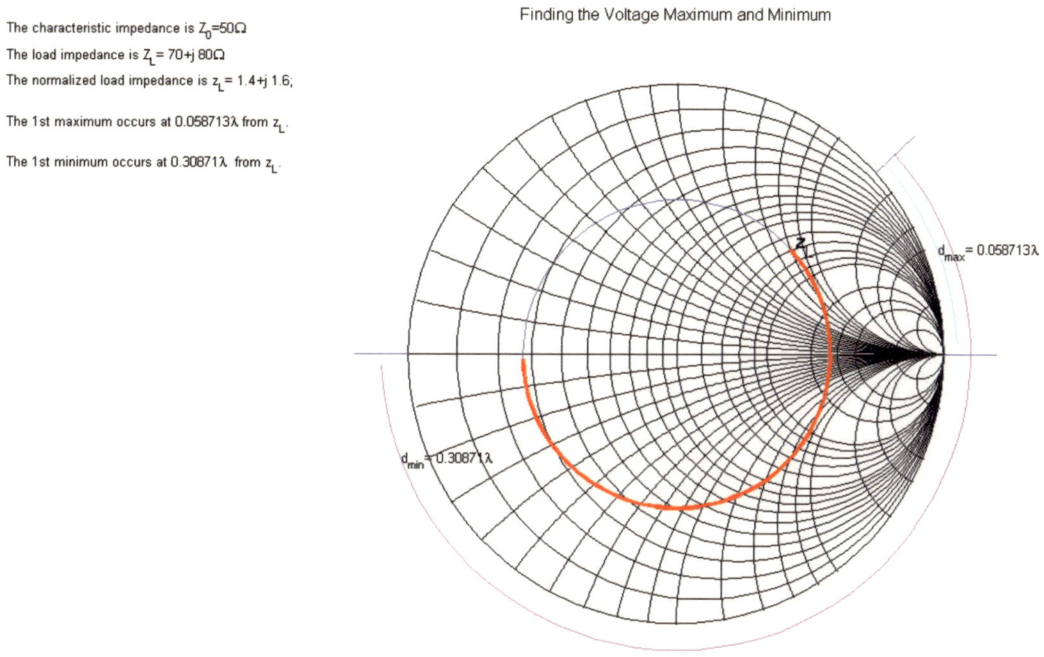

Fig. 7. Display given by SmithChart_InputZ_FindVmin_FindVmax_Eng_FV.m.

From Figure 7, one can perceive that travelling along the line, from the load toward the generator, the first particular point is a voltage maximum that occurs at a distance d=0.0587λ. This happens because the load is inductive. Continuing to travel along the line, after λ/4 a voltage minimum is found. As it is well known, the maxima are separated by λ/2. The same applies to the minima. This implies that a minimum is separated from the consecutive maxima by λ/4.
For a lossless line the absolute value of the reflection coefficient remains constant along the line, however its phase changes and therefore the impedance along the line also changes. Since a complete turn on the chart corresponds to travel λ/2, this means that after traveling λ/2, from the load to the generator, the load point is reached. This means that the impedance at a distance of λ/2 from the load is equal to the load. Therefore, for a lossless line, all the points separated by λ/2 have the same characteristics.

The authors developed a *MATLAB* script called *LosslessLine_Eng_FV.m* that graphically illustrates how the impedance along the line changes, as shown in figure 8. In this example a lossless line 0.35λ long with a characteristic impedance Z_0=50Ω, terminated with the load Z_L=100+j60 Ω, has an input impedance Z_{in}=21.88+j17.43 Ω. It is important to note the changes in nature of the impedance along the line when one moves from the load to the generator. At the load the impedance is inductive, then became real greater than Z_0. After that, and for the next λ/4, became capacitive and then again inductive until it reached the generator plane.

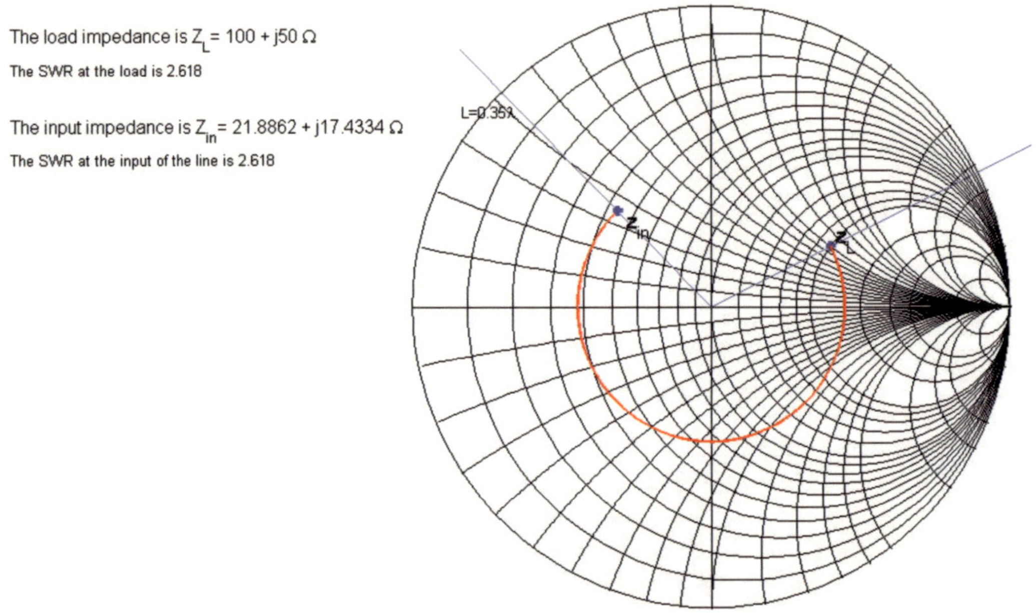

Fig. 8. Impedance variation along a lossless line 0.35λ long. Graphical solution given by the *LosslessLine_Eng_FV.m* script.

5. Applications examples

In this section, some examples that integrate transmission line concepts are presented. The following examples are explained: (1) Single stub matching, (2) Bandwidth of a single-stub impedance matching system, (3) Quarter wavelength impedance matching, (4) Analysis of lossy lines. The authors developed *MATLAB* scripts that display, step by step, the graphical procedures used to solve these problems.
An example illustrating the double-stub impedance matching problem was also developed by the authors, (Pereira & Pinho, 2010).

5.1 Single-stub impedance matching

In any Transmission Line course, the concept of impedance matching is a topic that must be addressed. In transmission line context, impedance matching occurs when the characteristic impedance Z_0 of the line is equal to the load impedance Z_L.When this happens, the characteristic impedance and load impedance are said to be matched. In this situation, the reflection coefficient is zero and no standing waves exist. In transmission line applications, it is desirable to achieve the matching condition.

There are several methods to achieve impedance matching. One of the simplest methods to match a transmission line to a given load is to connected a reactive element in parallel with the line at a point where the real part of the line admittance is equal to the characteristic admittance. This reactive element can be realized by a short piece of line, called stub. That is why this method is known by the single-stub impedance matching.

Although the location of the stub and its length can be found analytically using a computer or even a calculator, the authors believe that the use of the Smith chart to solve graphically this problem will give to the undergraduate students a much better insight of the aspects involved in this problem. The authors developed a *MATLAB* script called *SingleStubMatching_Eng_FV.m* that displays step by step, this graphical procedure. This script is available for download and should be used when reading this section.

The basic layout of the single-stub impedance matching is illustrated in Figure 9. The parameters to be evaluated are the distance *d*, measured from the load, at which the stub must be placed and, the stub length *Ls*. The stub is connected in parallel with the line. The stub can be short-circuited terminated or open-circuited terminated. Since the stub is connected in parallel with the line, the solution of this problem must be approached in terms of admittance. If the load is inputted as an impedance, then it is necessary to transform it in an admittance, using the graphical procedure explained before.

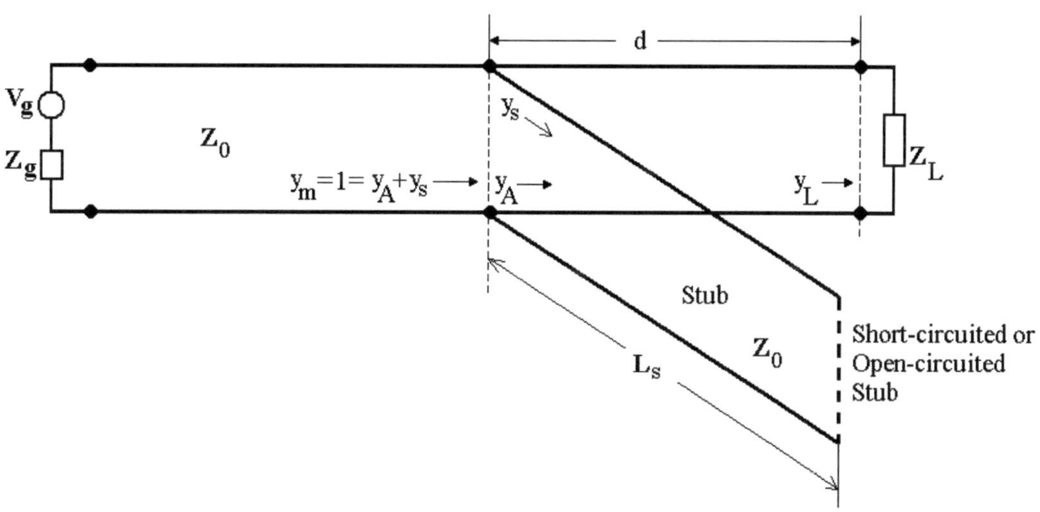

Fig. 9. Basic layout of the single-stub impedance matching.

The goal is to match the load Z_L to the line with characteristic impedance Z_0. Therefore the normalized admittance y_m, at the generator side of the stub, must be equal 1. On the other hand, this normalized admittance is equal to the sum of y_A and y_s. Since by definition, assuming lossless transmission lines, the input admittance of a stub has no real part, that is, $y_s = \pm jb_s$, that implies that the admittance y_A must be $y_A = 1 \pm jb_A$. Furthermore, the value of b_s must be the symmetrical of b_A in order to cancel each other out.

5.1.1 Graphical procedure

As explained above, the admittance at the load side of the stub must be $y_A = 1 \pm jb_A$. This means that the locus of y_A in the Smith chart is the $g = 1$ circle. Since lossless transmission lines are assumed, when travelling from the load toward the generator the absolute value of the reflection coefficient remains constant, that is, $|\rho| = |\rho_L|$.

Therefore, the possible values of y_A must be given by the intersection of the two circles: the $g = 1$ circle, and the ρ_L constant circle. Except for loads with real part equal to zero, there are two intersection points and therefore two solutions.

The solutions are found starting at the value of y_L in the Smith chart and moving toward the generator (clockwise), along the corresponding constant ρ_L circle, until the intersection with the $g = 1$ circle is obtained.

After choosing a solution for y_A, since $y_A = 1 \pm jb_A$ it is possible to get the corresponding value of $y_s = \mp jb_s = \pm jb_A$.

To determine the length of a short-circuited terminated stub, with an input admittance y_s, one should move, from the admittance SC point in the Smith chart, toward the generator (clockwise) to the point corresponding to the input admittance, along the $g = 0$ circle and read the required distance in wavelengths. To determine the length of an open-circuited terminated stub, with an input admittance y_s, one should move from the admittance OC point in the Smith chart, toward the generator (clockwise) to the point corresponding to the input admittance, along the $g = 0$ circle and read the required distance in wavelengths.

The authors developed a *MATLAB* script called *SingleStubMatching_Eng_FV.m* that displays step by step, the graphical procedure described above. Four cases are studied:

- Intersection with the upper half of the $g = 1$ circle and a short-circuited stub;
- Intersection with the lower half of the $g = 1$ circle, and a short-circuited stub;
- Intersection with the upper half of the $g = 1$ circle, and a open-circuited stub;
- Intersection with the lower half of the $g = 1$ circle, and a open-circuited stub;

The graphical solution given by this script for the first case, is shown in Figure 10, for a line with a characteristic impedance Z_0=50Ω and the load Z_L=100+j60 Ω.

Figure 10a) shows the first 7 steps:

1. Marking the normalized impedance z_L;
2. Drawing the ρ_L constant circle;
3. Transforming the normalized impedance in admittance, by inverting z_L to y_L;
4. Drawing the $g = 1$ constant circle;
5. Choosing one of the intersection points of the ρ_L constant circle with the $g = 1$ circle, (point A);
6. Finding the admittance y_A from the chosen intersection point;
7. Finding the distance *d*, in wavelengths, moving from y_L, toward the generator (clockwise) along the ρ_L constant circle, until y_A.

Figure 10b) shows the last 2 steps:

8. Getting the value of y_s from the value of y_A;
9. Determining the length *Ls* of the stub, in wavelengths, moving, from the admittance SC point in the Smith chart, toward the generator (clockwise) along the $g = 0$ circle to the point corresponding to the input admittance of the stub (point B).

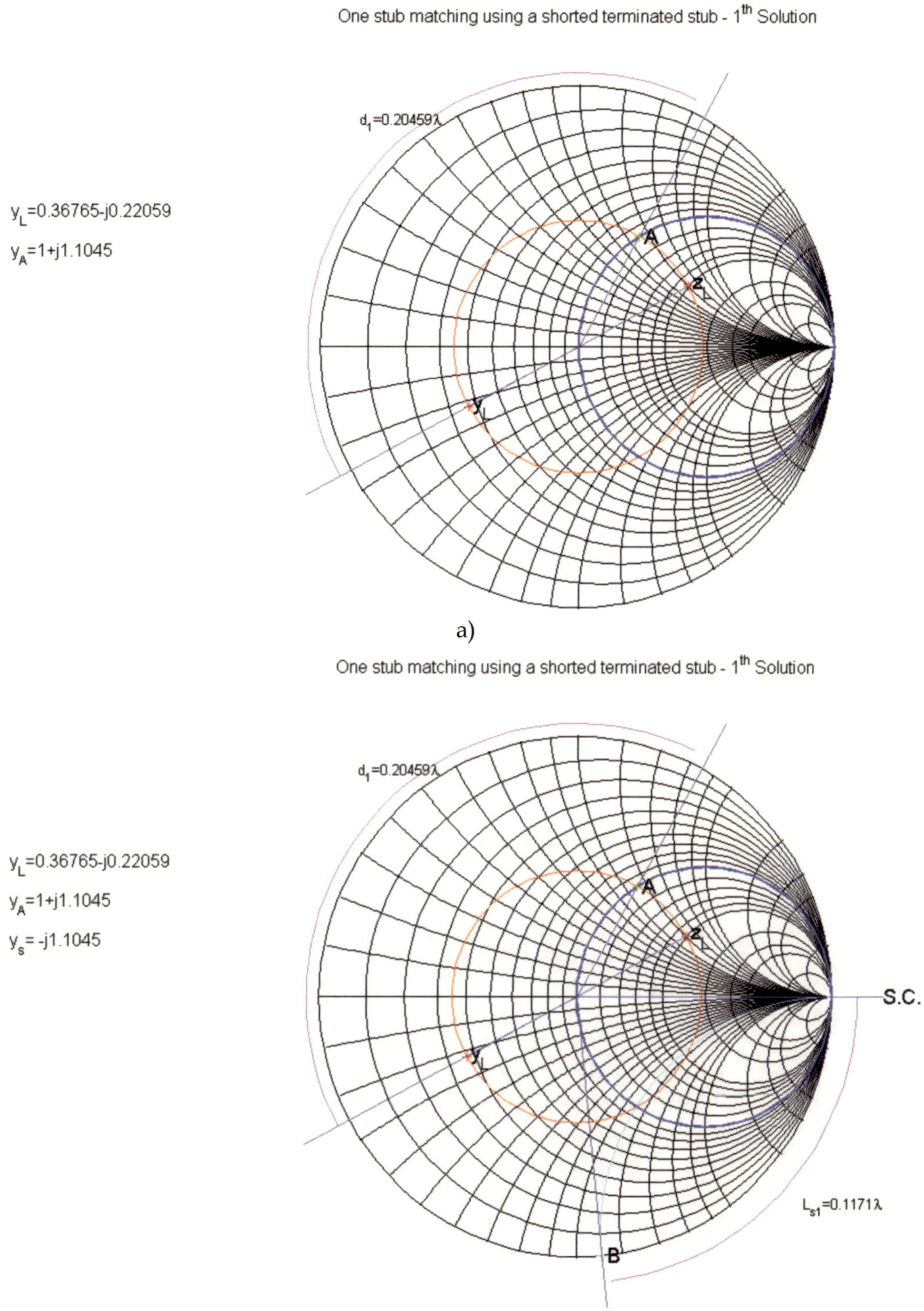

a)

b)

Fig. 10. Graphical solution given by the *SingleStubMatching_Eng_FV.m* script.

Following the display produced by this script, students should be able to solve in a paper chart any single-stub impedance matching problem using a ruler and a compass.
The other cases given by script *SingleStubMatching_Eng_FV.m* can be explored by the reader.

5.2 Bandwidth of a single-stub impedance matching system

Another important topic that should be explained to the undergraduate students is the concept of bandwidth of a system. The majority of the systems based in transmission lines are perfectly matched at just one frequency. However, since the system should be able to operate over a frequency band, it is important to find the frequency band for which the system is consider to be acceptable matched. This frequency band is called the bandwidth of the system. Usually the criterion used to consider a system matched is when the VSWR is less or equal to 2.
The lower and the upper frequencies of the bandwidth can be found analytically. However, the authors believe that using the Smith chart to find graphically the bandwidth, will give to the students a much better understanding of the effects on the admittance of the line, and therefore on the matching conditions, when the frequency changes. The authors developed two *MATLAB* scripts called *SingleStubMatching_Eng_BW_FV2a.m* and *SingleStubMatching_Eng_BW_FV2b.m* that displays graphically, step by step, the effects on the matching conditions, when the frequency changes. Both are for systems using short-circuited stubs. One of the scripts is for one of the two possible solutions and the other for the other solution. It is important for the students to verify that the bandwidth is not the same for the two solutions. These scripts is available for download and should be explored when reading this section.
The single-stub impedance matching system explained in the previous section, gives a perfect matching at one frequency. Once constructed, if the frequency changes so does the electric length of the distance d and length Ls, and therefore a perfect matching is no longer achieved.
It is important to study the evolution of the matching values for a single-stub matching system, when the frequency varies around the central value for which a perfect matching was achieved. To observe this evolution, the authors developed *MATLAB* scripts that graphically display this evolution and give the VSWR 2:1 bandwidth. After choosing short-circuited or open-circuited stubs, there are still two solutions for the single-stub matching system, the perfect matching can be achieved with two pairs of values of d and Ls and therefore two different evolution of the matching values are also obtained. The script called *SingleStubMatching_Eng_BW_FV2a.m* is intended for one of the solutions and script called *SingleStubMatching_Eng_BW_FV2b.m* is intended for the other. Both use short-circuited stubs. It is important to compare the VSWR 2:1 bandwidth obtained for both solutions.
Figure 11 shows the graphical evolution of the matching values given by the script *SingleStubMatching_Eng_BW_FV2a.m* for the example illustrated in Figure 10. In this script the chosen solution is the one that corresponds to the intersection with the upper half of the $g = 1$ circle.
Figure 11a) shows the graphical evolution of the matching values when the frequency decreases. When the frequency decreases, then the electrical sizes of d and Ls also decreases. Point A moves toward the load and point S toward SC. y_m moves away from the center of chart (perfect matching).
Figure 11b) shows the graphical evolution of the matching values when the frequency increases. When the frequency increases, then the electrical sizes of d and Ls also increases.

Point A moves away from the load and point S away from SC. y_m moves away from the center of chart (perfect matching). With this solution a VSWR 2:1 bandwidth of 38% is obtained.

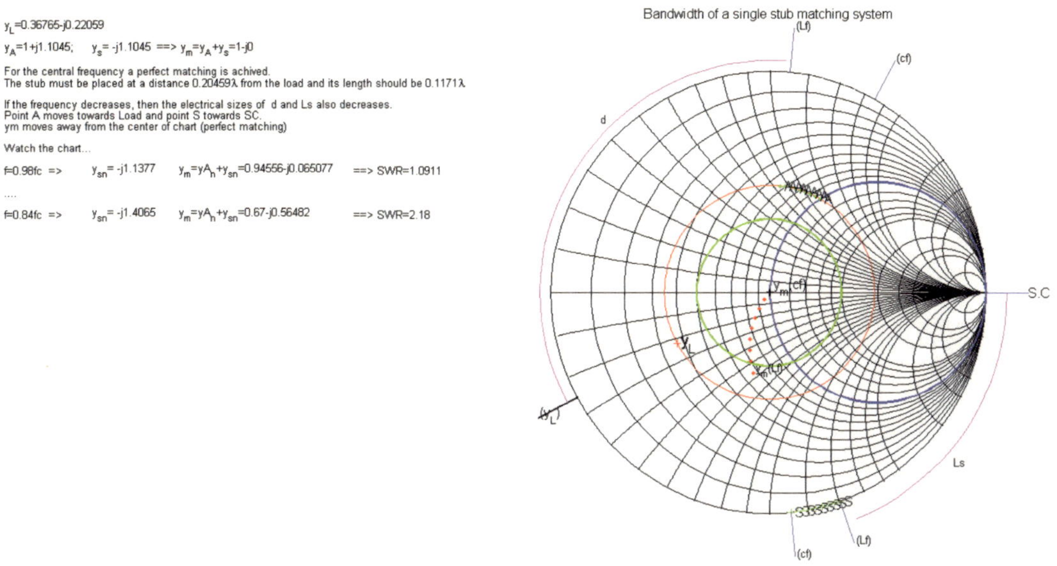

a)

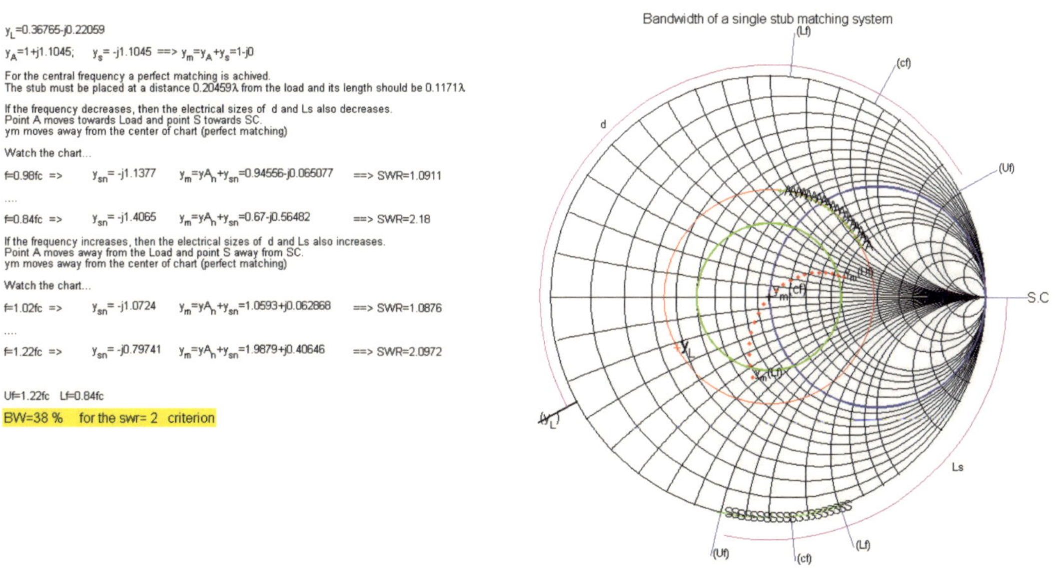

b)

Fig. 11. Graphical solution given by the *SingleStubMatching_Eng_BW_FV2a.m* script.

Figure 12 shows the graphical evolution of the matching values given by the script *SingleStubMatching_Eng_BW_FV2b.m* for the example illustrated in Figure 10. In this script

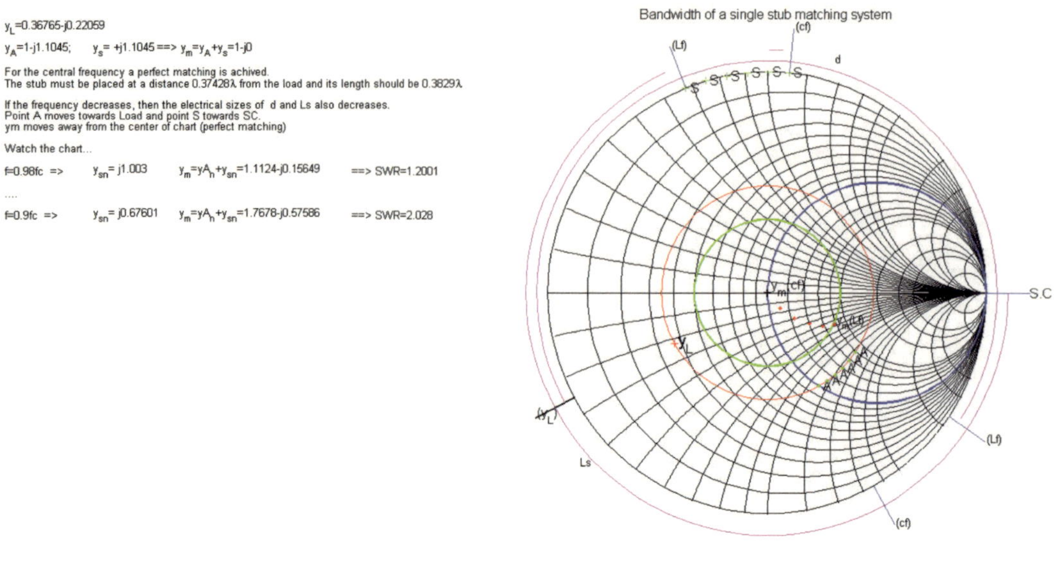

a)

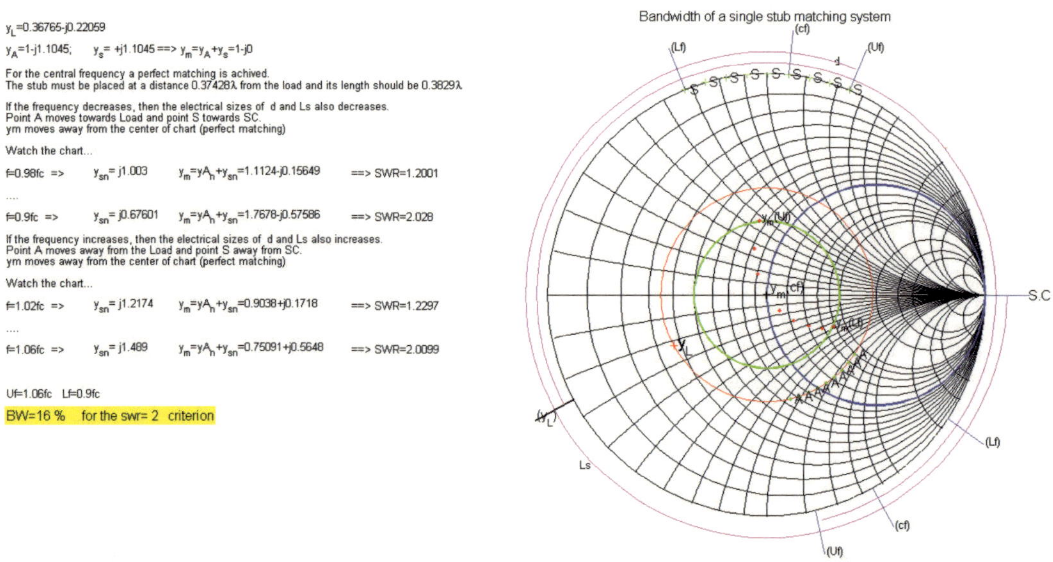

Fig. 12. Graphical solution given by the *SingleStubMatching_Eng_BW_FV2b.m* script.

the chosen solution is the one that corresponds to the intersection with the lower half of the $g = 1$ circle.

Figure 12a) shows the graphical evolution of the matching values when the frequency decreases. When the frequency decreases, the electrical sizes of d and Ls also decreases. Point A moves toward the load and point S toward SC. y_m moves away from the center of chart (perfect matching).

Figure 12b) shows the graphical evolution of the matching values when the frequency increases. When the frequency increases, the electrical sizes of d and Ls also increases. Point

A moves away from the load and point S away from SC. y_m moves away from the center of chart (perfect matching). With this solution a VSWR 2:1 bandwidth of 16% is obtained. So, as mentioned before, different bandwidth are obtained depending on the chosen for pair of values of *d* and *Ls*.

5.3 Quarter wavelength impedance matching system

As pointed out before, there are several methods to achieve impedance matching. One well known method consists in the insertion of a transmission line with a length of a quarter wavelength and an appropriate characteristic impedance, in a position where the impedance is real. This matching technique is known as a quarter wavelength impedance matching system or as the quarter wavelength transformer.

The characteristic impedance of this quarter wavelength transformer is given by $Z_1 = \sqrt{Z_{R1} Z_{R2}}$, where Z_{R1} is the impedance at the right side of the transformer and Z_{R2} is the impedance at the left side of the transformer. Since a common transmission line has a real characteristic impedance, Z_{R1} and Z_{R2} must both be real. If a line is terminated in a complex load, the quarter wavelength transformer cannot be inserted at the load plane. It is then necessary to move along the line, a distance *d*, toward the generator till a real impedance Z_{R1} is obtained. This is illustrated in Figure 13. Two values for Z_{R1} are possible. One greater than Z_0 and another less than Z_0, separated by $\lambda/4$. Once Z_{R1} is chosen, Z_1 can be calculated bearing in mind that Z_{R2} must be equal Z_0 to achieve a perfect matching.

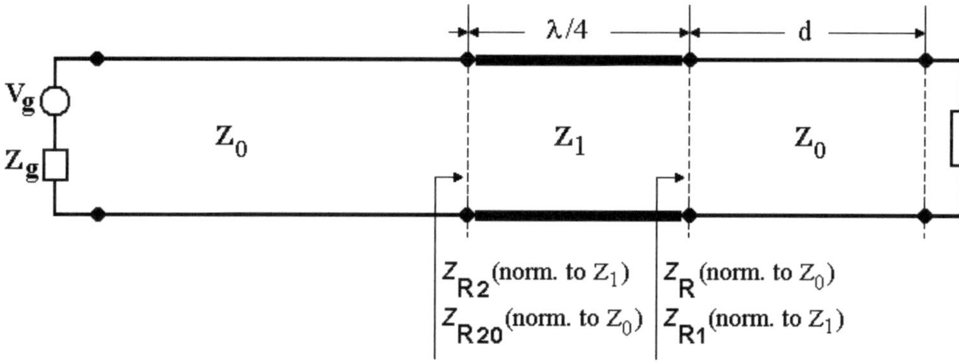

Fig. 13. Basic layout of the quarter wavelength impedance matching.

In general the students learn this method in a analytical way, by the direct computation of the required characteristic impedance of the quarter wavelength line and the location for its insertion. However, the authors believe that the use of the Smith chart to solve graphically this problem will give to the students a much better insight of the several impedance transformations involved in this problem to achieve an impedance equal to the characteristic impedance of the main line.

The authors developed a *MATLAB* script called *QuarterWavelengthTransformer_Eng_FV.m* that graphically explains, the quarter wavelength matching mechanism.

This is shown in Figure 14, for a line with a characteristic impedance Z_0=50Ω and a load Z_L=100+j60 Ω.

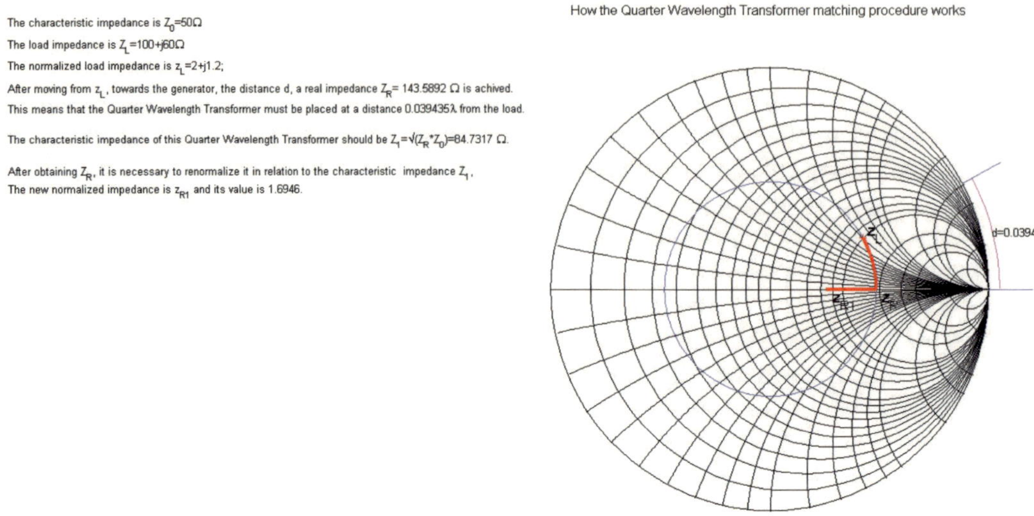

a)

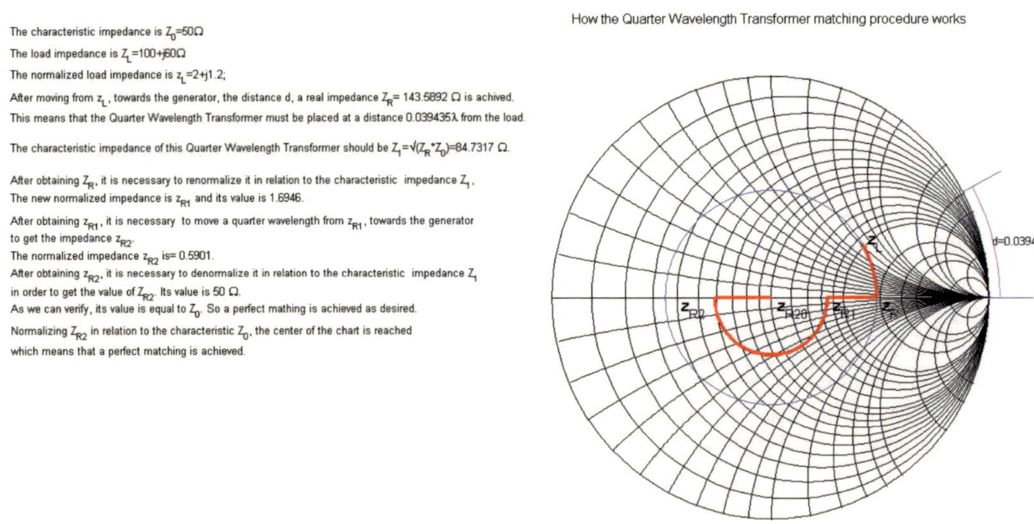

b)

Fig. 14. Graphical solution given by the *QuarterWavelengthTransformer_Eng_FV.m* script.

Figure 14a) shows the first 5 steps:

1. Marking the normalized impedance z_L;
2. Finding the distance *d*, in wavelengths, moving from z_L, toward the generator (clockwise) along the ρ_L constant circle, until the real normalized impedance z_R is obtained. In this example z_R greater than 1 was chosen;
3. Renormalize z_R impedance with reference to Z_0 in order to get Z_R;
4. Calculate $Z_1 = \sqrt{Z_R Z_0}$;
5. Normalize Z_R with reference to Z_1 obtaining z_{R1};

Figure 14b) shows the last 3 steps:

6. Moving from z_{R1}, toward the generator (clockwise) along the ρ constant circle, until the real normalized impedance z_{R2} is obtained;
7. Renormalizing z_{R2} impedance with reference to Z_1 an impedance $Z_{R2} = Z_0$ is obtained, meaning that a perfect matching is achieved;
8. Normalizing $Z_{R2} = Z_0$ with reference to Z_0 a normalized impedance of 1 is obtained, which means that the center of the chart is reached, confirming a perfect matching;

5.4 Analysis of lossy lines

In all the above examples, lossless transmission lines have been used. However all lines have some losses and this changes the results. One of the main influences of the losses is in the amplitude of the reflection coefficient and therefore in the impedance along the line. For a lossy line the reflection coefficient is given by equation 10.

$$\rho(d) = \rho_L e^{-2\alpha d} e^{-j2\beta d} \tag{10}$$

being d the distance measured from the load toward the generator, α the attenuation constant in Np/m and β the propagation constant in rad/m.

From equation 10, we notice that the phase changing of the reflection coefficient is equal to a lossless line, however the amplitude decreases from the load to the generator according with the equation 11.

$$|\rho(d)| = |\rho_L| e^{-2\alpha d} \tag{11}$$

Due to this amplitude decreasing, when travelling from the load to the generator the locus of ρ is a spiral approaching the center of the chart instead of a circle like in a lossless line. This means that at the input of a lossy line there is a better matching than at the load. Due to the loss of energy in the line, at the generator there is less returned energy to the generator and therefore a better matching. The authors developed a *MATLAB* script called *LossyLine_Eng_FV.m* that graphically explains these effects as illustrated in Figures 15 and 16. As shown in Figure 16 a long line terminated in a load with the high VSWR of 10.4, has at the input a very acceptable VSWR of 1.7.

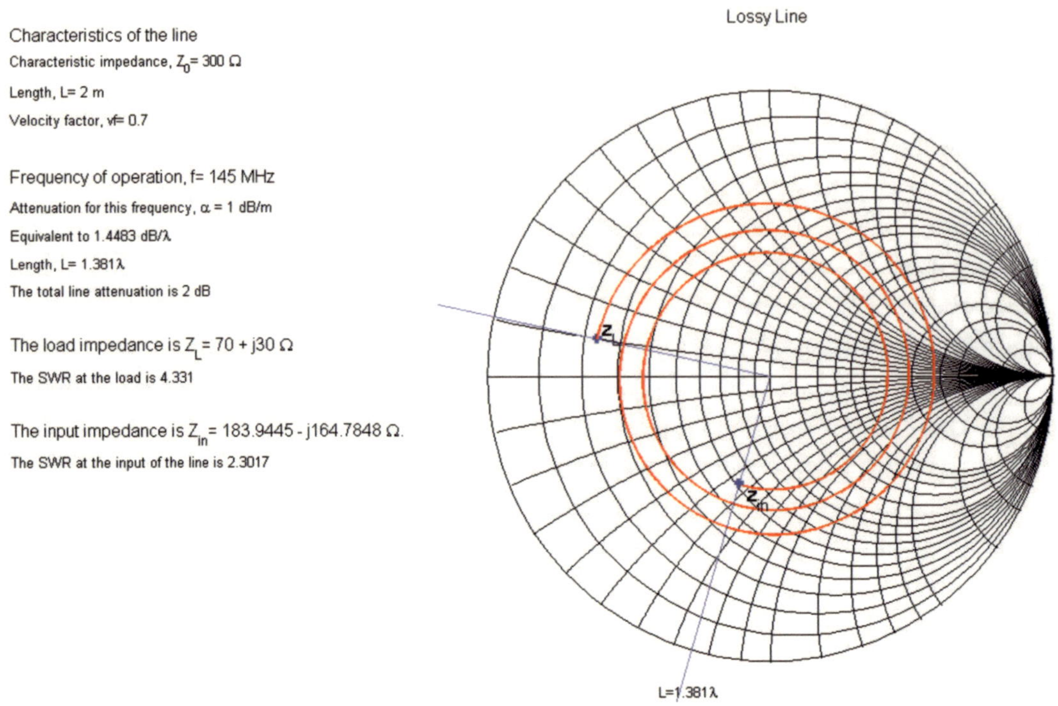

Fig. 15. Graphical solution given by the *LossyLine_Eng_FV.m* script for a short line.

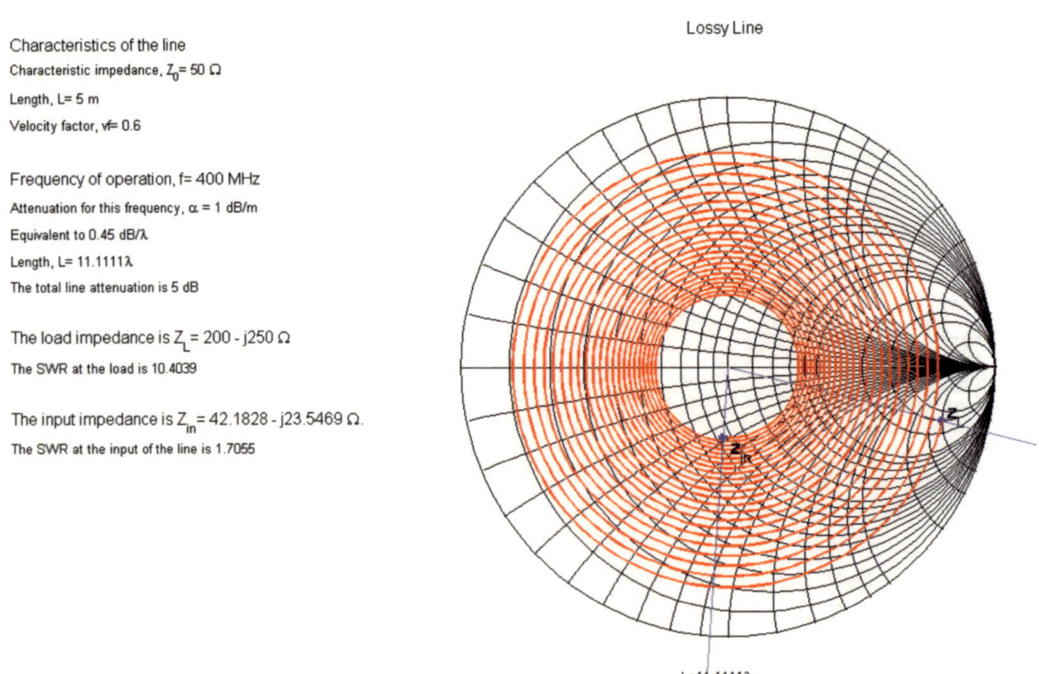

Fig. 16. Graphical solution given by the *LossyLine_Eng_FV.m* script for a long line.

If a long line is to be considered, it is important to know its attenuation constant and to evaluate its implications in the problem being considered.

6. Conclusion

It is well known that many transmission line problems can easily be solved using graphical procedures based on the Smith chart. The authors still believe that the use of the Smith chart by the students is an important pedagogical tool even knowing that personal computers and calculators are commonly available nowadays.

Since the main topic of this book is concerned with *e-learning*, the aim of this chapter is to help the reader understand and learn how to use the Smith chart following a step by step procedure based on *MATLAB* scripts, that should be used when reading this chapter. This approach should teach the students to solve several kinds of transmission line problems by themselves in a paper chart using a pencil, a ruler and a compass.

To exemplify this concept, the authors developed *MATLAB* scripts that display, step by step, the graphical procedure used in several applications. Using these scripts, many aspects of the transmission line theory such as: the voltage, current, impedance, Voltage Standing Wave Ratio (VSWR), reflection coefficient and matching design problems can be easily interpreted and well visualized using the Smith chart.

The chapter was organized as follows:

- History and use of the Smith chart and its importance in the resolution of classical transmission line problems.
- Construction of this chart from the basic equations and concepts.
- How to use the Smith chart.
- Presentation of some examples that integrates the transmission line concepts.

The authors developed a *MATLAB* scripts that display, step by step, the graphical procedure that must be used to solve these examples.

All the *MATLAB* scripts can be download from the link:

http://www.av.it.pt/rochap/MatlabScripts.zip

7. References

Inan, A. S. (2005). Remembering Phillip H. Smith on his 100th Birthday. *IEEE Antennas and Propagation Society International Symposium,* Vol. 3B, (July 2005), pp. 129-132, ISBN: 0-7803-8883-6

Marinčić, A. (1997). The Smith Chart, *Microwave Review,* Vol. 4, No.2, (December 1997), pp. 1-7

Mak, F. & Sundaram, R. (2008). A *MATLAB*-Based Teaching Of The Two-Stub Smith Chart Application For Electromagnetics Class, *38th ASEE/IEEE Frontiers in Education Conference,* pp. T2A-7-11, ISBN 978-1-4244-1969-2, Saratoga Springs, NY, October 22–25, 2008

MATLAB™, The MathWorks, Inc., http://www.mathworks.com

Pereira, J. R, & Pinho, P. (2010). Using Modern Tools to Explain the Use of the Smith Chart, *IEEE Antennas and Propagation Magazine*, Vol. 52, No. 2, (April 2010), pp. 145-150, ISSN 1045-9243

8

Intelligent Tutoring System with Associative Cellular Neural Network

Michihiro Namba
Department of Humanities, Yamanashi Eiwa College
Japan

1. Introduction

In self-directed learning such as e-learning, it is significant for learner to recongnize his understanding level. Wrong judgment would provide inefficient learning, and cause a lack of motivation. Test is widely used as an effective method evaluating learner's understanding level, and we often judge it based only on its score (accuracy rate). For easy system construction, many e-learning systems use a multiple-choice test, which often provides a right answer with no comprehension.

Studies on estimating learner's understanding level by using learning history and test have been reported. One of them is construction of learner model based on accuracy rate and answer time in test (Sobue et al., 2004). However, it requires an enormous amount of data and consideration of learner's uncertain elements.

Another solution is to use heuristic model. It is not appropriate to classify learners into at most two groups (either comprehend or not comprehend) due to effective instruction. Then, we add answer time as an objective criterion. Their combination can provide various understanding levels and more precise estimation. The problem that estimates leaner's understanding level based on objective information can be related to ambiguous classification. Heuristic model is effective for it.

Many intelligent tutoring system (ITS) (Gunel, 2010; Nkambou & Bourdeau, 2008) has been developed in recent years. Constructing an accurate learner model is an important element in ITS. The method that generates fuzzy rule and uses classification has been proposed (Takashi et al., 2006). However, it requires enormous data. The methods that use Bayesian Network which utilizes statistical approximation and Support Vector Machine (SVM) which has a high generalization ability have been reported (Okamoto & Kayama, 2008; Sumada et al., 2007). The models have significant problems with computational amount and learning time.

This study focuses on Cellular Neural Network (CNN) (Chua & Yang, 1988) which is one of neural network models because it has the following remarkable characteristics:

1. CNN can be easily implemented by arranging a simple analog circuit called cell.
2. Calculation efficiency of CNN is better than that of full-connected neural network as represented by Hopfield model because CNN has a local connectivity.
3. Behavior of CNN is expressed by first-order differential equations, and the input-output relation is represented by a linear function with saturated regions. The function provides a high computation accuracy.

In fact, CNN has been widely used in image processing, texture classification (Szianyi & Csapodi, 1998; Yang et al., 2001), time series processing, and so on.
In addition, it has been presented that CNN is useful for associative memory (Liu & Michel, 1993). The method is to relate stored patterns to asymptotically stable equilibrium points of dynamics. It enables us that verifying incomplete recall and improving efficiency are easy in pattern classification since information of stored patterns are aggregated in template which represents a connection between each cell and its neighbors. So far, we have presented some associative CNN systems of diagnosing liver diseases, recognizing Chinese characters and detecting abnormal automobiles' sounds, and so on (Namba, 2005; 2006; Zhang et al., 2005).
This study aims to construct an ITS with associatve CNN which diagnoses learner's understanding level and give appropriate feedback to him. As described above, since associative CNN is useful in classifying ambiguous data, we will apply associative CNN to the diagnosis system.
This chapter describes a new diagnosis method with Binary Output CNN(BCNN) (Namba, 2008; Namba2, 2008). As classification information, accuracy rate and answer time are used. The usefulness is verified by using experimental result of Java programming test (15 learners). The classification results and the validity is discussed.
Furthermore, in order to improve versatility of the system, CNN is extended to Tri-valued Output CNN (TCNN) (Namba, 2010; Namba2, 2010; Namba, 2011). By extending CNN function, more kinds of diagnosis information can be used, and representable understanding levels can be increased. Hence, more exact instructions can be realized. Then, a method with associative TCNN is described. In order to evaluate usefulness of the system, associative TCNN estimates understanding levels of 20 learners. The classification results and the validity is also discussed. In addition, in order to evaluate diagnosis ability of associative TCNN, comparison experiment is performed with linear function which is conventional estimation method.

2. Associative Cellular Neural Network

2.1 Cellular Neural Network

CNN is composed of simple analog circuits called cell. Each cell is connected with $r-$neighbors, which means a local connectivity. Fig.1 shows 7×7 and $r = 2$ CNN. In this figure, the black cell is C(4,5), and gray cells are the neighborhood. In $r-$neighborhood $m \times n$ CNN, the i-th row, j-th column($i = 1, 2, \cdots, m; j = 1, 2, \cdots, n$) cell $C(i, j)$ is represented by

$$\dot{x}_{ij} = -x_{ij} + T_{ij} * y_{ij} + S_{ij} * u_{ij} + I_{ij} \tag{1}$$

,where x_{ij}, y_{ij}, u_{ij} and I_{ij} show a state, an output, input variable, and a threshold, respectively. T_{ij} and S_{ij} are connection coefficients which show influence from the neighbor cells. $*$ means the following opeation:

$$T_{ij} * y_{ij} = \sum_{u=-r}^{r} \sum_{v=-r}^{r} t_{ij(u,v)} y_{i+u,j+v}. \tag{2}$$

For example, the dynamics of cell C(4,5) in $r = 2, 7 \times 7$ CNN is represented as the following:

$$\dot{x}_{45} = -x_{45} + \sum_{u=-2}^{2} \sum_{v=-2}^{2} t_{45(u,v)} y_{4+u,5+v} + I_{45}, \tag{3}$$

and the matrix $\boldsymbol{t}_{45}$ is described as Table 1.

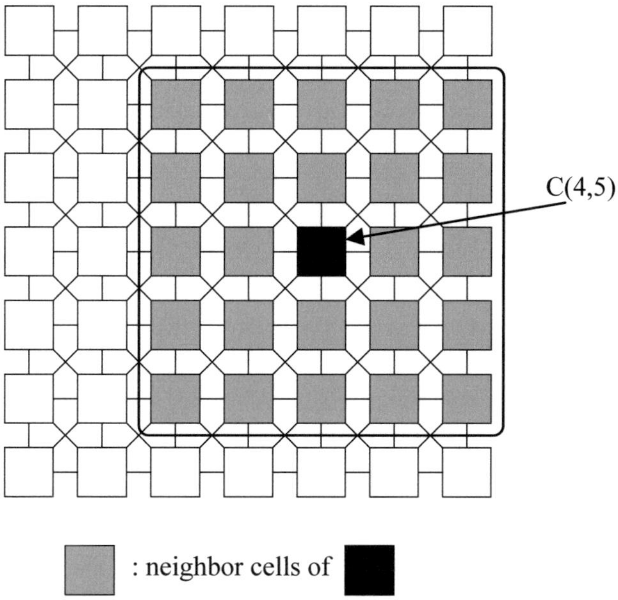

Fig. 1. 7×7 and $r = 2$ CNN

0	0	0	0	0	0	0
0	0	$t_{45(-2,-2)}$	$t_{45(-2,-1)}$	$t_{45(-2,0)}$	$t_{45(-2,1)}$	$t_{45(-2,2)}$
0	0	$t_{45(-1,-2)}$	$t_{45(-1,-1)}$	$t_{45(-1,0)}$	$t_{45(-1,1)}$	$t_{45(-1,2)}$
0	0	$t_{45(0,-2)}$	$t_{45(0,-1)}$	$t_{45(0,0)}$	$t_{45(0,1)}$	$t_{45(0,2)}$
0	0	$t_{45(1,-2)}$	$t_{45(1,-1)}$	$t_{45(1,0)}$	$t_{45(1,1)}$	$t_{45(1,2)}$
0	0	$t_{45(2,-2)}$	$t_{45(2,-1)}$	$t_{45(2,0)}$	$t_{45(2,1)}$	$t_{45(2,2)}$
0	0	0	0	0	0	0

Table 1. The matrix $\boldsymbol{t}_{45}$

CNN used in this study is $u_{ij} = 0$ for simplicity. Hence, the dynamics is

$$\dot{x}_{ij} = -x_{ij} + T_{ij} * y_{ij} + I_{ij}. \tag{4}$$

Moreover, y_{ij} is a function of x_{ij} as the following:

$$y_{ij} = \frac{1}{2}(|x_{ij} + 1| - |x_{ij} - 1|). \tag{5}$$

Fig.2 shows the binary output function. Eq.(5) guarantees a high computation accuracy. By using vector notation, the differential equation of $m \times n$ CNN can be represented as

$$\dot{\boldsymbol{x}} = -\boldsymbol{x} + \boldsymbol{T}\boldsymbol{y} + \boldsymbol{I} \tag{6}$$

,where $\boldsymbol{x}, \boldsymbol{y}$ and $\boldsymbol{I}$ show a state, an output, and a threshold vector, respectively. $\boldsymbol{T}$ is a template matrix.

$$\left.\begin{aligned} \boldsymbol{x} &= (x_{11}, x_{12}, \cdots, x_{1n}, \cdots, x_{m1}, \cdots, x_{mn})^T \\ \boldsymbol{y} &= (y_{11}, y_{12}, \cdots, y_{1n}, \cdots, y_{m1}, \cdots, y_{mn})^T \\ \boldsymbol{I} &= (I_{11}, I_{12}, \cdots, I_{1n}, \cdots, I_{m1}, \cdots, I_{mn})^T \end{aligned}\right\}$$

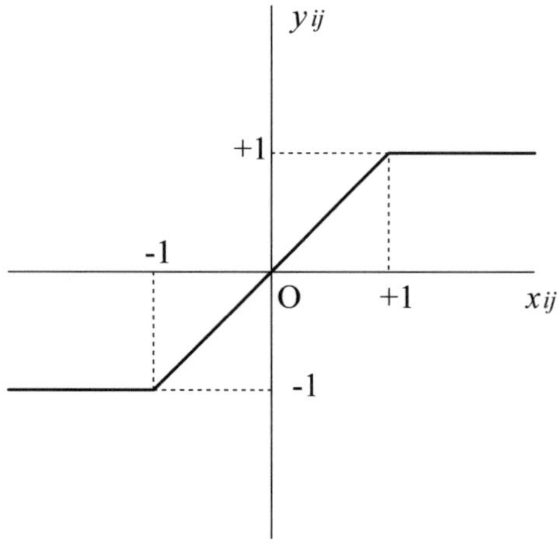

Fig. 2. Binary output function

2.2 Design of associative BCNN

Associative BCNN can store a lot of patterns because they are related to asymptotically stable equilibrium points of dynamics. We prepare p state vectors $\boldsymbol{\beta}_1, \boldsymbol{\beta}_2, \cdots, \boldsymbol{\beta}_p$ multiplied p stored vectors $\boldsymbol{\alpha}_i (i = 1, 2, \cdots, p)$ whose element is ± 1 by constant $c(c > 1)$. In other words, we can obtain Eq.(7).

$$\boldsymbol{\beta}_i = c\boldsymbol{\alpha}_i \tag{7}$$

It is evident that $\boldsymbol{\alpha}_i, \boldsymbol{\beta}_i, \boldsymbol{T}$ and $\boldsymbol{I}$ concurrently satisfy the following equations:

$$\left.\begin{array}{l} -\boldsymbol{\beta}_1 + \boldsymbol{T}\boldsymbol{\alpha}_1 + \boldsymbol{I} = 0 \\ -\boldsymbol{\beta}_2 + \boldsymbol{T}\boldsymbol{\alpha}_2 + \boldsymbol{I} = 0 \\ \cdots \\ -\boldsymbol{\beta}_p + \boldsymbol{T}\boldsymbol{\alpha}_p + \boldsymbol{I} = 0 \end{array}\right\}. \tag{8}$$

Let matrices $\boldsymbol{A}$ and $\boldsymbol{B}$ be

$$\left.\begin{array}{l} \boldsymbol{A} = (\boldsymbol{\alpha}_1 - \boldsymbol{\alpha}_p, \boldsymbol{\alpha}_2 - \boldsymbol{\alpha}_p, \cdots, \boldsymbol{\alpha}_{p-1} - \boldsymbol{\alpha}_p) \\ \boldsymbol{B} = (\boldsymbol{\beta}_1 - \boldsymbol{\beta}_p, \boldsymbol{\beta}_2 - \boldsymbol{\beta}_p, \cdots, \boldsymbol{\beta}_{p-1} - \boldsymbol{\beta}_p) \end{array}\right\}. \tag{9}$$

We are able to obtain the following equations:

$$\left.\begin{array}{l} \boldsymbol{B} = \boldsymbol{T}\boldsymbol{A} \\ \boldsymbol{I} = \boldsymbol{\beta}_p - \boldsymbol{T}\boldsymbol{\alpha}_p \end{array}\right\}. \tag{10}$$

$\boldsymbol{T}$ and $\boldsymbol{I}$ which satisfy these expressions must exist in order for the CNN to have $\boldsymbol{\alpha}_i$ as stored vectors. We are easily able to find $\boldsymbol{T}$ and $\boldsymbol{I}$ by adopting the following method.
If we focus on the computing at $k-$th cell in CNN($k = n(i-1) + j$), its conditional equation is given by

$$\boldsymbol{b}_k = \boldsymbol{t}_k \boldsymbol{A} \tag{11}$$

,where $\boldsymbol{b}_k$ and $\boldsymbol{t}_k$ are the $k-$th row vector of matrix $\boldsymbol{B}$ and $\boldsymbol{T}$. A large number of null elements are included in the vector $\boldsymbol{t}_k$. Using the property of the $r-$neighborhood, we obtain Eq.(12) by removing from $\boldsymbol{b}_k$,$\boldsymbol{t}_k$ and $\boldsymbol{A}$:

$$\boldsymbol{b}_k^r = \boldsymbol{t}_k^r \boldsymbol{A}^r \tag{12}$$

,where $\boldsymbol{A}^r$ is a matrix having removed the elements not belonging to $r-$neighborhood of the $k-$th cell from matrix $\boldsymbol{A}$. $\boldsymbol{b}_k$ and $\boldsymbol{t}_k$ are the similar meaning vectors. The amount of computing can be decreased by these procedures. Generally, the matrix $\boldsymbol{A}^r$ is not a square matrix. Hence, we solve $\boldsymbol{t}_k^r$ by using a singular value decomposition as the following:

$$\boldsymbol{A}^r = \boldsymbol{U}_k [\boldsymbol{\lambda}]^{1/2} \boldsymbol{V}_k^T. \tag{13}$$

Hence we have

$$\boldsymbol{t}_k^r = \boldsymbol{b}_k^r \boldsymbol{V}_k [\boldsymbol{\lambda}]^{-1/2} \boldsymbol{U}_k^T. \tag{14}$$

This solution is the minimal norm of Eq.(12). $[\boldsymbol{\lambda}]^{1/2}$ is a diagonally dominant matrix consisting of square root of the eigenvalue of matrix $[\boldsymbol{A}^r]^T \boldsymbol{A}^r$. $\boldsymbol{U}_k$ and $\boldsymbol{V}_k$ are the orthogonal matrices, respectively.
In the CNN designed by the method described above, stored patterns theoretically correspond to each equilibrium point of dynamics. CNN can recall a pattern by solving Eq.(6) when an initial state is given. In other words, it will converge on the stable equilibrium point of the optimal solution of differential equations.

3. Design of associative CNN diagnosis system

3.1 Overview

Fig.3 shows the overview of associative CNN diagnosis system. In advance, we define understanding levels, and correspond them to stored patterns in associative CNN. Learner pattern is generated from his test data. After that, a stored pattern can be obtained by the self-recall process of associative CNN. The understanding level which corresponds to the pattern is the diagnosis result. Due to the characterisic of associative CNN, stored patterns are not always recalled. This means that the system can't diagnose his understanding level.

3.2 Expressing cell and answer pattern

We here relate understanding levels to stored patterns of associative CNN. In order to design the diagnosis system, we use prior knowledge as the following:

- High understanding level has high accuracy.
- Higher understanding level has high accuracy and short time.
- Low accuracy and short answer time may mean that he makes a careless mistake.

They can be expressed by combination of cells. We allocate information of a question to two cells which means answer and time. Each cell denotes the following:

1. Answer cell means that an answer is right/wrong (Discrete).
2. Time cell means that an answer time is short/long (Continuous).

Table 2 shows understanding levels defined per question. Moreover, by aggregating them to the number of questions, answer pattern can be generated. Fig.4 shows the expression method.

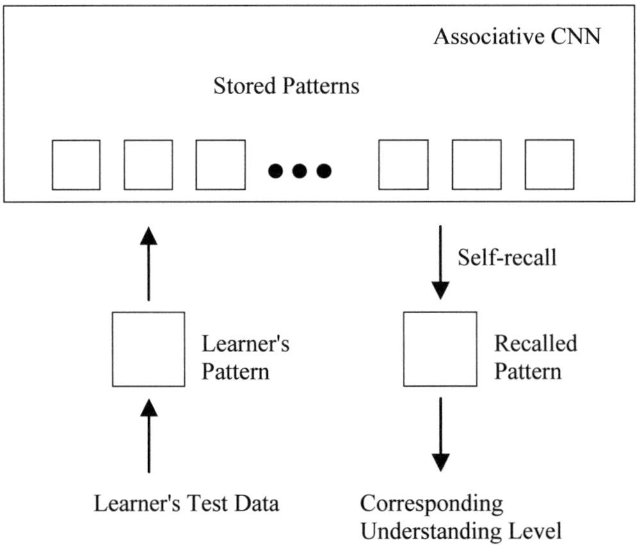

Fig. 3. Overview of our system

Label	Answer	Time	Understanding level
A	Right	Short	Higher
B	Right	Long	High
C	Wrong	Short	Low
D	Wrong	Long	Low

Table 2. Understanding levels defined per question

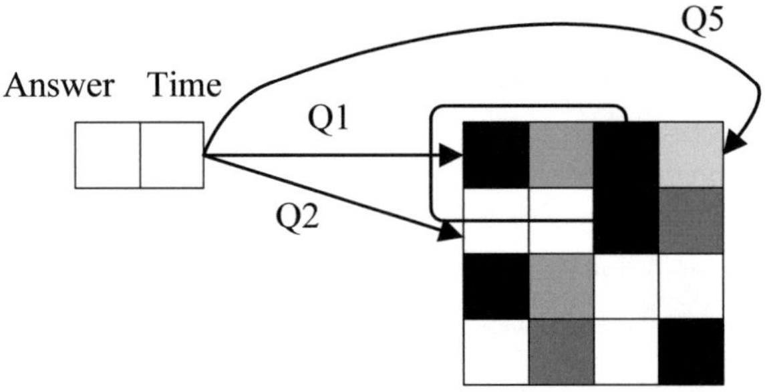

Fig. 4. Expression of answer pattern by associative CNN

3.3 Stored patterns

This study defines three understanding levels, and design four stored patterns corrresponding to them. Fig.5 shows them, and Labels A-D correspond to those of Table 2.

3.4 Generating input pattern

The answer time is transformed into $-1 \sim +1$ for input to associative CNN (scaling). Hence, in order to transform an actual answer time d_k into normalized one q_k in the $k-$th question,

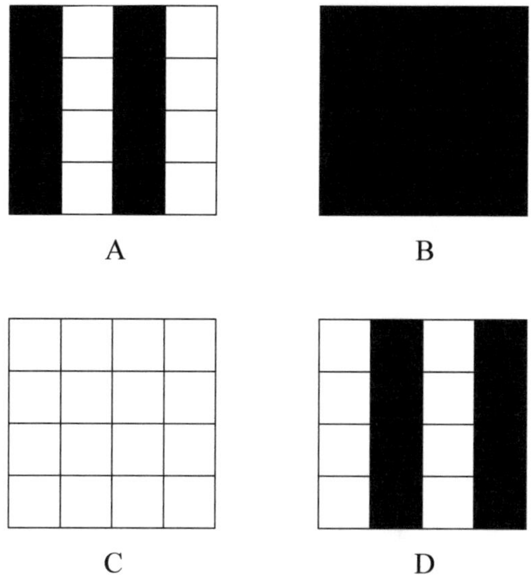

Fig. 5. Stored patterns

Level	Accuracy Rate(%)	Category	Number
I	80−100	Easy	19
II	40−80	Standard	20
III	0−40	Difficult	11

Table 3. Question level defined in the experiment

we use

$$q_k = \frac{1}{\sigma_k}(d_k - \bar{t_k}) \tag{15}$$

,where σ_k and $\bar{t_k}$ are standard deviation and average of all learners in the $k-$th question.

4. Experimental results by associative BCNN

15 learners who studied Java programming were experimented. They were randomly divided into two groups (ten and five students), and experimented in each group. The former belongs to Group X, and the latter belongs to Group Y.

4.1 Experiment 1 – Group X

The learners in Group X were experimented. At first, all 50 questions were divided into three levels according to accuracy rate of Group X. As shown in Table 3, question level was defined, and all questions were classified. Moreover, the average and standard deviation of answer time in Group X were obtained, and all data were transformed by using Eq.(15). The diagnosis results are shown in Table 4.

"Others" in Table 4 indicates that the output was not any stored patterns, in other words, CNN couldn't diagnose. In the experiment, diagnosis rate, which means that CNN recalled a stored pattern, was about 93.3 %. It is recognized that learner patterns are classified into A,B in easy questions (Level I) and C,D in difficult (Level III). Hence, this result can be appropriate.

Level	No.	A	B	C	D	Others
I	10	7	3	0	0	0
II	10	2	3	2	1	2
III	10	0	0	5	5	0

Table 4. Diagnosis Result of Group X

Level	No.	A	B	C	D	Others
I	5	4	1	0	0	0
II	5	3	1	0	1	0
III	5	1	0	1	3	0

Table 5. Diagnosis Result of Group Y

(a) Group X

Level	No.	A	B	C	D	Others
I	10	2	2	0	0	6
II	10	1	0	0	0	9
III	10	1	0	1	3	5

(b) Group Y

Level	No.	A	B	C	D	Others
I	5	2	1	0	0	2
II	5	1	0	0	1	3
III	5	0	0	0	1	4

Table 6. Diagnosis Result by MLP

4.2 Experiment 2 – Group Y

We next made a similar experiment in Group Y. The same value as $\bar{t_k}$ and σ_k of Group X were used. Experimental results are shown in Table 5. In this experiment, diagnosis rate was 100 %.

Associative CNN has a classification function of ambiguous data, and doesn't require a great number of data such as a fuzzy rule. Hence, it can be an useful model for such a problem.

Moreover, a system should immediately provide learners with feedback in real-time environment such as WBT (Web Based Training) system. As Experiment 2, if the system could classify without recalculating $\bar{t_k}$ and σ_k, its usefulness would be much higher.

4.3 Experiment 3 – Comparison experiment

In this section, multi-layered perceptron (MLP) which is one of representative neural network model was applied to this diagnosis problem in order to compare with associative CNN performance. The typical three-layered perceptron with Back Propagation Algorithm was used. Fig.6 shows MLP model used in the experiment. Training data were four stored patterns as shown in Fig.5. Learning was iterated until the mean square error between training data and the output was less than 0.001. When a value of output unit was more than 0.75, the pattern corresponding to it was the estimation result. Tables 6 (a) and (b) show the results. Most of patterns were classified as "Others", in other words, "not diagnosed". To compare with the diagnosis result by associative CNN (Tables 4 and 5), it is evident that diagnosis rate of associative CNN is superior to that of MLP in both cases.

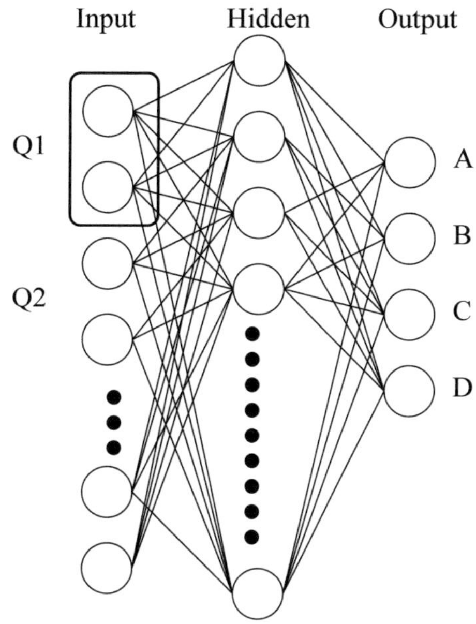

Fig. 6. Diagnosis Module by MLP

Associative BCNN is effective to diagnose learner's understanding level because it has a high diagnosis capability. However, it has a significant problem with lack of representable understanding levels. Though we can basically overcome it by increasing cells, and computational amount is also be increased.

5. Extended associative CNN – TCNN

As described above, Associative BCNN is effective for diagnosis of understanding level. However, it has a difficulty of few understanding levels. In order to overcome it, extended Associative CNN is designed, and more versatile system is constructed.

5.1 Tri-valued output associative CNN

The principle of Tri-valued output CNN (TCNN) is similar with that of BCNN, and we can easily realize by redesigning output function as

$$y_{ij} = \begin{cases} 1 & \text{if } s + L \leq x \\ \dfrac{x_{ij} - s}{L} & \text{if } s < x < s + L \\ 0 & \text{if } -s \leq x < s \\ \dfrac{x_{ij} + s}{L} & \text{if } -(s + L) < x < -s \\ -1 & \text{if } x \leq -(s + L). \end{cases} \tag{16}$$

The parameter s provides a new saturated region, and L enables us to adjust saturated regions. If $s = 0$ and $L = 0$, the function is conventional BCNN. Fig.7 shows the output function. Design method of associative TCNN is also similar with that of associative BCNN. All you have to do is to change each element of α_i in Eq.(7) is $-1, 0, +1$.

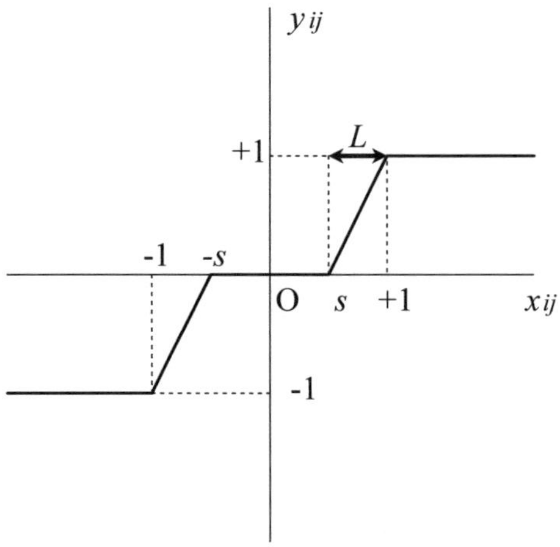

Fig. 7. Output function with three saturated regions

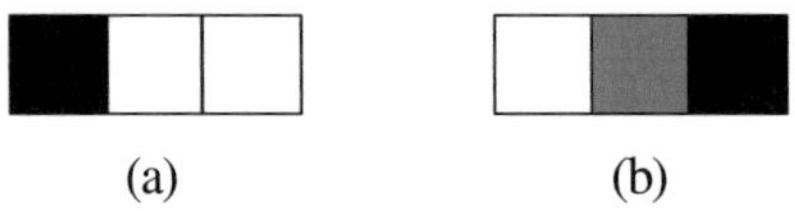

Fig. 8. Examples of answer pattern per question

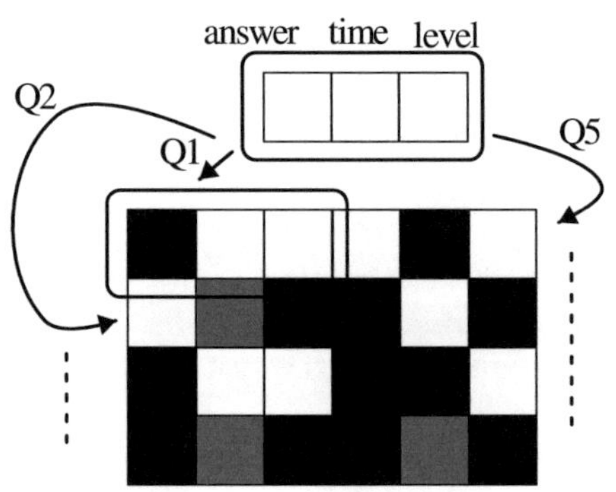

Fig. 9. Expression of answer pattern by Associative TCNN

5.2 Design of associative TCNN diagnosis module

By extending associative CNN to tri-valued output, the number of representable information for diagnosis can be increased. In other words, more prior knowledge can be realized in cell expression. Then, question level (difficulty) is newly added. That is,

1. Answer cell means that an answer is right/wrong (Discrete).
2. Time cell means that an answer time is short/long (Continuous).
3. Level cell means that a question is easy/standard/difficult (Discrete).

Fig.8 shows examples of answer pattern per question. (a) means right/short/easy, and (b) indicates wrong/medium/difficult. Moreover, we can make a total answer pattern by arranging all answer patterns as shown in Fig.9 as is the case with associative BCNN.
We next generate stored patterns which correspond to understanding levels. This study defines six grades (four understanding levels) in a question as shown in Table 7. We define

Label	Answer	Time	Understanding level
a	Right	Short	Highest
b	Right	Medium	High
c	Right	Long	Medium
d	Wrong	Short	Low
e	Wrong	Medium	Low
f	Wrong	Long	Low

Table 7. Understanding levels defined per question

Pattern	Easy	Medium	Difficult
A	a	a	a
	b	b	b
B	c	c	b
	c	c	c
	c	b	c
C	a	a	f
	b	b	f
	c	c	f
D	a	f	f
	b	f	f
	c	f	f
E	d	d	d
	e	e	e
	f	f	f

Table 8. Understanding levels

understanding levels in accordance with combination of label and level as shown in Table 8, and design stored patterns which correspond to them.

6. Evaluation experiments and results

The purpose of experiments is to evaluate how exactly associative TCNN can diagnose learner's understanding level. Experiment condition is described as follows:

1. All tests are used in CBT (Computer Based Testing).
2. All 38 questions are multiple choice (eight choices).
3. 20 learners are tested in experiments.
4. Test is used in a unit ("Probablities").

6.1 Design of associative TCNN

Design of associative TCNN is described as follows:

1. We design stored patterns which correspond to expected understanding levels in accordance with prior knowledge.
2. We use $s = 0.3$ and $L = 0.5$ in Eq.(16), which is general value.
3. We normalize experiment data, and make answer patterns.

Level	-	A	B	C	D	E	Others	All
-	Numbers	3	0	3	3	11	0	20
I (Easy)	Accuracy	85.7	-	71.4	71.4	29.9	-	50.7
	Time	60.2	-	60.1	75.8	87.3	-	77.4
II (Standard)	Accuracy	81.0	-	71.4	19.0	15.6	-	34.3
	Time	98.3	-	133.9	68.2	89.0	-	94.0
III (Difficult)	Accuracy	66.7	-	26.7	6.7	5.5	-	18.0
	Time	134.1	-	261.8	45.1	60.2	-	99.3

Table 9. Diagnosis results (Accuracy:%,Time:s)

6.2 Experiment results and discussion

Table 9 shows diagnosis results. All values in the table are average. This result shows that associative TCNN could completely diagnose all learners. We next evaluate the validity of diagnosis result. For instance, learners in the cluster "A" should have higher understanding level in all levels. It has high accuracy and short time compared with averages of all in any level. Hence, the diagnosis result of cluster "A" is valid. Learners in cluster "C" should have high or higher understanding level in Standard and Easy (Level II and I), and low in Difficult (Level III). Learners in cluster "D" should have high or higher understanding level in Easy, and low in Difficult and Standard. Learners in cluster "E" should have low understanding level in all levels. We can similarly conclude that the diagnosis results of clusters C,D, and E are valid.

6.3 Comparison experiment

In order to evaluate the accuracy of our system, we make a comparison experiment. We use a linear function according to the related work (Sumada et al., 2007) as the following:

$$U = kL_t + (1 - k)L_a \tag{17}$$

,where L_t, L_a are answer time and accuracy, respectively. U is understanding level. This equation is also based on our prior knowledge. It is appropriate as a comparison model with ours.

Comparison experiment is performed as the following:

1. All 38 questions are divided into two groups so that their difficulties will be the same. One is estimation part, and the other is evaluation part.
2. Accuracy and answer time are obtained from estimation part in order to be used in estimating understanding level.
3. Accuracy and answer time are obtained from evaluation part in order to be used in evaluating estimation results.
4. True understanding level is obtained from 3.
5. Precision of associative TCNN and that of linear function are considered by comparing with true understanding level obtained in 4.

In case of estimation by linear funcion, k is changed from 0.1 to 0.9, and the best is adopted as the estimation result.

Table 10 shows a comparison of precision. The precision of associative TCNN is superior to that of linear function. These results represent that synthetical diagnosis of associative TCNN is better than partial estimation of linear function.

Associative TCNN	Linear Model
95.0%	52.6%

Table 10. Comparison of precision

7. Conclusion

The early half of chapter described a new diagnosis system of learner's understanding level by using associative Binary Cellular Neural Network (BCNN). The results obtained are as follows:

1. At first, ten learners (Group X) were divided all questions into three levels (difficulties) in accordance with accuracy rate. Their understanding levels could be appropriately diagnosed by the system in each difficulty. As a result, diagnosis rate was about 93.3%. It implies that the result can be appropriate according to the relation between question level and result of understanding level.
2. Moreover, we made a similar experiment on five learners (Group Y). Consequently, diagnosis rate was 100%. It implies that associative BCNN is useful as an diagnosis module in terms of versatility.
3. The similar diagnosis experiments were performed by Multi-Layered Perceptron (MLP). Consequently, the diagnosis performance of associative BCNN is better than that of MLP.

BCNN has an important problem with lack of representable understanding levels. Then, the latter half of chapter described an improved diagnosis system by using associative Tri-valued Cellular Neural Network (TCNN). The results obtained are as follows:

1. We first defined five understanding levels, and designed associative TCNN according to them.
2. We next made a diagnosis experiment with associative TCNN. Participants were 20 learners who studied "Probabilities". Consequently, associative TCNN could completely diagnose all of them into expected understanding levels. It was recognized that the diagnosis results were valid in accordance with accuracy and answer time.
3. In order to compare our system with conventional method, we also made a diagnosis experiment by linear function. From comparison of precision, we confirmed that associative TCNN which comprehensively diagnoses was better than linear function which partly estimates.

The diagnosis by associative TCNN plays a role in rough-classification in pattern recognition. Standard associative TCNN is used in the experiment. Hence, optimized associative TCNN will probably provide better results. Our future work is to improve diagnosis performance with optimized associative TCNN.

8. Acknowledgment

Part of this research was supported by a Grant-in-Aid for Scientific Research from the Ministry of Education, Culture, Sports, Science and Technology (21700829), Japan.

9. References

Chua, L.O. and Yang, Y. (1988). Cellular Neural Networks. *IEEE Transaction on Circuit & Systems*, pp.1257-1290.

Gunel, K (2010). Intelligent Tutoring Systems. *LAMBERT Academic Publishing*, pp.1-15.

Liu, D. and Michel, A.N. (1993). Cellular Neural Networks for Associative Memory. *IEEE Transaction on Circuit & Systems*, CAS-40, pp.119-121.

Namba, M. & Zhang, Z. (2006). The Proposal of Cellular Neural Network with Multiple Memory Tables. *Proceedings of Cellular Neural Networks and their Applications*, pp.240-247.

Namba, M. & Zhang, Z. (2006). Cellular Neural Network for Associative Memory and Its Application to Braille Image Recognition. *Proceedings of World Congress on Computational Intelligence*, pp.4716-4721.

Namba, M. (2008). Estimating Learner's Comprehension by Cellular Neural Networks for Associative Memory. *Proceedings of International Conference on Cellular Neural Networks and their Applications*, pp.97-100.

Namba, M. (2008). Estimating Learner's Comprehension with Cellular Neural Network for Associative Memory. *Japan Journal of Educational Technology*, Vol.32, Suppl., pp.150-153.

Namba, M. (2010). Tri-valued Output Cellular Neural Network for Associative Memory to Estimate Understanding Level. *Proceedings of International Conference on Computers and Advanced Technology in Education*, pp.88-93.

Namba, M. (2010). Design of Tri-Valued Output Cellular Neural Network for Associative Memory for Self-Directed E-learning. *ICIC Express Letters*, Vol.2, No.3(B), pp.552-558.

Namba, M. (2011). Associative Cellular Neural Network and Its Application to Intelligent Tutoring System. *Proceedings of International Conference on Computers and Advanced Technology in Education*, Paper No.734-016.

Nkambou, R. & Bourdeau, J. (2010). Advances in Intelligent Tutoring Systems. *Springer*, ISBN 978-3-642-14362-5.

Okamoto, T. & Kayama, M. (2008). Artificial Intelligence and Educational Engineering. *Ohm-sha*, Japan, pp.249-252.

Sobue, Y.; Matsumoto, T. ; *et al* (2004). Construction of the Statistical Student Model Using Learning History on Web-Based Learning System. *IEICE Technical Report*, Vol.103, No.697 ,ET2003-113, pp. 89–94.

Sumada, T.; Matsumoto, T. ; *et al.* (2007). Estimation of Learner's Properties Using Bayesian Network. *IEICE Technical Report*, ET2006-141, pp.203-208.

Szianyi, T. & Csapodi, M. (1998). Texture Classification and Segmentation by Cellular Neural Networks. *Computer Vision and Image Understanding*, Vol.71, No.3, pp.255-270.

Takashi, O.; Tominaga, H. ; *et al* (2006). AQuAs:Personal Adaptive Quiz with A-Question-and-an-Answer for Interactive Lesson Support. *IEICE Technical Report*, ET2005-89, pp.7-12.

Yang, Z. ; Nishio Y. ; *et al.* (2001). A Two Layer CNN in Image Processing Applications. *Proceedings of International Symposium on Nonlinear Theory and its Applications*, Vol.1, pp.67-70.

Zhang, Z. ; Namba, M. ; *et al* (2005). Cellular Neural Networks and Its Application to Abnormal Detection. *Journal of Information*, Vol.8,No.4, pp.587-604.

9

Proposing Two Algorithms to Acquire Learning Knowledge in Problem-Based Learning Environment

Akcell Chiang
Department of Digital Media Design,
Tungnan University, Taipei,
Taiwan, R.O.C.

1. Introduction

Discussion-based Internet forums or interactive chat rooms are an effective educational help system for both individuals and teams of learners. Many companies, particularly computer vendors (ComputerHope, 2004; IBM, 2004; Microsoft, 2004), adopt this technology to provide product training, learning or Q&A on their web sites. Nevertheless, the current state of chat forum technology only provides a platform for information exchange and organization (K.Kaye & J.Johnson, 2004). It is still unable to stimulate the users to learn from looking at the problem from different perspectives (Roberts & Ousey, 2003). The work reported in this chapter extends this technology further by incorporating critical thinking as a stimulus in teamwork discussions at algorithm one. We claim that such a method would sharpen web-based educational services. Separating the discussion topic from instant chat would further enhance the system into a comprehensive problem-based learning environment.

Problem-based learning (PBL) (Torp & Sage, 2002) and critical thinking (Fisher, 2001) skills have been used widely in education. These features are particularly noticeable in nursing education (Conway & Sharkey, 2002; Cooke & Moyle, 2002). This problem-based discipline can also apply to vocational education programs, such as, computer troubleshooting, which could be taught as a case study through Internet discussion. As we know, a trainee in a professional discipline, such as a computer technician, is more than just a passive learner but also an active problem-solver in real world situations. When a problem is encountered first in a learning process, it can be used as an initiative to build up learners' problem solving or reasoning skills. In the process, learners would appreciate this learning discussion and then embrace this added responsibility.

Essentially, there is a fundamental difference in the philosophy between nursing education and IT education (K.Kaye & J.Johnson, 2004; Lewis, Davies, Jenkins, & Tait, 2001). The difference in value between a life vs. a machine is such that discussion is not needed. A nursing-problem learning is very conservative in its approach; they often faced with poorly defined problems, incomplete information and etc. But a computer can be reloaded or reformated without any problems. It means we can redo the troubleshooting on a machine again without any major loss. Therefore one of our system design philosophies is to grant

more control to the system, by using statistics for decision-making. Thus the learning system becomes more intelligent and reduces the workload of educator. On the other hand, we relegate some of the problem-based learning principles into the development of the on-line intelligent learning tool.
Internet forums allow users to post their topics/learning-issues for discussion. In a well facilitated web site, after having chosen a topic, users can post their suggestions or switch to chat room for on-line discussion. Our system is designed to accept a broader view of problems within the learning domain and deeper discussion. This means that we can allow different problem-descriptions to be posted from individual learners within the set up learning domain. We are not confined to single problem and may achieve superior understanding of the problem in the discussions.
This chapter introduces two algorithms/models to design the MALESA learning system – one is MALESAbrain for learning discussion and another is MALESAassessment for learning assessment. The former is a discussion system in facilitating a PBL classroom. It encourages learners to judge or criticize the solutions posted by others before exploring further knowledge-content. The system then sums up the judgment scores as its knowledge-weight in order to pass the thresholds set up for ranking/arranging the learning issues. The latter MALESAassessment is an assessment system for evaluating learners' performances after learning discussion. It uses a real world practical problem to assess the learners' solving-plan and fixing-processes as the educator's marking standard. These two systems co-operate to transform chat forum technologies for the problem-based learning in IT education.

2. MALESA learning system

The first system learning design has borrowed the threshold and knowledge-weight concepts from machine learning (Mitchell, 1997) to build up the intelligent learning tool. The educator needs only to give a learning domain and a few beginning questions (even beginning questions are not compulsory) to the system before the learning discussion starts. The system then asks learners to judge (or criticize) other's proposed solutions. Through threshold evaluation of the knowledge-weights, knowledge pieces are automatically ranked and arranged by the intelligent learning system. This kind of teamwork learning would then integrate and synthesize previous and current learning to increase the knowledge base.

2.1 The learning model of MALESAbrain[1]

The algorithm one is called MALESAbrain. The design of its learning model is to form a critical thinking methodology for problem-based discussion. Accordingly, we develop an intelligent system to help learners think critically and learn topics like computer troubleshooting through an Internet workshop. The model takes an active role in sharpening the learners' contributions towards viewpoints on the discussion issues. In discussion, the learning system would highlight the importance of those issues which help the learners pay more attention to consensus solutions for better discussion and problem solution. The model consists of three main stages (Fig. 1) to facilitate learners in problem-based discussion:

---

[1] The acronym for "Machine-Learning-Expert-System Algorithm for brainstorming"

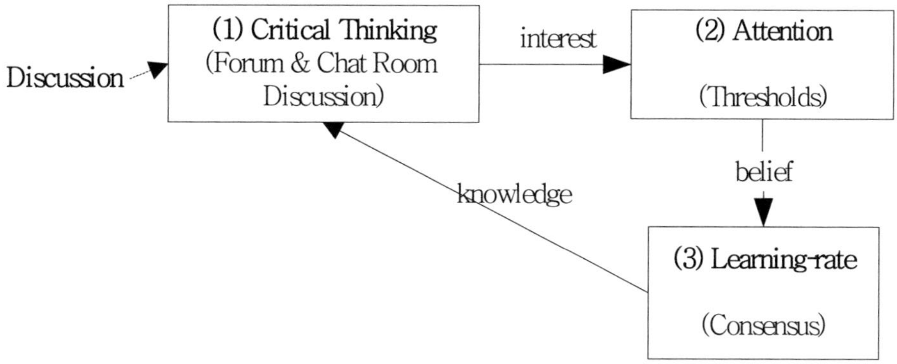

Fig. 1. The design model.

1. The first stage redesigns chat room and forum by adding the critical thinking function (Cooke & Moyle, 2002). This stage stimulates the learners to think about alternative aspects of the problem. They need to judge others' posted solutions by
   - giving personal preference or judgment on solutions posted by others;
   - contributing personal problem-solution suggestions for the feedback of preference from the judgments of others.
2. The second stage is to help learners to pay "attention" (S. Paul, Haseman, & Ramamurthy, 2004) to important issues.
   - Learners need to pay attention and think about why certain issues accumulate higher scores than others.
   - The highly-scored issues are highlighted by the system to stimulate more discussions on them.
   - Those extensively discussed issues therefore end up with more meaningful content to help solve the problems.
3. The third stage is to help learners and educator understand the current "learning-rate" (Culvenor, 2003). It indicates how many problems have consensus solutions, and how many problems are without consensus. The without consensus issues will become the learning issues that the learners still need to further investigate or research.
   - An indicator will show in the learning tool to help the educator and learners perceive what percentage of the discussion-problems has resulted in consensus;
   - also how many discussion-problems did not result in consensus.
   - How many discussion-problems with consensus results enable the educator and learners to understand the progress of the discussion and the learning issues on demand.

2.2 The assessment model of MALESAassessment[2]

The second algorithm is called MALESAassessment. The principle of the system design is to reuse learners' discussion knowledge, which retained in MALESAbrain learning system, for answering the follow-up performance test. In this chapter the assessment system consults the learners for organizing their own problem-solving plan for answering their test

[2] The acronym for "Machine-Learning-Expert-System Algorithm for learning assessment"

problems. It is not just to give a simple solution from the computer suggestion. The answer must be planned by learners and consulted by MALESAassessment.
Fig. 2 shows a rapid prototyping and user testing model, called "task-artifact cycle" (Finneran & Zhang, 2003; Vicente, 1999). MALESAassessment borrows the iterative improvement and concepts-in-action design (Sutcliffe & Carroll, 1999) to develop its assessment interface. It iteratively stimulates learners to improve their tasks (troubleshooting plans) and their actions (fixing problems). The four-stage continuous cycles, in MALESAassessment, help the learners to exercise a proto-type in ways that can contribute as much as possible. The open-ended design allows the learners to exercise their plans, rather than provide a raw solution which may be useless in a practical problem. The interface (see Fig. 13) offers advice to the learners to help them to build up a viable working plan to cope with the difficulty of solving a testing problem.

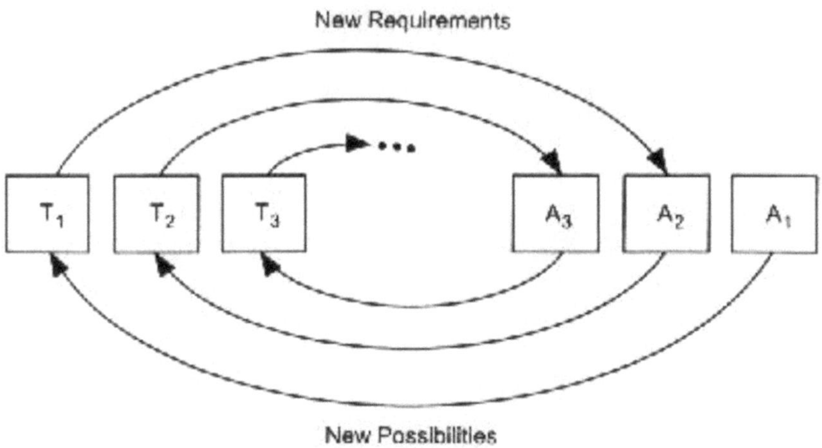

Fig. 2. Iterating through the task artifact cycle (reprinted from Fig 4.3 Vicente (1999) with permission).

In the following sections, we further discuss these two algorithms. Each algorithm is separated into two sections. The first section applies our experiment result as example to picturize a whole concept to the readers. The second section offers the definitions, the algorithm and the knowledge retained in the system to clarify the previous example. After the algorithm discussions, we evaluate the system based on the participants' comments. At last, we conclude and highlight the contributions of these two algorithms.

3. Using MALESAbrain in problem-based discussion

To illuminate the learning algorithm in MALESAbrain, we use an example to explain the problem-based discussion guided by the learning system. In this section, we explain how an educator set up the learning thresholds, and then discuss the functions in the learning system.

3.1 Learning thresholds set up

Before discussion, the educator needs to set up learning thresholds to enable MALESAbrain to recognize the importance of the discussion-issues. In Fig. 3, the educator has set up "2" as *knowledge qualification-threshold*, when knowledge-weight ≥ 2 then the knowledge becomes a qualified knowledge, which is the minimum requirement to join the competition for promotion to a higher order of discussion position; "-3.2" is a *knowledge rejection-threshold,* when knowledge-weight < *-3.2* MALESAbrain would then delete the knowledge; "4.2" is a *solution-maturity threshold,* when the solution-weight ≥ 4.2, then MALESAbrain would consider this solution is able to solve a discussion-problem; "-3" is a *solution-disagreement threshold,* if solution-weight < -3 then MALESAbrain would delete the solution. However, to help MALESAbrain decide when to suggest learners to stop the discussion, the educator also needs to set up *learning-rate* "70%" and due-date "4/9/2010".

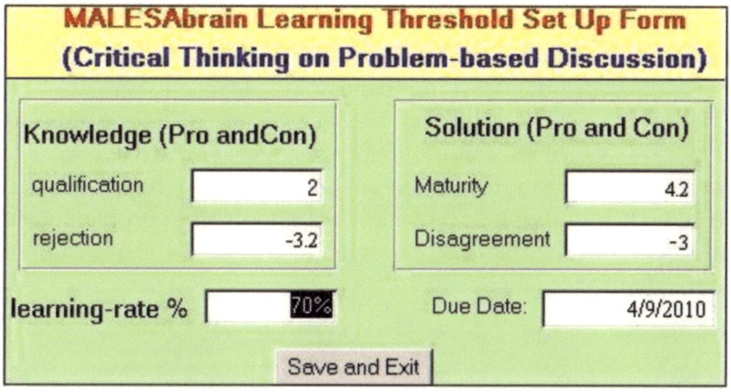

Fig. 3. Educator set up learning thresholds.

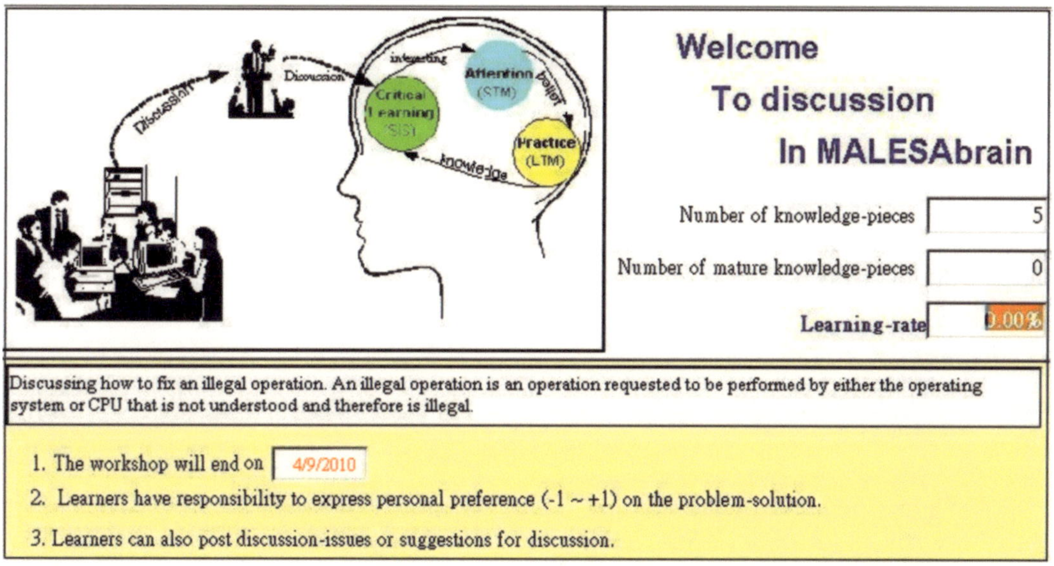

Fig. 4. Welcome page encourages learners to follow the learning rules for discussion.

As shown in Fig. 4, MALESAbrain will keep assessing current learning-rate "0.00%" and checking the due-date "4/9/2010". During discussion, there are three figures shown on the welcome page (see Fig. 4), which help the educator to assess the current retained number of knowledge pieces "5", the current matured number of knowledge pieces "0" and the current learning rate "0.00%". They help the educator and learners to understand the progress of the discussion. Nevertheless, at the due date "4/9/2010", if the learning-rate is still lower than the setup learning-rate 70% then the educator will need to decide whether to extend the discussion. The educator may calibrate the learning factors by re-setting the *knowledge-qualification-threshold, knowledge-rejection-threshold, solution-maturity-threshold, solution-disagreemen- threshold* or *learning-rate* (see Fig.2) and arrange another discussion by extending the due-date. At the end of the learning discussion, the educator will stop the discussion and then assesses the achievement of total retained knowledge and individual learners' contribution for which their suggestions have succeeded in the important area of the learning issues.

3.2 Problem-based learning discussion

After the educator sets up the learning thresholds, learners can start to discuss their problems. Fig. 5 shows a learner entering his/her problem descriptions by completing a 'question enquiry form'. Once submitted, the query will be matched with MALESAbrain's retained knowledge according to the chosen keywords. Firstly the query will be matched by the keywords. If none is found, it will be seconded to match the problem description details. As a result, the locations of the matched knowledge will be the output to which the learner is being advised to advance.

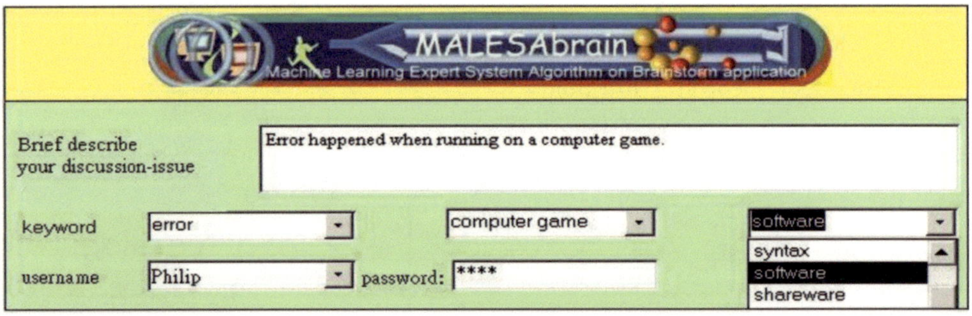

Fig. 5. A learner "Philip" enters his discussion-issue for joining MALESAbrain discussion.

In Fig. 6, the system suggests some locations for learners to join discussion. The suggestion location "0.1.3" weight "5.3" is on the lower/next level of location "0.1". Learners can click

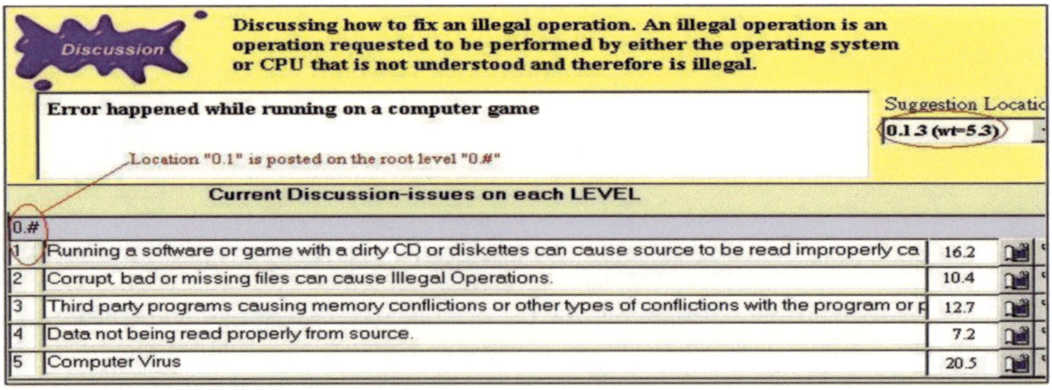

Fig. 6. After matching, the system suggests some locations for learners to join discussion.

location "0.1" to browse next level "0.1.#" which includes location "0.1.3" or directly click suggestion location "0.1.3". Simply speaking, "0.1.3" is an example of a location address - about different level separated with "." Like the "dot" in Internet address, "0.1.3" is an address in MALESAbrain: "0" is the root level address that learner much choose 1 to go to "0.1" and then choose 3 to go to "0.1.3".

In Fig. 7, the system asks the learner about his/her preference. The learner then express his/her preference score "0.9" from his own judgment before being allowed to enter chat room for discussion. During exploration, MALESAbrain actively questions the learners about their *preferences* - a numerical measure of the learner's degree of support (or lack of support) for a posted-solution to the problem. Learners should answer these questions prior to moving on to the next piece of content or chat room for discussion. The preference value ranges from 1 for total agreement, to 0 for no comment, and to -1 for total disagreement. Learners must judge or criticize another's proposed solution, for its ability to solve a problem.

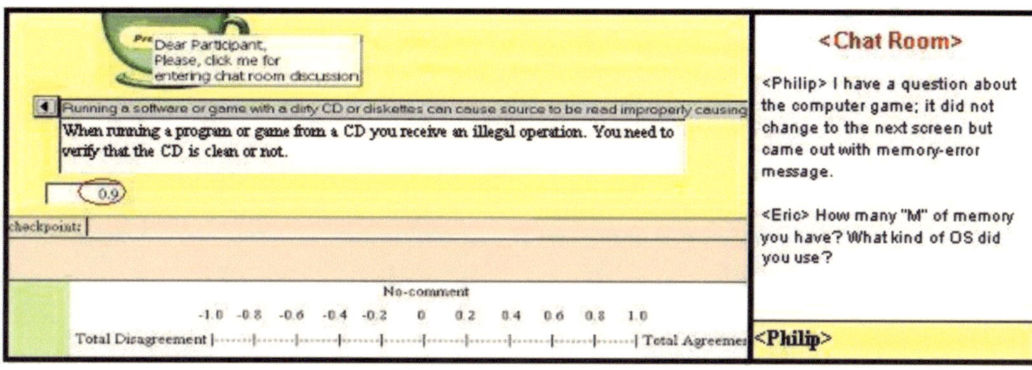

Fig. 7. In response to the learner's chosen issue, the system would actively ask its user about his/her preference.

Subsequently, learners can understand each issue better in the chat forum for their discussions. Such a device provides a window of opportunity for individual learners to review other problems from different perspectives and subjectively evaluate the advantages and disadvantages of other learners' works. It is an important mechanism installed on the model, which encourages learners to critically think about a problem-solution from others' suggestions and carefully judge their own preference scores. In certain situations, the educator will encourage each of the learners to pick up a learning issue for further investigation and research, such as, go to library, discuss with an expert, use Internet searching or test an experiment on the laboratory before going back for further discussion.

In Fig. 8, the user browses deeper into a few levels from a suggested location, and check a problem of interest, such as, "Funny things happened when exchanging screens or dragging stuff from one position to another" which attached a solution of "Incorrect video driver may cause illegal operations when playing a game". By this kind of critical thinking and browsing others' posted problem-solutions, learners would build up their knowledge regardless of the previous learned or current development.

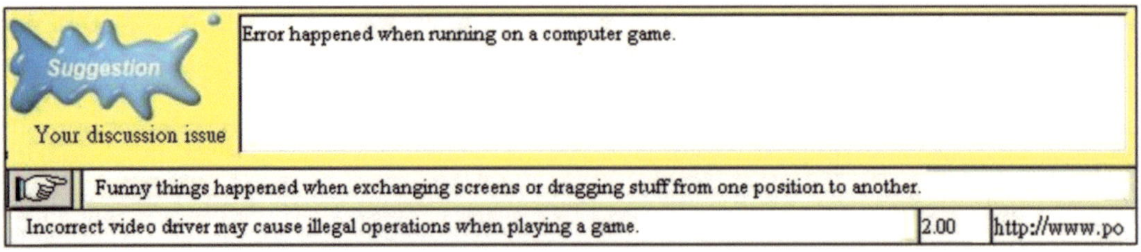

Fig. 8. shows a learner browsing deeper into a few levels from a suggested location.

However, if there are no suitable learning issues for their discussions, learners might post their own problems. Fig. 9 shows a learner posting his/her own problem, about "Error happened when running on a computer game. It did not change to the next screen but came out with memory-error message".

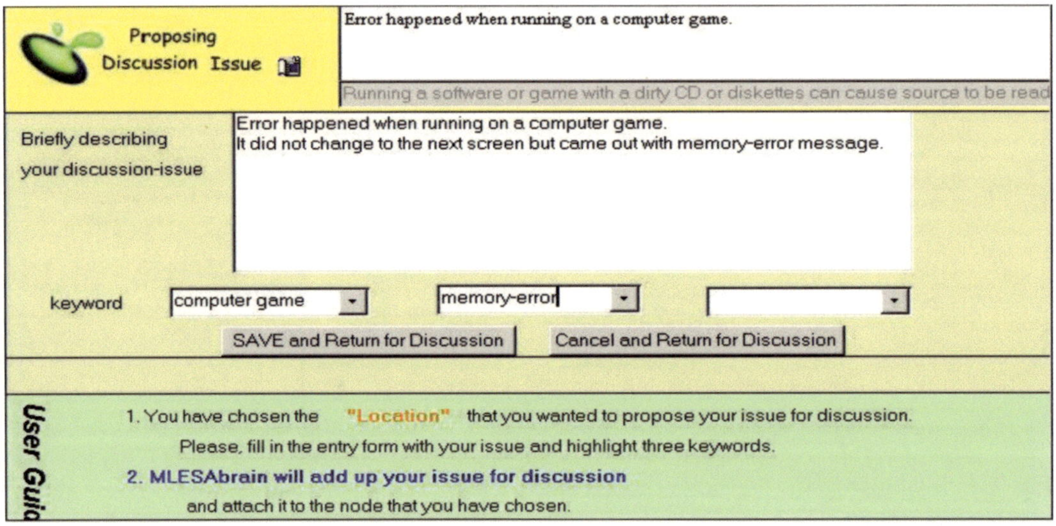

Fig. 9. A learner posts his/her own problem for joining discussion.

Fig. 10 shows MALESAbrain sending the user's posted problem to other learners. This is a *broadcasting function* that gives the posted problems a chance to be discussed from other learners' viewpoints or judgments. In this process of a problem-solution discussion, the learners who do not agree with a problem might propose another problem to clarify the original problem; and those who do not agree with a solution might contribute another solution to clarify or specify the original solution. However, when any new knowledge is added, MALESAbrain would notify other learners to encourage them to join the discussion.

This broadcasting function can also be considered as a feedback mechanism, which stimulates the learners to brainstorm more knowledge among participants. In Fig. 11, the system adds the problem to the location "0.1.4". The user now needs to wait for the feedback from the other learners' judgments on his/her proposal. These broadcasts and discussions will continue until MALESAbrain can identify the knowledge according to the set up thresholds. The more discussions which are returned the more changes occur in individual knowledge-weights because of the contribution from the learners' preferences.

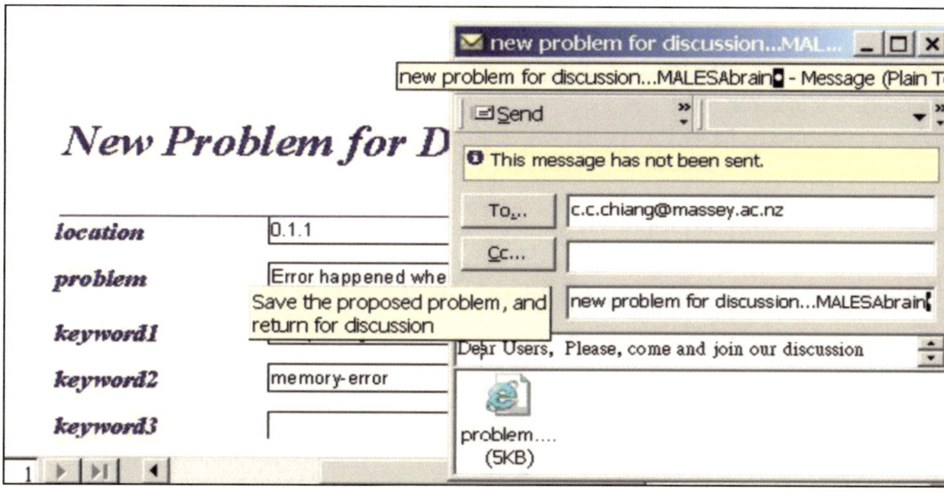

Fig. 10. MALESAbrain sends the user's posted problem to other learners.

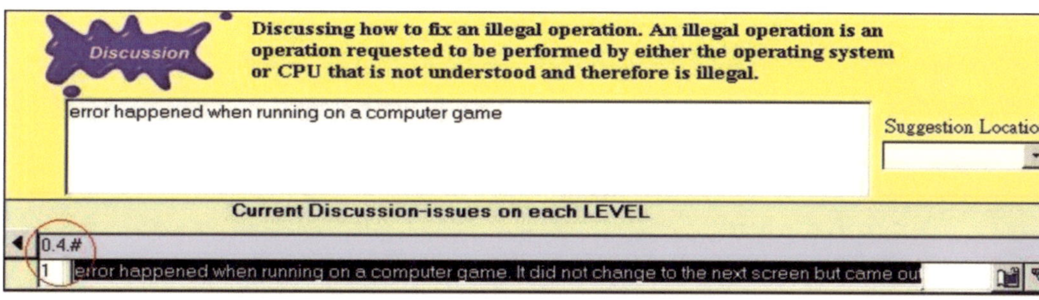

Fig. 11. The system adds the problem to the location "0.1.4".

4. The algorithm of MALESAbrain

In this section, we explain the first algorithm - MALESAbrain. The definitions precisely define the symbols used in the algorithm. The algorithm shows how an educator set up the learning thresholds; and how MALESAbrain facilitates an on-line discussion for knowledge acquisition. The calculation example discusses the knowledge-weights of the retained knowledge.

4.1 Definitions of MALESAbrain

Definition 1-1. A piece of *knowledge-content* φ_i in MALESAbrain for problem-based discussion is defined as a pair of problem and solutions:
$\varphi_i = (p_i, \bigcup_j s_{i,j})$ where p_i is a *problem* $\bigcup_j s_{i,j}$ is the collection of suggested solutions associated with p_i

Definition 1-2. The knowledge *preferences* ***Pref*** in MALESAbrain is defined as a continuous function of real value ranged from -1 to +1

$$\textbf{\textit{Pref}}:(\,learner_k\,,\, s_{i,j}\,) \rightarrow agreement_{k,i,j}\ (\text{-}1 \sim +1)$$

where $(\,learner_k\,,\, s_{i,j}\,)$ is a pair such that

$learner_k$ = a learner,

$s_{i,j}$ = a solution in MALESAbrain (see the defined solution $s_{i,j}$ in Definition 1-1).

$agreement_{k,i,j}$ = the preference score of an learner's, $learner_k$, judgment of a solution $s_{i,j}$ (value from –1 ~ +1).

Definition 1-3 The *knowledge-weight* w_i in MALESAbrain is defined as

$w_i = \sum_{j=1}^{m} w_{i,j} \cdot |\, s_{i,j}\,|$ where $w_{i,j}$ is the summation of all learner $learner_k$ preferences towards $s_{i,j}$

$$w_{i,j} = \sum_k agreement_{k,i,j}$$ (see Definition 1-2 ***Pref***: < $learner_k$, $s_{i,j}$ > → $agreement_{k,i,j}$)

Note: we define a symbol "| |" here, which will be used to test the existence of a solution, for transfer the existence of a solution into the value "0" or "1", to allow the knowledge-weight w_i calculation. $|x| = \begin{cases} 0 & when\ (\neg\exists x) \\ 1 & when\ (\exists x) \end{cases}$ where χ is a solution. (see Example 1: the calculation of knowledge weight)

Definition 1-4. An *artificial-knowledge-CELL* (AK-cell) k_i in MALESAbrain is a combination definition of Definition 1-1 and Definition 1-3, which is defined as a pair of knowledge-content and knowledge-weight:

$k_i = <\varphi_i, w_i>$ where

φ_i is the knowledge-content (see Definition 1-1 $\varphi_i = (p_i\,,\ \bigcup_j s_{i,j})$) and

w_i is the corresponding knowledge-weight (see Definition 1-3 $w_i = \sum_{j=1}^{m} w_{i,j} \cdot |\, s_{i,j}\,|$)

Definition 1-5. The *learning threshold* θ is defined as a collection of two decision pairs $\theta = \{<\theta_{kq}, \theta_{kr}>, <\theta_{sm}, \theta_{sd}>\}$, for comparing the retained AK-cells and their respective solutions, where

θ_{kq} is an *AK-cell qualification threshold*, when $w_i \geq \theta_{kq}$ then k_i becomes a qualified AK-cell, which is the minimum requirement to join the competition for promotion to a higher order of discussion position

θ_{kr} is an *AK-cell rejection threshold*, when $w_i < \theta_{kr}$ then delete the AK-cell k_i

θ_{sm} is a *solution maturity threshold*, when $w_{i,j} \geq \theta_{sm}$, the learning group agrees the solution $s_{i,j}$ is able to solve the problem p_i .

θ_{sd} is a *solution disagreement threshold*, if $w_{i,j} < \theta_{sd}$ then delete the solution $s_{i,j}$

Whenever any of the thresholds are triggered by an AK-cell or a solution, MALESAbrain will re-organize the knowledge structure.

Definition 1-6. The *growth-factor* γ, an integer number, in MALESAbrain is defined as the limit for constraining the posted number of AK-cells at each level, which converts the architecture of knowledge base from linear structure into a hierarchical structure, of γ-branch tree, in the forum.

Definition 1-7. The *learning-rate function* $\frac{|M|}{|K|} \geq \alpha$ is defined to help the educator and learners to understand the progress of the discussion, where the *convergent-factor* "α" is the educator's training target set up and

the learning-rate $\frac{|M|}{|K|}$ is a percentage of the discussion-problems resulted in consensus, where

$|M|$ is the number of mature AK-cells, where $M = \{k_i \mid k_i \in \text{MALESAbrain} \wedge \exists s_{i,j}$ where $w_{i,j} \geq \theta_{sm}\}$

$|K|$ is the number of current retained AK-cells , where $K = \{k_i \in \text{MALESAbrain}\}$

4.2 Algorithm of MALESAbrain

To trace the algorithm, we suggest readers browsing the definitions first. Then reading the instructions, comments in the algorithm and checking definitions when tracing. Afterwards compare the algorithm with the example in previous section.

MALESAbrain(θ_{kq},θ_{kr} ,θ_{sm},θ_{sd},γ,α,due-date)

SET θ_{kq} / * the minimum requirement of an AK-cell to join the competition for promotion to a higher discussion position - called *qualification threshold* (Definition 1-5)*/

SET θ_{kr}, / * the worthless AK-cells will be deleted whenever lower than the *rejection threshold* (Definition 1-5) */

SET θ_{sm} / * a consensus of the learning group agrees the solution is able to solve the problem whenever a solution reached the *solution maturity threshold* (Definition 1-5)*/

SET θ_{sd} / * the worthless solutions will be deleted whenever lower than the *solution disagreement threshold* (Definition 1-5) */

SET γ / * *growth-factor* limits the posted number of AK-cells at each level, which converts the architecture of knowledge base from linear structure into a hierarchical structure of γ-branch tree in the forum. (Definition 1-6) */

SET α / * *convergent-factor* is used to decide whether the percentage of mature AK-cells has achieved the educator's training target (Definition 1-7) */

SET due-date / * *due-date* is an expected date to end the discussion */

REPEAT

/* ***Critical thinking*** */

COMPARE personal viewpoint "x" with retained knowledge pieces "k_i" in MALESAbrain $K = \{k_i \in$ MALESAbrain$\}$ /* Definition 1-4 */

Learners INPUT their ***Pref***:($learner_k$, $s_{i,j}$) → $agreement_{k,i,j}$ (-1 ~ +1) /* learners' show their judgment score to others' problem-solutions while browse the forum (Definition 1-2) */

IF (***Pref*** between -1 ~ +1 but not nil) THEN allow ENTER chat-room or MOVE to next pieces of knowledge /* Learners must give their preference scores prior to moving on to chat room or next pieces of knowledge for discussion (Definition 1-2) */

MALESAbrain COMPUTE the *knowledge-weight* $w_i = \sum_{j=1}^{m} w_{i,j} \cdot | s_{i,j} |$ /* Definition 1-3 */

MALESAbrain DISPLAY (or POST) *learners' discussion issues based on "growth-factor γ"* /* Definition 1-6 */

/* ***Attention*** */
IF $w_i \geq \theta_{kq}$ THEN /* the AK-cell is a qualified AK-cell (Definition 1-5,7)*/
    INCREMENT a "qualified-mark" AK-cell k_i to knowledge base $\boldsymbol{K} = \{k_i \in$ MALESAbrain$\}$
    IF w_i > parent(w_i) THEN /* higher weight AK-cell should be in the front level */
        SWAP(k_i,parent(k_i))
    END IF
END IF

IF $w_i < \theta_{kr}$ THEN /* the AK-cell is a worthless knowledge-piece (Definition 1-5)*/
    DELETE k_i
END IF

IF $w_{i,j} \geq \theta_{sm}$ THEN /* the AK-cell becomes an matured AK-cell in the knowledge base (Definition 1-5,7)*/
    DISPLAY a "mature-mark" on solution $s_{i,j}$
    INCREMENT a "mature-mark" AK-cell k_i to $\boldsymbol{M} = \{k_i \mid k_i \in$ MALESAbrain $\wedge \exists s_{i,j}$ where $w_{i,j} \geq \theta_{sm}\}$
END IF

IF $w_{i,j} < \theta_{sd}$ THEN /* the solution is worthless solution (Definition 1-5)*/
    DELETE $s_{i,j}$
END IF

IF (dd:mm:yy = due-date) THEN
    IF ($\frac{|\boldsymbol{M}|}{|\boldsymbol{K}|} \geq \alpha$) THEN /* if learning-rate $\frac{|\boldsymbol{M}|}{|\boldsymbol{K}|}$ is greater or equal to convergent-factor "α" then end discussion (Definition 1-7) */
        PRINT (MALESAbrain meeting with $\frac{|\boldsymbol{M}|}{|\boldsymbol{K}|}$ % learning-rate)
        endDiscussion = TRUE /* stop the meeting */
    ELSE
        endDiscussion = FALSE
        CALL MALESAbrain(θ_{kq},θ_{kr},θ_{sm},θ_{sd},γ,α,due-date) /* re-calibrate the learning thresholds and start another session of discussion whenever the learning-rate lower than α when time is due */
    END IF
END IF

UNTIL (endDiscussion = TRUE) /* ***learning-rate*** */
END MALESAbrain

4.3 A calculation example

In this subsection, we use a knowledge retained snapshot and a calculation example to look into the internal storage structure of the knowledge base of MALESAbrain.

X: Discussion topic "How to Fix an Illegal Operation" - An operation requested to be performed by either the Operating System or CPU, which is not understood and therefore is illegal.

- K_1 Running a software or game when memory shortage can cause illegal operations. ($w_1 = 3.1$)
- K_2 Running a source with a dirty CD or diskettes can cause data to be read improperly causing illegal operations. ($w_2 = 2.9$)
  - $K_{2.1}$ Corrupt, bad or missing files can cause illegal operations. ($\varphi_{2.1} = (p_{2.1}, \bigcup_j s_{2.1,j})$, $w_{2.1} = 2.1$)
    - $s_{2.1,1}$ Finding program bugs in the program and fix them. ($s_{2.1,1}$, $w_{2.1,1}$=0.7)
    - $s_{2.1,2}$ It is recommended that you attempt to uninstall and or reinstall the program causing the illegal operation to verify that any corrupt, bad or missing files are replaced or repaired during the reinstallation. ($s_{2.1,2}$, $w_{2.1,2}$=1.4)

Fig. 12. A snapshot of the retained knowledge pieces in MALESAbrain's knowledge base.

Fig. 12 shows a snapshot of knowledge pieces retained in the knowledge base. The knowledge posted by the learners has been organized in a tree-like manner according to the respective weights of individual nodes. In this example shown, the AK-cell $K_i = K_{2.1}$ includes a *knowledge-content* $\varphi_i = \varphi_{2.1}$ and a *knowledge-weight* $w_i = w_{2.1}$. For illustration the calculation on the knowledge-weight $w_i = w_{2.1}$ bonds with solution $s_{i,j} = s_{2.1,1}$ and solution $s_{i,j} = s_{2.1,2}$. Let us assume three visited learners have given their preferences on solution $s_{2.1,1}$ as 0.9, 0.5 and -0.7; and two visitors have given their preferences on solution $s_{2.1,2}$ as 0.6 and 0.8.

By Definition 1-3 $w_{i,j}$ is the learners' judgment scores towards $s_{i,j}$

$\because$ $s_{2.1,1}$ has three visited learners' judgment scores (0.9, 0.5 and -0.7)

$\therefore w_{2.1,1} = 0.9 + 0.5 + (-0.7) = 0.7 \ldots$ ①

$\because$ $s_{2.1,2}$ has two visited learners' judgment scores (0.6 and 0.8)

$\therefore w_{2.1,2} = 0.6 + 0.8 = 1.4 \ldots$ ②

$\varphi_{2.1}$ includes the problem $p_{2.1}$ and two solution $s_{2.1,1}$ and $s_{2.1,2}$ (because the number of solutions is two, therefore $m = 2$), so the knowledge-weight is:

$$w_{2.1} = \sum_{j=1}^{m} w_{2.1,j} \cdot |s_{2.1,j}| = \sum_{j=1}^{2} w_{2.1,j} \cdot |s_{2.1,j}|$$

$$= w_{2.1,1} \cdot |s_{2.1,1}| + w_{2.1,2} \cdot |s_{2.1,2}|$$

$$= 0.7 \cdot |s_{2.1,1}| + (1.4) \cdot |s_{2.1,2}| \quad (\because \text{①} \text{ and } \text{②})$$

$$= 0.7 \cdot (1) + (1.4) \cdot (1) = 2.1 \quad \left(\because |x| = \begin{cases} 0 & when\ (\neg\exists x) \\ 1 & when\ (\exists x) \end{cases} \text{ see Definition 1-3}\right)$$

Example 1. The calculation of knowledge weight ($w_{2.1}$).

This value of 2.1 represents the weight ($w_{2.1}$) of the knowledge-content ($\varphi_{2.1}$) in the knowledge (AK-cell $K_{2.1}$), which provides a quantitative measure of the synergic viewpoint on $\varphi_{2.1}$ obtained from the discussion and it forms the basis for MALESAbrain's knowledge judgment capability. In the example the qualification threshold θ_{kq} is set to "2" (see Fig. 3). Then any AK-cell weights higher than 2 point will be qualified to join the competition for promotion (see Definition 1-5). This means that the moment the knowledge-weights "3.1" of K_1 and "2.9" K_2 are greater than $K_{2.1}$ "2.1" (see Fig. 12); otherwise the system will swap the positions of the lower-weighted AK-cell with the higher-weighted AK-cell. Furthermore, the *AK-cell rejection threshold* θ_{kr} is set up as "-3.2" and the knowledge-weight $w_{2.1}$=2.1, therefore $K_{2.1}$ will not be deleted. The *solution maturity threshold* θ_{sm} is set up as "4.2" and the solution-weight $w_{i,j} = w_{2.1,2}$ = 1.4, therefore the learning system does not agree the solution $s_{2.1,2}$ is able to solve the problem $p_{2.1}$. The *solution disagreement threshold* θ_{sd} is set up as "-3" and the solution-weight $w_{2.1,1}$ = 0.7, therefore the solution $s_{2.1,1}$ will not be deleted by the system.

There is one definition worth to memtion here, the growth-factor, in definition 1-6, is introduced to convert the linear structure into a hierarchical structure of discussion-issues posted on the forum. The hierarchical structure helps our learners decide on different important positions, the learning-issues posted on the forum must not appear as a linear structure on the separate pages on the web site, but as hierarchical on demand. The growth factor normally is set up before discussion; however, it can also be changed after discussion if the educator wants to view the forum from a different angle. If the growth-factor has been set to 3 then the decision tree will be turned into three AK-cells on the top level and become a three-branch tree; if it has been switched to 5 then the decision tree will be turned into five best AK-cells on the top level for the learning decision and become a five-branch tree; if set up as one AK-cell then there is only one best decision to be made and become a linear-tree.

5. Using MALESAassessment in a test

The second algorithm - MALESAassessment - is to test students' performance after MALESAbrain's learning discussion. In this section, we use an example to explain how learners apply MALESAassessment for answering the testing problem.

After completing learning discussion, the educator will re-assign suitable keywords to each AK-cell according to his/her own understanding and viewpoint. This operation causes knowledge base reconstruction and turns it into a CBR expert system - called MALESAassessment. According to the matching of the reassigned-keywords, similar cases would be retrieved whenever users enter their inquiry. The similar cases retrieved are the AK-cells with attached knowledge-weight as the users' reference.

After set up CBR expert system, the educator will explain important cases to the learners with MALESAassessment. In the discussion the educator gives learners an understanding of what kind of cases that s/he considers good discussion-issues. It then gives a demonstration of how to use MALESAassessment to answer the questions in the assessment test.

After the demonstration, the educator will give learners a practical test to assess their understanding when handling a testing problem. For example, the educator can take off some memory from a motherboard and then run a heavy memory consuming game in a computer laboratory. S/he would ask the learners to make their own troubleshooting-plans and then to fix the problem. To make a troubleshooting plan the learners can seek advice from MALESAassessment. They can get the consultation cases from the original discussions, this helps them understand and cope with the testing problem. Their answers (troubleshooting plan) and thinking processes (log file) will also be recorded in the system to help educator in marking.

Fig. 13 shows the assessment interfaces in MALESAassessment. The CBR expert system consults the learners when making their troubleshooting-plans for answering the test. There are four screens or interfaces for consulting the learners to arrange their troubleshooting plans. First, the "*Inquiry*" screen can enter clients' query problem. Secondly, the "*consultation*" screen will offer the advice. Thirdly, the "*attention*" screen can help clients pay attention to their chosen cases/AK-cells. And the last/forth "*plan*" screen will help the learners make their problem-solving plan.

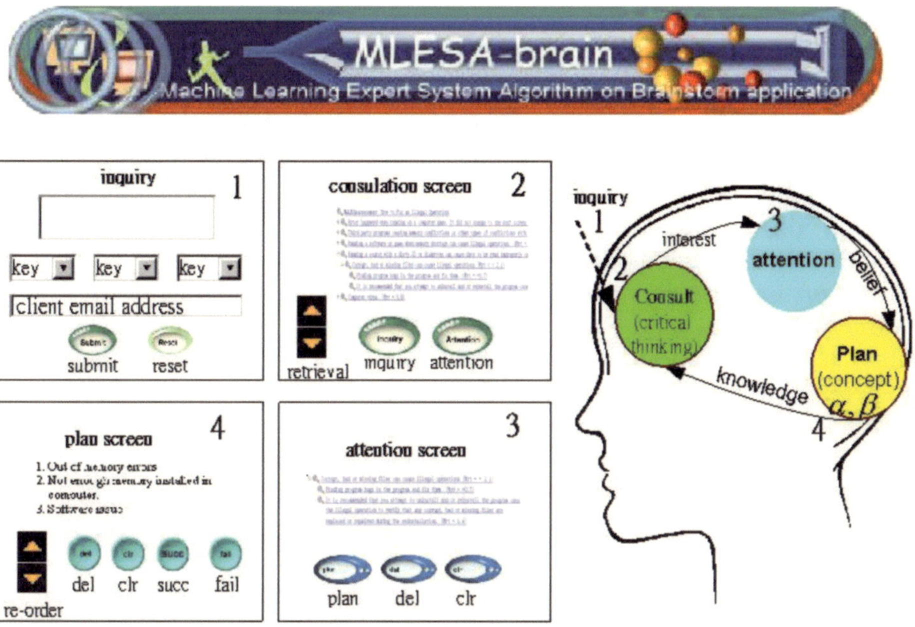

Fig. 13. The interfaces of assessment model in MALESAassessment.

5.1 Inquiry screen

The inquiry screen (1) shows that the learner enters his/her problem in order to seek advice. The learner types his/her question on the inquiry-board, choose one to three keywords, and input his/her contact email address if s/he wants the feedback from the educator after assessment; then submits or resets his/her request. In the mean time, behind the screen, MALESAassessment will retrieve the keyword-matched AK-cell from its CBR knowledge base; and output them to the consultation screen (2).

5.2 Consultation screen

When the learner changes his/her screen to consultation screen (2), the system will provide some preliminary suggestions to the learner according to the request on the inquiry screen (1). The retrieved cases are sorted according to their similarity and knowledge-weight. The learner still has to revise them to construct his/her own troubleshooting plan as the testing request. S/he will be encouraged to choose his/her interested AK-cells from screen (2); and output them into attention screen (3) for reuse and study. Whenever s/he clicks an AK-cell, it will change the AK-cell as a target for CBR and retrieve those cases of interest to the learner. These kinds of learner-browsing and system-retrieving operations will be repeated until s/he can find interested AK-cell on the screen.

Fig 13 shows there are two control buttons and two adjustment arrows on the consultation screen (2). To show his/her interest in an AK-cell, s/he can click "attention" button to put the chosen AK-cell to the attention screen (3). To re-enter his/her inquiring problem, s/he can click "inquiry" button for restarting a query. To change the number of AK-cells on the screen, the learner can also click either the "up" or "down" arrow to increase or decrease the number of the AK-cells on the screen.

This process of selecting interested AK-cells will be continued until the learner is satisfied with the selection of interested AK-cells on the attention screen (3).

5.3 Attention screen

After successfully collecting a list of interested AK-cells, the learner then exits consultation screen (2) and pays attention to the interested knowledge pieces on attention screen (3) for study and revision. This screen shows a list of interested AK-cells from learner's choices. Each AK-cell also includes a list of suggested solutions, obtained from the learning discussions. To answer the assessment test, learner now needs to pay attention to these solution-lists to discover suitable solutions to fix the real world problem.

There are three buttons on this screen. First, the learner can choose a solution then click a "plan" button, which will append the selected solution to the plan screen (4). Secondly, s/he can choose an unwanted AK-cell then click "delete" button for deleting the uninteresting AK-cell at the screen. Thirdly, if the learner cannot make a plan on the screen, s/he might click "clear" button to clear the whole screen and returns to consultation screen (2) for restarting and choosing more practical AK-cells.

5.4 Plan screen

After obtaining some solutions from the attention screen (3), the learner now revises and re-arranges the order of executive steps on the plan screen (4). On this screen, there are two arrows for "ascending" or "descending" the position of a selected solution, which helps the learner to organize his/her plan. There are also four other buttons on the plan screen with different usages. The "deleting" button is for deleting a selected solution. The "clearing" button is for clearing the whole screen and switching back to the attention screen (3) for restarting the selections again. The "successful" exit button is for the learner who has successfully made his/her troubleshooting plan and fixed the assessment problem. The "fail" exit button is for the learner who cannot establish a plan or cannot fix the assessment problem.

Behind the screen there is one thing worth noting. No matter whether the learner clicks "successful" exit or "fail" exit, the assessment reports will be sent to the educator for marking. The assessment reports include two parts:

i. the troubleshooting plan, and
ii. the log file which records whole learner's planning tasks with time stamps.

The educator then marks the assessment reports based on these two documents. When it is a successful case, the educator can concentrate on his/her troubleshooting plan for marking. When it is a failure case, the educator can concentrate on the log file and give him/her some proper advice for improving. Lastly, the marked reports would be retained in another CBR knowledge base as a refined second version expert system.

6. The algorithm of MALESAassessment

This section explains the second algorithm - MALESAassessment. It applies six definitions to clarify the symbols used in the instructions. The algorithm shows how the educator re-assigns suitable keywords to each AK-cell to reconstruct the system to a CBR expert system; and how learners apply MALESAassessment to answer the testing question. At last, we provide a successful retained case in the system during the experiment.

6.1 The definitions of MALESAassessment

Definition 2-1. The *re-organize(**K**)* action is used to reorganize the knowledge base, which includes two steps, are defined as follow:

1. keywords(educator, k_i), means the educator would re-assign the keywords to each AK-cell k_i in the knowledge base $\boldsymbol{K}$
2. CBR($\boldsymbol{K}$), means MALESAbrain $\boldsymbol{K}$ has been re-constructed as CBR expert system - called MALESAassessment.

Definition 2-2. The *inquiry(x)* function is defined as

$$Inquiry{:}x \xrightarrow[matching]{} \bigcup_{i=0}^{n} k_i \quad \text{where}$$

- x is participant's inquiring-input which includes inquiring-question, keywords and participant-email
- $\bigcup_{i=0}^{n} k_i$ is retrieved AK-cells as CBR output to the consultation screen.

Definition 2-3-1. The *retrievalQuantity(σ±ε)* is defined as the number of AK-cells being retrieved into consultation screen where

$$\left| \bigcup_{i=0}^{n} k_i \right| \leq \sigma \pm \varepsilon \text{ where}$$

- is the default retrieval number of AK-cells
- $\pm\varepsilon$ is an offset to adapt the retrieval quantity

Definition 2-3-2. A *consultation-action(c_i)* is defined as an action chosen by the participants on consultation screen, where

$$c_i = \begin{cases} inquiry(x)\ ;\ or \\ attention(k_i) \end{cases} \quad \text{where,}$$

- *inquiry(x)* , means participant do not satisfy with the inquiry result on the consultation screen and want to re-enter another inquiry again.
- *attention(k_i)*, means participant chosen an AK-cell for reuse, and MALESAassessment then append it to the attention screen.

Definition 2-4. A *attention-action(a_i)* is defined as

$$a_i = \begin{cases} plan(s_{i,j})\ ;\ or \\ delete(k_i)\ ;\ or \\ clearAttentionScreen \end{cases} \quad \text{where}$$

- *plan($s_{i,j}$)*, means participant chosen a solution on the attention screen for revision, and MALESAassessment then append it to the plan screen.
- *delete (k_i)*, means participant want to delete a chosen AK-cell on the attention screen.
- *clearAttentionScreen*, means participant does not satisfy with the whole attention screen and want to clear them.

Definition 2-5. A *plan-action(p_i)* is defined as

$$p_i = \begin{cases} position(s_{i,j})\ ;\ or \\ delete(s_{i,j})\ ;\ or \\ clearPlanScreen\ ;\ or \\ exit(successful)\ ;\ or \\ exit(fail) \end{cases} \quad \text{where}$$

- *position($s_{i,j}$)*, means participant want to organize solution's execution steps; by either click ascending or descending on a chosen solution to the right execution step.
- *delete($s_{i,j}$)* , means participant want to delete a chosen solution on the plan screen.
- *clearPlanScreen*, means participant does not satisfy with the whole plan screen and want to clear it.
- *exit(successful)*, means participant have successfully made the plan and fixed the problem. MALESAassessment then retains the log file and the successful plan into a new CBR knowledge base as a successful case when s/he exits.
- *exit(fail)*, means participant cannot establish a plan or cannot fix the problem. MALESAassessment then retains the log file and the failure plan into a new CBR knowledge base as a failure case when s/he exits.

6.2 The algorithm of MALESAassessment

re-organise(**K**) /* *Preparation* Definition 2-1 */

INPUT keywords(educator, k_i)

CONSTRCT CBR(***K***)

END re-organise

MALESAassessment(participant$_i$,***K***)

CASE screen chosen by participant$_i$ OF /* the participants can choose one of the four screens */

```
        Inquiry screen (1): GOTO inquiry(x)   /* Inquiry screen definition 2-2*/
        Consultation screen (2): GOTO consultation-action(ci)  /* Consultation screen
        definition 2-3*/
        Attention screen (3): GOTO attention-action(ai)  /* Attention screen definition 2-4*/
        Plan screen (4):   GOTO plan-action(pi)  /* Plan screen definition 2-5*/
    ENDCASE
END MALESAassessment

inquiry(x)  /* Inquiry Definition 2-2 */
        INPUT inquiring-question
        INPUT keywords
        INPUT participant-email
END inquiry

consultation-action(ci)  /* Consultation Definition 2-3*/
    CASE operation chosen by participanti  OF  /* the participants can choose one of the
    four operations */
        "inquiry":      GOTO inquiry(x)  /*Definition 2-2*/
        "attention":    DISPLAY-IN attention(ki)  /*Definition 2-3-2 */
        "up":           INCREMENT retrievalQuantity(σ + ε)  /*Definition 2-3-1 */
        "down":         DECREMENT retrievalQuantity(σ - ε)  /*Definition 2-3-1 */
    ENDCASE
END consultation-action

attention-action(ai)  /* Attention  Definition 2-4*/
    CASE operation chosen by participanti  OF  /* the participants can choose one of the
    three operations */
        "plan" :        DISPLAY-IN plan(si,j)
        "delete":       DELETE delete(ki)
        "clear":        CLEAR clearAttentionScreen
    ENDCASE
END attention-action

plan-action(pi)  /* Plan  Definition 2-5*/
    CASE operation chosen by participanti  OF  /* the participants can choose one of the
    five operations */
        "position":     DETERMINE position(si,j),
        "delete":       DELETE delete (si,j)
        "clear":        CLEAR clearPlanScreen
        "successful":   EXIT exit(successful)
        "fail":         EXIT exit(fail)
    ENDCASE
END plan-action
```

7. Discussion

IT education is in a state of change. Similar to nursing education, IT courses have a high content load to teach in the state of the art. However, the large student numbers and limited staff in the computer class often hinder interested educators combining PBL with structured teaching in their curricula. The question is "without an effective and efficient tool, it seems impractical to ask an educator handle with large number of group discussions in the discipline of PBL".

In this experiment, we test whether these two algorithms in the learning system can support PBL discussion in IT curricula or not? We want to know:

- Does the system help students organize and synthesize knowledge in discussion?
- Does the system save educator the efforts in helping discussion group effectively?
- Does the system efficiently save educator the efforts on the student performance test?

The first algorithm, MALESAbrain has been tested in our graduate laboratory, with "70%" learning rate setup and for two-week time of discussion. This experiment invited six of the postgraduate students to discuss the question: "How to fix an illegal operation? An illegal operation is an operation requested to be performed by either the Operating System or CPU that is not understood and therefore is illegal".

The evaluation after the experiment, with "56%" learning rate on the due date; and MALESAbrain has received some comments from the participants:

In considering of the methodology, the learning system

1. helps the students to think about the pros and cons of the proposed issues before they go into chat room for discussion.
2. highlights the issues with different levels of importance to help the students to identify the significance of the learning issues in the problem. .

In considering of the educators' benefits, the learning system

1. allows educator to monitor learner-groups' discussions on his/her screen to save the shortage of manpower and time limitation.
2. allows the educator to coach the meeting progressing and to guide learners in the right direction for discussion.
3. allows educator to encourage each of the students to pick up a learning issue for further investigation and research.

However, the strategies to set up the "learning thresholds" in MALESAbrain still remain to be evaluated and estimated. There are two reasons:

1. Firstly, it is because we are trying to change the learning thresholds setup by observing the number of learners in discussion at that time. In the Internet discussion, sometimes, it is not easy to control the number of participants who are really keen to learn and join discussion. Based on observing the number of participants and the discussion situation, we changed the learning thresholds to control the remaining learning issues to a number.
2. Second, we do not use "rejection threshold" to prune out worthless issues during discussion until due date for calculating the leaning-rate. It is because we do not want to lose any proposed issues. General speaking, it looks fine in this experiment. However, we are not sure it is still a proper procedure on the other experiment?

In the experiment, the thresholds' setup proves to be challenged by the participants - "why not let them decide the thresholds before the meeting, because it is their discussions and is their responsibility to answer the educator's request". This means we cannot approve a best thresholds setup at this stage. However, the following table is their suggestion setup.

MALESAbrain learning Threshold θ				
Threshold	*qualification threshold*	*rejection threshold*	*maturity threshold*	*disagreement threshold*
Symbol	θ_{kq}	θ_{kr}	θ_{sm}	θ_{sd}
Setup Value	2 points	-3.2 points	4.2 points	-3 points

Table 1. A suggestion learning thresholds set up in MALESAbrain with 6 participants.

The second experiment, of MALESAassessment, found the keywords in the AK-cells are not well matched the problem issues. It is because learners' assign keywords, during MALESAbrain discussion, will have individuals' viewpoints without integrated into an overview for reusing. It affects the searching results in the test. After we re-assign keywords to each AK-cell, MALESAassessment becomes quite significant for reusing the learned knowledge. The Assessment Report and log file, in section 6.3, show one of the successful retained cases after test. This means there are no difficulties to give a proper mark to a successful answered student and give a proper advice to a failure answered student in this experiment.

8. Conclusion

In this chapter, we propose two intelligent algorithms to save the educator the time for acquiring learning knowledge in PBL environment. The first algorithm builds up MALESAbrain as an intelligent system to acquire students' knowledge in PBL discussion. It will help students integrate their knowledge by critical thinking on different angles of a problem through on-line discussion. The second algorithm builds up MALESAassessment as an evaluation system to test students' performance after PBL discussion. These two algorithms work together to reduce educator's efforts for connecting PBL to IT education.

MALESAbrain algorithm saves the educator the effort of searching for important knowledge pieces generated by students' discussions through its automatic calculations. It reduces the pressure of time in the teaching schedule for coaching PBL discussions in the IT course. Consequently, MALESAbrain has contributed three notions to make the PBL discussion more effective and efficient for knowledge acquisition:

1. The first notion is the created data structure - coined as "AK-cell" (see Definition 1-4) - for cooperative learning, which combines knowledge-content and knowledge-weight. It allows the discussion-knowledge to become calculable in a threshold system. The knowledge-contents become mobile because of the combination of knowledge-weight and knowledge-content in the data structure. Knowledge-weight ranks AK-cells into different important locations, based on learners' judgments and the thresholds set up. It helps learners pay attention to consensus knowledge for more discussion; and to think about why certain issues accumulate different scores from other issues.
2. The second notion is the autonomous decision-making mechanism - called "learning threshold" (see Definition 1-5). It helps the learning system automatically arrange and order construction of a hierarchical knowledge base. It helps students to identify the importance of the issues in a problem.
3. The third notion is the dynamic structure of the knowledge base - called "growth-factor" (see Definition 1-6). It helps the data structure AK-cell to be constructed according to the educator's viewpoint; whatever is right in his/her coaching for knowledge acquisition.

The value of the second algorithm MALESAassessment is the assessment design, which uses the student performance test to refine the learned knowledge. It offers learners a chance to retrospect their learned knowledge and refine them to solve another problem in test. The test assesses learners' concept in making an action plan and examines their abilities to solve a physical troubleshooting problem.

The design feature of MALESAassessment is based on the principles described on the chapter "From case-based reasoning to problem-based learning" (Eshach & Bitterman, 2003) and four-stage CBR-cycle design on the book of "Applying Case-Based Reasoning: Techniques for Enterprise Systems" (Watson, 1997) (see Fig. 13). The four-stage open-ended cycle and concepts-in-action designs help to refine an existing case and construct a new case from the raw/previous cases. In the assessment, learners retrieve the similar cases from the CBR knowledge base; reuse the cases to attempt to solve the existing problem; revise the proposed solutions to solve the new problem; and retain the new solution as their answer to solve the test problem.

9. References

Biljon, J. A. v., Tolmie, C. J., & Plessis, J. P. d. (1999). MagixDan ICAE system for Problem-Based Learning. *Computers & Education, 32*, 65-81.

ComputerHope. (2004). *Computer Hope.com*, [web site]. Available: http://www.computerhope.com/ [15/4/2004].

Conway, J., & Sharkey, R. (2002). Integrating on campus problem based learning and practice based learning: issues and challenges in using computer mediated communication. *Nurse Education Today, 22*, 552-562.

Cooke, M., & Moyle, K. (2002). Students' evaluation of problem-based learning. *Nurse Education Today, 22*, 330-339.

Culvenor, J. (2003). Comparison of team and individual judgments of solutions to safety problems. *Safety Science, 41*, 543 –556.

Eshach, H., & Bitterman, H. (2003). From case-based reasoning to problem-based learning. *Academic Medicine, 78*, 491-496.

Fisher, A. (2001). *Critical Thinking an Introduction* University of Cambridge.

IBM. (2004). *IBM Education: Solutions and resources for IT and business professionals, educators and students*, [web site].
Available: http://www-306.ibm.com/software/info/education/ [16/4/2004].

K.Kaye, B., & J.Johnson, T. (2004). A Web for all reasons: uses and gratifications of Internet components for political information. *Telematics and Informatics, 21*, 197-223.

Lewis, M. J., Davies, R., Jenkins, D., & Tait, M. I. (2001). A review of evaluative studies of computer-based learning in nursing education. *Nurse Education Today, 21*(1), 26-37.

Microsoft. (2004). *Microsoft.com*, [web site]. Available: http://www.microsoft.com/homepage/nav.asp?pid=1 [16/4/2004].

Mitchell, T. M. (1997). *Machine Learning* McGraw-Hill.

Paul, S., Haseman, W. D., & Ramamurthy, K. (2004). Collective memory support and cognitive-conflict group decision-making: an experimental investigation. *Decision Support Systems, 36*(3), 261-281.

Roberts, D., & Ousey, K. (2003). Problem based learning: developing the triggers. Experiences from a first wave site. *Nurse Education in Practice*, (3), 1-5.

Torp, L., & Sage, S. (2002). *Problems as Possibilities: Problem-Based Learning for K–16 Education* Association for Supervision & Curriculum Development.

Watson, I. (1997). *Applying Case-Based Reasoning: Techniques for Enterprise Systems* Morgan Kaufmann Publisers.

10

E-Learning in Architecture: Professional and Lifelong Learning Prospects

Matevz Juvancic[1], Michael Mullins[2] and Tadeja Zupancic[1]
[1]*University of Ljubljana*
[2]*Aalborg University*
[1]*Slovenia*
[2]*Denmark*

1. Introduction

E-learning in architectural and spatially related fields can be examined from two different perspectives, each having quite specific and complex implications. By discussing e-learning *in* architecture we inspect the scope of e-learning tools and practices within the architectural domain, the visual nature of education and professional training of architects, and the state of the art of e-learning implementations, together with their practicality and limitations. While these are the first areas that come to mind when considering e-learning in relation to architecture, there is another also very relevant and sometimes overlooked aspect: that of e-learning *about* architecture. In the latter, we introduce not only the professional but also the broader, non-expert public into the process of acting within, and shaping of, their spatial environments. This aspect raises burning questions regarding the communication abilities of the actors involved, holding their attention, ingraining sustainable principles and getting the messages across the invisible, but perennial expert / non-expert divide. E-learning *in* and *about* architecture not only offers opportunities for both sides to learn but also to get to know each other better.

The chapter first introduces and highlights the common aspects of e-learning within the architectural domain, followed by e-learning for experts, through what we have named e-learning *in* architecture, describing specifics and presenting an example of one of the e-learning initiatives. It is followed by a subchapter describing aspects of e-learning *about* architecture and sustainable principles of space interventions for broader audience of non-experts involved in the lifelong learning processes (LLP). Similarly, the subchapter concludes with an example of an e-learning tool in action and the reflections on the research presented. The chapter concludes with discussions of 'lessons learned' and ranking of new opportunities in professional and lifelong e-learning prospects in architecture and its related fields.

2. Aspects of e-learning within the architectural domain

Architectural education is centrally concerned with individual design creativity among its students and encompasses an important aspect of visual acuity or training in interpretation of visual representation. These are aspects of human articulation, neither easily taught in the lecture theatre nor transmitted in the computer laboratory.

Education in architecture, be it for experts or non-experts, is also a communication process with an exchange of mainly visual messages. As such it follows (in general) the established Laswell's mass communication model (Severin & Thankard, 1992): *Who? Says what? In which channel? To whom? With what effect?* It is especially useful for articulation of many important aspects of architectural e-learning at the start of our journey and is here used because of its convenient, almost self-explanatory simplicity. 'Who' is usually an expert, a teacher but, as we will see later, can also represent a fellow learner or the learner himself exchanging (feedback) information in the learning process. 'Says what' is the message and in architectural learning it is most probably of a visual nature and of specific content, which has again its implications. 'In which channel', we interpret here as the way the learning is organized (curriculum, learning setting, environment, media used, teaching methods, teaching tools, etc). 'To whom', depends on the targeted learners as discussed in the introduction above, in the distinction between learning *in* and learning *about* architecture. 'With what effect', denotes the learning outcomes and includes the assessment methods. It is now easier to envision the components of the process and our aims to describe them in architectural learning context.

Learning about how to do architecture and how to 'think' architecture requires a great deal of cognitive processing, the manipulation of mental images, understanding of complex cause and effect relationships, functional, technical, performance, aesthetic, cultural and physical aspects. Visuospatial thinking theories are especially suited for the purpose of learning *in* and *about* architecture which both rely heavily on the notion that thinking consists of mental images and principled manipulation of mental images (Mayer, 2005) on the premise that: "a) appropriate visuospatial thinking during learning can enhance the learner's understanding, and b) multimedia presentation can be designed to prime appropriate visuospatial thinking during learning" (Mayer, 2005).

2.1 Blended learning and constructivist approach: a viable solution for learning *in* and *about* architecture

Instead of strictly using *e-* for electronic learning, implying that (ICT) e-learning platform is in the heart of learners' experience, the learning *in* and *about* architecture is more aligned with blended learning practices. Blended learning spans over face-to-face (f2f) and e-learning connecting them, combining learning on site with distant learning under the joint name of distributed learning (Mason & Rennie, 2006). The exchange of messages provides the necessary learning environment and scaffolding to higher-order thinking (Slavik, 1994 as cited in Mason & Rennie, 2006). Blended learning with f2f component can produce a stronger sense of community among participants than fully online course (Rovai & Jordan, 2004 as cited in Mason & Rennie, 2006), socio-cultural context for learning environment and helps maintain the link with traditional design studio practices in the field of architecture.

Architectural learning requires a practical component of 'learning by doing', traditionally in a studio environment, through which students acquire experience and knowledge of professional practice in a social context of peers, thus aligning them with the constructivist learning models. This aspect of learning in realistic settings reflects the view of learning as an active construction of knowledge by the learner who makes his or her own sense of authentic tasks set by the instructor. The learner will in theory engage a variety of cognitive processes including processing relevant information, organising that information into coherent representations and integrating these representations with existing knowledge in order to create solutions to the challenges presented. The term 'constructivist' thus refers to the idea that learners construct knowledge for themselves individually and socially in the process of learning: "If the view is adopted that 'knowledge' is the conceptual means to make sense of experience rather than the 'representation' of something that is supposed to lie beyond it, this shift of perspective brings with it an important corollary: the concepts and relations in terms of which we perceive and conceive the experiential world are necessarily generated by ourselves. In this sense we are responsible for the world we are experiencing" (von Glaserfield, 1991). The instructors primary task is thus to create environments in which the learner can interact meaningfully with a set of 'real-life' challenges.

Constructivist models, often used in e-applications and learning - situated learning, PBL and simulation - are very much attuned to traditional design studio learning with the benefits (and disadvantages) of ICT environments and capabilities. While these principles have been embraced in architectural schools, particularly in 'problem-based learning' methods, architectural education has also in the past decades sought to experiment with and apply the tools of information and computer technology. These ICT tools represent a relatively new context in which the architectural creative process is increasingly carried out in project groups rather than by independent designers, affording cross-disciplinary, global teamwork, and which leads in consequence to situations where negotiation is required in exploring alternatives to solve problems, often probing the boundaries between disciplines (Fruchter, 2006). ICT has the effect of bringing together for limited periods of time, previously disparate communities of practice for the purpose of solving particular problems. The focus is shifted from individual learning about practice, to extracting the full potential of learning through practice in a community. As Etienne Wenger has observed, when the core of central expertise held by individual communities of practice meets other communities with their cores of expertise, radically new insights can arise at the boundary between the communities (Wenger, 1998). It is often this meeting of apparently very different ways of viewing the world whereby the creativity of new ideas and solutions is encouraged.

In as much as the perspective of learning shifts from the individual to a larger system of the individual's participation in a community of practice, it is more relevant to consider e-learning as a situative context of interaction in which individuals participate and coordinate their activities to achieve meaningful objectives (Greeno, 1998). This strategy implies a focus on the informational contents of the activities undertaken, and a study of how such a dynamic system functions. The task of the instructor can on this basis be formulated to be that of facilitating the active membership of a community of practice that engages for a limited time in joint activities with others to create solutions for authentic problems through adaptation, commitment and social relationships. Specifically, the successful development of community of practice requires the provision of guidance and resources that encourage the negotiation by the participants of a joint project through mutual engagement in a well-functioning social entity. Thereby, participants are afforded the opportunity to mutually construct meaning through presentations, manipulation of design objects, discussions and interactions which allow them to reach mutual understanding through the interpretations of visual and written materials.

E-learning programs which complement or replace traditional architectural education should seek to blend self-study, face-to-face meetings, to stimulate social context and facilitate cooperative work of 'real-life' professional experience. This approach goes beyond merely acquiring knowledge of the technology involved: effectiveness of e-learning is not merely a function of new technology, but rather is achieved through the "adaptation of the learning environment to a changing context which presents new opportunities for an investigation and formation of 'place', as that difficult concept is understood in schools of architecture" (Strojan & Mullins, 2002).

Learning *about* architecture (for non-experts) can follow the same blended and constructivist approaches although the levels need to be adapted in terms of existing non-expert knowledge pool, skills and their understanding of visual language.

2.2 Visuospatial thinking, multimedia and visual language skills

What is specific to architectural learning is its reliance on the exchange of mainly visual messages in the process. This requires learners to understand and interpret them in a meaningful, accepted and consistent way. It also requires the participants to respond in kind, with the visual messages composed on their own that also convey an intended message in a meaningful and consistent way. Research has demonstrated the apparent differences how architects as experts and laypersons as non-experts perceive and understand visual representations (Bates-Brkljac, 2007). Introducing architectural or spatial issues, and with that sometimes very specific visual messages, opens new questions of 'reading' and 'writing' of visual messages by different participants involved in the learning process. In general we discern between three groups of participants in terms of visual reading-writing abilities in the architectural planning process [and consequentially learning in- and about- architecture]: 1) the group of experts that is able to read and write visual messages, but less able to express themselves by writing (architects, urban planners, designers, civil engineers, etc), 2) the group who express themselves primarily in writing but are also able to understand ('read') expert visualizations, but much less able to compose them and 3) the largest group of non-experts which is very limited in reading and writing abilities when it comes to visual messages, exchanged in architectural domain (Juvancic et al., 2011).

The e-learning *in* and *about* architecture profits from the graphic capabilities of ICT in the communication process already mentioned, which mainly uses visual messages to represent space and relations in space in two dimensions, while often through means of perspective or isometric, emulates also the third dimension. Readers being aware of immersive environments capabilities and features (i.e. in games and pervasive digital worlds), we will not go into the matter further here.

E-learning, which through ICT supports and includes multimedia possibilities, can offer an especially suitable learning environment for learning *in* and *about* architecture, but it needs to be further extended with specialized learning tools if it wants to satisfy the specifics of expert and non-expert architectural learning (as we will see later in the two showcases). The design principles for fostering visuospatial thinking in multimedia learning as suggested by Mayer (2005): multimedia, contiguity, coherence, modality, redundancy, personalization, interactivity and signalling principles hold true for learning *in* and *about* architecture as well. Some of them were proven through the experimental use of prototypical architectural educational interfaces (see subchapter 4.8) others were and are used assuming their importance as proven for other fields. Although Mayer does not specifically refer to manipulation of objects and presentations within his span of multimedia learning it needs to be emphasized that the principle cannot be overlooked, especially in the light of the situative perspective of dynamic learning (Greeno, 1998) and constructivist learning.

2.3 E-learning platforms, educational interfaces and the acquisition of new knowledge

E-learning extends beyond multimedia learning – it integrates a curriculum, course design, contents (presented in different forms through presentations), learning outcomes, assessment, specialized tools and not least, usually relies on e-learning platform that serves as a medium, a meeting point, a link and a repository for the learning resources and a community forum for the learners. The e-learning platforms, nowadays most often called Learning Management Systems (LMS), come in many varieties, sharing common aspects and elements that are suitable for a cross-section of common e-learning activities and tools for running and managing (blended) courses (i.e. Moodle is a good example applied to many levels of teaching and used for different topics and in different settings). The common and general e-learning platforms provide modular structure to facilitate specific needs and specialization. Knewton (Fischman, 2011) is an example that can take on different contents provided it follows more or less the same structure and can be framed within the multimedia options available in the system but still adapt the pace of learning to an individual learner.

Multipurpose e-learning platforms might satisfy the management needs of architectural expert and non-expert courses (and activities) but when it comes to learning they need further extensions with special modules and functionalities to provide for suitable interactive and engaging environment. For expert learning, the multidimensional environments and integration of tools used in architectural practices are of the essence, with further extensions of scripting and parametric design highly recommended (i.e. 3D Lab in VIPA case, described later). For non-expert learning, the much needed user friendly upgrades are educational interfaces that can show complex spatial phenomena through different presentation means and engage the learner in constructivist learning activities. Much more about the functionalities, extensions and aims of e-learning platforms in architecture is highlighted through two different examples later in the chapter (see subchapters 3.1 and 4.8).

Not only can the distinction between expert and non-expert learners be drawn on the basis of different levels of 'reading-writing, visual-message' skills and on the expectations regarding the understanding of complex spatial phenomena, but also on the basis of formal knowledge expected from them. While future experts possess certain formal knowledge in the field and need to acquire and complement it through the learning process, non-experts can rely only on their informal and tacit knowledge when dealing with architectural and environmental tasks.

While the future expert learner will, with the help of e-learning, cross the gulf of expertise (Quintana et al., 2002), gaining knowledge and skills to do his job successfully, the non-expert will have to cross the gulf of knowledge in the field of architecture and gain insight into the field he is not familiar with and will not spent his life professionally practicing within its domain. However at the same time, his understanding of the field will play a crucial role in his decision making process and space interventions he will encounter during his lifespan of builder, active and passive actor in spatial environment and its 'inhabitant'. Given the sheer number of non-experts physically ('architecturally') intervening daily in their environments and deciding about it (through democratic processes), the non-experts are the major influencing factor in the environmental equation. This is where common aspects end and the e-learning prospects divide to two separate, equally important directions - for experts and non-experts - each with its own goals and agendas.

3. E-learning in professional architectural training and education

Teaching architecture is not primarily an instructional process but rather a process of interaction and experience. An evaluation of the effectiveness of e-learning cannot only focus on the technology itself but should also examine the potential of technology as a tool for learning and design. Software for 3D modelling, rendering and animation and so on, should be combined with multi-user, interactive environments which support a social learning context. It is not that the 'virtual space' in which learning and teaching occurs should only represent the vibrancy of an architectural studio when it is best, but that its application offers new potential for architectural curricula. Architecture can be described as a combination of practical, functional and technical solutions to a spatial problem, which gives or explores an aesthetic reflection of the society in which it occurs. It relies on an interdisciplinary teamwork of different professions, each with different visual language abilities and expertise, towards achieving a common goal - a building, an urban design, or settlement - in a non-linear way. Sometimes very technical and sometimes very intuitive, this process is a difficult task to mould into a constructivist e-learning environment.

While the theory of learning in such an environment has been established in the preceding theoretical framework, for application to the scaffolding provided by instructors or mentors, the actual context of the learning environment must receive closer attention. Prevailing learning management and content management systems (LMS & CMS), such as Moodle, lack the integrated tools for visual and 3D based communication exchange in architectural education. The problems of useful, economically viable, and most of all effortless integration of communication, learning management and design tools is such that the field of architecture has yet to find the 'magic' e-learning solution. However, by addressing specific tasks with suitable tools effective, albeit partial, solutions can be developed.

Architecture has also transcended its historically physical domain into the virtual, shaping insistent immersive environments, not only crossing the digital divide but also redefining notions traditionally held to be self-evident, such as the nature of digital tectonics, the simulation or otherwise of gravity constraints, scale, and presence.

3.1 Showcase example: Virtual campus for virtual space design provided for european architects (VIPA)

As an example of an e-learning project, VIPA (Kipcak, 2007) is of particular interest. It has been developed through an EU project to address many relevant issues of e-learning in architecture, using traditional LMS e-learning tools and integrating new ones. The showcased example being complex enough to point out the specifics of e-learning *in* architecture (and the content is, we will assume, more or less known to the reader) we will follow the case and underlying notions simultaneously.

3.1.1 The objectives of VIPA

The overall objective of the project is to expand and enhance education in the field of architecture within a virtual campus through development of pedagogical courseware and appropriate technological platforms. Project goals include:

- A virtual campus integrating administrative, curricular and communicative infrastructures for schools of architecture.
- Competence development in the design of virtual and augmented reality for architecture students.
- Development and coordination of the training of European architecture students in the field of 3D-design
- Use of industrial know-how in the field of interactive 3D-authoring for the training of architects
- Content and conception input for these industries from the field of architecture
- Coordination and research at European architecture universities in this field
- An internationalisation of curricula into joint or double degree developments for architectural students and/or graduates.

- Additional and more intensive cooperation between the respective educational institutions across Europe.

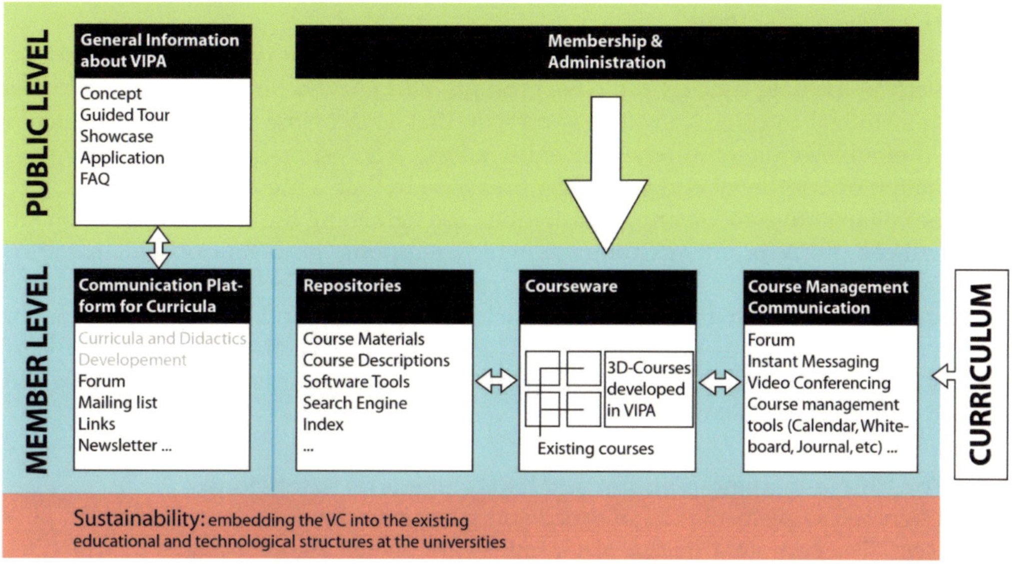

Fig. 1. The organizational and structural layout of VIPA virtual campus (Kipcak, 2007).

University curricula have developed out of local core competences, teachers and researchers. These local factors are woven into the fabric of a transnational VIPA curriculum and supported with organizational layout, platform, user interfaces and their features. It has been therefore proposed that all participants offer their existing courses in virtual space design, as well as developing new ones. This offers the option for both present and future participants to adjust the VIPA courseware to suit local curricula demands, while offering a large range of courses and knowledge. The professional fields that students of these curricula may enter range from well-established fields like architectural design to emerging fields like information design and the provision of virtual environments as extensions to existing institutions of complex social networks. An additional feature of VIPA is thus as a platform for curricula development for virtual space design to cope with the demands of a highly multi-disciplinary and emerging field of knowledge.

3.1.2 Reluctance of e-learning use in architectural schools

Virtual campuses are already established at most universities in the European Community, yet surprisingly e-learning is not yet widespread in architectural schools in Europe and is arguably still in its initial research phase. Although there are best practice examples where e-learning is replacing traditional study forms in other teaching disciplines, it has been found in the participating architectural faculties that there is a considerable resistance to e-learning. Among various other concerns, there is a common doubt that e-learning can be as equally effective as traditional face-to-face architectural studio teaching and culture. This is not a problem related only to architectural education and has been addressed in other projects such as OMAET, a pioneer in offering online degree programs for mid-career education professionals (Stager, 2005). Here, learner-centred theories and practices built upon the writings of Vygotsky, Lave, Wenger, Piaget & Papert stress that the course compensates for the lack of face-to-face contact between students and faculty "in ways that actually lead to greater intimacy and access" (Stager, 2005).

3.1.3 The didactics of VIPA

The concept of VIPA didactics is based on the constructivist e-learning model. The constructivist learning concept provides prompts, stimuli, coaching and support instead of guiding a student through knowledge and is in that aspect close to established teaching in the field of architecture (and other related sciences). VIPA supports blended learning - the combination of traditional and e-learning practices. In that sense it combines local specifics with the collaborative and sharing possibilities, strengthening the sense of affiliation among its members. VIPA is an environment which supports problem-oriented, experiential, collaborative learning with media-rich contents based on grounded pedagogical methodologies, with a high grade of interactivity. Learning and teaching of virtual space design stand in the focus of VIPA effort. Combining constructivist and blended learning models, the main virtual campus features are oriented towards creative, intuitive, user-friendly didactical environments and tools.

3.1.4 The VIPA e-learning platform and its architectural extensions

The design and implementation of space and place is no longer wholly reliant on physical processes. The conceptual design of virtual spaces is creating new places in which to live and work. In consequence, new opportunities for work and employment are opening up for architects as well as for architectural educators. In response to this challenge, VIPA contains an e-learning and research platform for European architectural schools with a focus on virtual space design. The virtual campus integrates administrative, curricular, and communicative infrastructures, interactive, multimedia 3-D contents, and pedagogical considerations in respect of the aims, content and technologies employed.

VIPA effort is oriented towards development of tools for Virtual Space Design and teaching in that environment. Special emphasis is put on longer term aspects of virtual space, as students will be encouraged to experiment with, design and develop virtual space as a new emerging environment. Virtual lab is considered to be one of the crucial VIPA strengths and is the focus of the VIPA curriculum. The course should present and enable students to create personal environments, make generic spaces and forms, collaborate, interact and communicate, and experiment with forms and environment responses to user actions.

The strongest points of VIPA platform are: extensibility, modularity, comprehensive services and means of communication among users, towards future oriented tools for e-learning (especially for virtual space design), where partner universities and partners from the private sector may profit by sharing resources, competencies and contact networks. VIPA is at present a prototype that tests the feasibility of the curricular, didactical and technical concepts. Issues partially addressed and the ones to be developed still further include its development into a working model and include:

- Different types of degrees/coursework offered
- Part or whole of a MSc.
- Coursework in the doctoral degree
- MPhil or PhD research platform
- Quality control where VIPA combines courses from various schools
- Quality criteria

- Choice of evaluators
- The organisation of VIPA as an institution in the future
- The CLUSTER consortium is a possible model (www.cluster.org)
- The appointment of teaching staff
- European accreditation of titles, modules

Tools for Course Management - learning management system (LMS)	**Repository of course materials and Software Tools - content management system (CMS)**
• modular student/teachers features • calendar • journal/web log • wiki • course summary • online users • glossary • topics of the week/course • recent activity • upcoming events • courses • tools for teachers administering their class • registration of students to courses • tools for assessment/grading	• database structure: course materials, course descriptions, software tools, shared documents • tools for manipulation of files (up/down-load, deletion, modification, track changes, notes, etc) • search engine • automatic indexing of databases / lists according to search criteria (thematically, successively, alphabetically, similar media)
Communication	**Cooperation platform for didactics and curricula**
• video conferencing tools (possible use of existing external applications) • audio conferencing tools (possible use of existing external applications) • instant messaging (possible use of existing external applications) • forum • mailing lists	• forum • document up/down-load • mailing list • links
Virtual design laboratory	
• creating of 3D primitives, mapping • scripting • manipulation and modification of objects • changing the virtual space parameters and behaviour • collaborative interaction and modification of spaces and forms • simple modular integration of additional tools • working on different levels (novice, expert users) • personalization of the environment • interaction with other documents and programs • import of data (especially 3D) from established programs for 3D modelling and design (dxf, 3ds, dwg, etc.) • the virtual lab has to be prepared with both end users and developers in mind (basic functionalities have to be already present after installation and easily used in VIPA courses)	

Table 1. VIPA e-learning platform components and functionalities.

4. E-learning about architecture and sustainable spatial practices for non-experts

Architecture as profession has been recently dealing not only with the design and planning but more and more frequently engaging in awareness-raising and education about spatial values and sustainable practices as well. In these processes different participants that act in existing natural and cultural contexts are addressed. The participation always brings to the surface the questions of who the participants are and what, if any, intersection of knowledge, (visual) communication skills, attitudes and values they share.

The proverbial lack of common visions regarding architecture, eco-spatial values and spatial interventions does not arise merely from misunderstandings and expression disabilities, as already highlighted at the introduction. The national surveys (in Slovenia) indicate (Tos, 2004) that there is a wide overlap of professional and general public values regarding natural and built environmental issues. But as in many similar cases the divide between declarative statements of respondents and their actions and interventions when it comes to materialization becomes painfully obvious as they start solving their everyday living and housing needs.

The Lifelong Learning Process (LLP) presents an opportunity to address such problems before they emerge (prevention), it presents them to wider audience (who is not always even aware of wrong-doing) at different stages in life, especially at times when changing attitudes does not re-quire as much effort as in later years.

The basic presumption when addressing the LLP, architecture and space is axiomatic: the awareness and education of the non-experts and the inclusion of sustainable spatial topics into the process of LLP can improve the comprehension of professional baselines and values. Furthermore they may contribute to more prudent space management and spatial interventions as well as in decrease of spatially related problems and conflicts. By means of education and educational system it is sensible not only to administer the values and motives which underlie the legal acts and experts' positions but also to explain them. Assuming comprehension is the solid foundation for acting, building and the decision making regarding space the actual behaviour of individuals in space is influenced by more factors than knowledge alone (affect, values vs. needs, etc) - blind belief the education is the cure for every perennial spatial issue is thus contra productive and exaggerates its potential and we are giving it some thought later on (see subchapter 4.7).

Overcoming the first barrier - learning the visual language or offering a suitable alternative and support to participate and to express oneself in visual debate can be facilitated through means of e-Learning and ICT. 56% of households in Slovenia have a broadband internet access[1]. With 98% regular users among the population between 10 and 24 years of age this constitutes ever more suitable environment for distance learning: ICT seasoned users and widespread and fast network access. Through e-learning in particular we can reach the ICT 'fluent' generations who know how to use the ICT to their advantage in everyday life and when solving different tasks: not merely as passive users but as creative, responsive and reflecting individuals. Using the required visual-, desired parametric-, logic-, networking- and multiple feedback communication- possibilities of e-learning (existing and future) tools allow us to make the transition, from merely transmitting the knowledge and information to a wider audience, to engaging the non-experts, making the participants and collaborators

[1] Source: Eurostat, 2010

out of a passive audience, which is deemed crucial when it comes to questions of responsible spatial interventions and sustainable spatial behaviour.

4.1 The range of spatial topics to be conveyed to non-experts through e-learning

Learning *about* architecture can take different approaches. The historic, timescale approach comes first to mind. As it can be insightful and informative it also takes a very long time and a reflective individual to draw conclusions and implications for the present state of affairs in built environments. The historic approach can prove to be burdened with counterproductive issues such as style, taste, etc. that sometimes overshadow the conceptual underlays and bias the perception when looked at from present-centric perspective and context, which is often the case how non-experts react, especially younger generation. Rather than discussing what is tasteful and beautiful, which varies greatly between individuals, societies, cultures and where consensus is very hard to reach (and even if reached does not help much) the topics of what is respectful of its surrounding environment, what is efficient, what is functional can be addressed.

Learning about architecture and its context in the present state, pointing and searching for cause-effect relationships and impacts leaps over the historic perspective but offers the connection to sustainability issues and can address actual and burning spatial problems and practices. Combining architecture and responsible spatial behaviour is ever more viable in the recent push to reduce our impact on the environment. The human need 'to inhabit' (be it in terms of residence, working environment, leisure activities, education) has broad-ranging impact on the environment and can consequently play a major role in sustainable efforts (Gauzin-Müller, 2002). Focusing on the 'inhabiting' also represents a viable and meaningful intersection between architectural practices, emerging and existing spatial problems, the role of actors in space and efforts towards more sustainable development.

Content Elements	Characteristics - ways of presenting content elements
• burning architectural-spatial problems • problems indicated by the existent development trends • specific indicators of sustainable development	• the sustainability begins in local environment • focusing of the concept of spatial sustainability around notions of 'living and dwelling' and operating with spatial qualities rather than spatial values • an equal treatment of all three sustainability 'columns' (social, environmental, economic) • the absence of interference and non-materialization are the interventions that should also be taken into consideration

Table 2. Lifelong learning about sustainability focuses around content elements and aspects.

There are many interpretations and dimensions of sustainable spatial development and responsible acting in different environments. Some are leaning towards energy efficiency, others focus on natural aspects, and less often the cultural aspects of sustainability are taken into an account: Stibbe & Luna (2009) go a step further, arguing for sustainability literacy skills that foster a deeper look into the social, cultural and economic systems that gave rise to environmental problems. Combining declared attitudes and values into operative, concise, near-everyday-life experience terms ('spatial qualities'; see Verovsek & Juvancic,

2009) and into useful, rounded, concise topics of content demands a systematic approach that on one hand determines the content elements and on the other the aspects/focus through which the contents should be conveyed (Table 2).

Content elements cover topics connected to sustainable handling of space that the experts want to point at, or change behaviour patterns of non-experts to be more in sync with professional efforts. The elements can deal with burning spatial problems - scattered settlements, unfinished buildings, decaying and energy inefficient facades, building on slopes, greenery and housing, etc. Additionally, the elements can warn against harmful spatial trends and practices that will lead to problems in the future. Not least, the elements can consist of individual indicators of sustainable development (i.e. Able, 1997).

When presenting the spatially related sustainable issues the topics can be highlighted through four crucial aspects:

1. "All sustainability is local" (McDonough, 1998) - the main questions here are: where am I? What natural, cultural and socio-economic environments encompass me? Connect the individual and efforts 'from the doorstep' to broader issues of sustainable development, from top-down to more personalized and on individual actions focused bottom-up perspective.
2. Focusing of sustainability around the notion of residing, settling, dwelling, inhabiting - this changes the optics of spatial intervening to individual actors, where one easily recognizes himself, pictures oneself in that role. The approach jumps scale from global - far away and far above - to concrete, local environment and touches individual everyday actions.
3. Equal treatment of 'tree trunks' of sustainable development, including those that are harder to measure and not prone to statistical analysis, and that are less present in peoples' minds or because their characteristics are harder to generalize.
4. The absence of interference and non-materialization are the interventions that should also be taken into consideration when pondering sustainable behaviour: before the material intervention the questions should be asked regarding its necessity, its timing, ripeness of available technologies and its scale/range.

While the characteristics or ways of presenting content elements remain focused around the four points in every situation, the content elements change depending on target population, age and educational structure, local environment and aims the learning strives to achieve. The same principles of presenting spatial issues around four focuses were later also used in the research study, titled "Education on the built environment for sustainable development" (Zupancic et al, 2009), which has been carried out in the framework of the national Targeted research programme Slovenian competitiveness 2006-2013.

4.2 Communication and interface aspects - feedback, multiple-way communication, interaction: luxury or necessity in e-learning?

As elaborated in the introduction the learning process is, in a way, also a communication process where, in our architectural case, mainly visual messages are exchanged. Dealing with e-learning applications and ICT, where not only pedagogical methods and theoretical approaches apply, but also where the multi-layering and complexity of hardware and software solutions have to be reckoned with, there are many factors that influence the outcome of the learner's experience and knowledge acquired.

Teachers, mediators and experts can and do influence the outcomes of traditional learning by choosing the topics, pedagogical approach, exemplary cases, ways of narration, engagement with the audience, etc. With the introduction of ICT and e-learning their roles and influence change to some extent (i.e. teachers as advisors, mediators, facilitators; Neville, 1999), and while still being important even more 'mediators' that influence the outcome of the learning come into play. Some of them are experts who specialize in ICT or other participants who make specialized contributions (i.e. professional actors for the re-enacting the scenes, narrators, who excel in narration, artists and illustrators, who specialize in graphic representations), other mediators are artificial (i.e. graphic user interfaces) and usually come in the form of the learning environment, communication tools, etc. As we are dealing with e-learning, and will later be inspecting educational interfaces that can be used without (or minimal) teacher's involvement, we will be highlighting the later - artificial mediators. The statement should not be understood in terms that teachers are redundant with the introduction of e-learning about architecture or that e-learning for non-experts should follow the path of excluding human mediators (although some experimental practices are leaning in that direction, i.e. Knewton[2]). In fact the showcase will prove to the contrary - the combination of f2f and ICT - blended learning - gives the best results at the moment. However for the purposes of the research, educational interfaces had to be isolated as sole mediators for the testing of the different elements and characteristics.

The parts can be arranged systematically, similarly to content part, into (visual) *elements* of interfaces and *characteristics* of interfaces the user is confronted with. The table (Table 3) applies to user interfaces and user experience with the system, which we focus on here. Although many characteristics are joined into five bigger groups that encompass the majority of particular characteristics, there are so many found in the literature (i.e. Shneiderman, 1998; Manovich, 2001; Rhee, Moon & Choe, 2006) some overlapping, some denoting similar things with different terminology, the effort to address them all seems futile. The interface characteristics are the ways the user manipulates the contents and the interface, the exchange of information between the user and the system, the ways of modification, the ways of being immersed in his actions and learning environment, etc.

While we focus on the interface part of the system and the *learner – interface – content experience*, additional parts of e-learning systems that are not addressed here but are relevant for the other actors involved would include characteristics of: experts, teachers or mediators managing the content - content management systems (CMS), learning management systems (LMS) and their interfaces, administrators managing the networks and support systems, and not least, the ICT experts creating the software solutions.

Interface elements	Interface Characteristics
• system/interaction management elements (menus, entry fields, slider, buttons, pointers etc) • 'visual' elements (presentations, icons, windows, descriptions, titles etc) • contents	• ways of navigation • ways of content presentation/narration • ways of interaction with elements • system openness rate • immersion rate and manner

Table 3. Learner–interface–content experience is dependent on elements and characteristics.

[2] http://www.knewton.com/

1. *The elements* represent the 'building blocks' that previous studies about interfaces (i.e. Shneiderman, 1998) in general or presentation techniques (i.e. Uccelli et al., 1999); Mullins et al., 2002, etc.) have already looked into: system/interaction management elements (menus, entering fields, slides, buttons, indicators, etc) and visual formulation elements (presentations, icons, windows, descriptions, addresses), as well as content formatted as multimedia itself.
2. *The characteristics* that can influence effectiveness of interfaces have been isolated and are the following:

- *ways of navigation* – how the user 'moves' through the system (discrete or continuous movement). According to Manovich (2001) the navigation within the system is not neutral but already sets and influences a narrative,
- *ways of content presentation/narration* – how the content is transmitted (on demand, automatically, combination of narration and presentation techniques used, etc), some referred to by Mayer (2005) within his principles for fostering visuospatial thinking in multimedia learning
- *ways of interaction with elements* – how the user interacts with the systems (manipulation of objects/contents, reversibility of actions, visual feedback of actions, etc),
- *system openness rate* – how the user can modify the system (openness of systems to modifications, possibility that users add own content or modify the existing one)
- *rate and manner of user immersion* in the system and its environment (Sherman & Craig, 2003)

4.3 Challenging and engaging the learners: Why it needs not only be conveying of facts but also fun to learn about?

Especially younger generations, the population that is already engaging or will soon engage in spatial interventions related to 'inhabiting' needs, has been brought up not as followers of the media only (passive receivers) but learned to engage in the process of active participation (also as contributors) through the widespread availability of ICT solutions (mainly, but not solely, internet). Students enter higher education with greater ICT abilities than their lecturers (Eklund et al., 2003 as cited in Mason & Rennie, 2006). The wide range of complex computer based games (i.e. Sim City, The Sims and Civilization to mention just a few which are directly relating to 'inhabiting' issues) and pervasive digital environments (i.e. Second Life) in combination with development of graphic capabilities of computers and availability of networking within them raised the bar of standards which are tacitly expected from educational software to succeed. As we will later see in the presented case, the more complex and challenging the task is, the more it attracts the learners and holds their attention in trying to achieve the optimum results. Merely translating traditional teaching tools and media into digital form thus not satisfies the usual learner, who is very aware what the present state ICT is capable of and resents to be vowed by 'digitality' only. E-learning about architecture profits greatly from use of ICT firstly because of complex sets of parameters (multiple cause and effect combinations) in architectural and urban settings that can be modelled into the educational software, computed and presented in real-time (Verovsek et al., 2011). For example: by tweaking of the different initial variables of the given urban setting, such as: pedestrian reserved spaces, greenery elements, elements for sojourning (benches, tables, chairs, etc), public transport opportunities, etc the future trends, perennial problems, conflicts and solutions can be tried out by the users themselves, gaining much more complex insight into the relationship than possible through traditional means of teaching. Knowledge gained in such a constructivist manner has also a much more durable lifespan than factual learning (Dondi et al., 2004; Prensky, 2001). For the educational software to be successful it also needs to be visually challenging and up to the standards of entertainment, social and other commonly used applications.

4.4 Networking and collaboration between learners (and teachers) in e-learning about architecture

Being able to communicate during the learning process with peers and teachers is an important part of the experience of learning. E-learning *about* architecture should be no different in that sense, facilitating the communication through different ICT possibilities (more integrated into the learning e-learning environment the better). Communicating with fellow learners enriches the experience with the social context (Stacey, 1998 as cited in Mason & Rennie, 2006) and when distance learning this can influence the motivation (Rovai & Jordan, 2004 as cited in Mason & Rennie, 2006) and the feeling of belonging to a group of learners.

While expert e-learning *in* architecture uses the networking and communication possibilities for a crucial collaboration on a common task, simulating everyday experience of working in a team of interdisciplinary experts, the non-expert learners can benefit from networking in another common experience: simulating everyday negotiations and consensus reaching, incorporating the effect of the behaviour of groups and crowds in the decision making process, coming to potential clashes of interests between different users of space and within individual priorities (i.e. economic vs. sustainable, self interest vs. interest of the common good, practical vs. moral). Through that the mediator can emphasize how actions of an individual can influence a wider range of people that are touched through individual's actions and the socio-spatial consequences that ensue. Another option is showing the limitations of individual actions (even sustainable) if the group avoids involvement or acts differently. And yet another is highlighting the force of a joint action in positive and negative endeavours viewed from the perspective of sustainable spatial interventions (i.e. asking students to choose a building spot for their fictional house in an fictional but close-to-reality environment, which can lead to dispersed settling and thus showing the problematical issues or it can be coordinated to more sustainable solutions).

4.5 Adaptation to learners and their knowledge level

Learners engaging in LLP learning about spatial sustainability and spatial issues differ in several aspects that influence their reference frame, experience, world view, knowledge base, skills and psycho-physical performance. The ones important for our discussion are: i) the age in combination with psycho-physical performance levels (Svetina et al., 2011) ii) level of formal education achieved (Chou & Hsiao, 2007), iii) interests and motivations. Their abilities to read the visual messages and respond in kind also vary, as mentioned earlier (in sub-chapter 2.2). The elements of contents and the use of e-learning tools thus needs to be adapted to the (envisioned, if not known) least able participants in the learning process from the outset. The showcased example presented in the next subchapter focused on specific population and tried to adapt to its awaited specifics. The survey conducted on younger generations that spanned the broader range of ages and levels (Zupancic et al., 2009) about their spatial sustainable awareness is a good example of how to modify the contents in a way that it adapts to different ages (through the questions and manner of questions asked, complexity of language, use of capital letters, depth of questions, etc). The teaching plans often point to suitable manners of how to tackle different issues and hint to base knowledge already acquired. However (in Slovenia) architectural and space related sustainable issues are (at the moment) not to be found there directly but are only tacitly implicated in them (Zupancic et al., 2010).

With the initial and general adaptation to the awaited group of learners set aside, the e-learning tools can offer a 'mass-customization' to individual learners by adapting to the individual learner with the setting of learning pace, introduction of additional contents once the base knowledge is acquired, helping and repeating where the learner struggles, offering an in-depth explanations and so forth (i.e., Knewton as reported in Fischman, 2011). Although the notion is more suitable for expert learning *in* architecture there are opportunities available for that kind of adaptation principle in e-learning *about* architecture also, but have yet to be seen in practice.

4.6 Assessment of knowledge gained

Referring to (in subchapter 2.2) discussed visuospatial thinking and multimedia learning, the way to assess the learners' understanding is to ask them to use what they have learned to solve a new problem (Mayer, 2005). This principle was used as the assessment tool in the educational interface showcased later in the chapter. From the strict scientific rigour perspective the results can be misleading as the learner's previous knowledge is only assumed and the level of knowing and ability to learn varies among the individuals in a group of learners. The initial pre-testing is a solution to measure the scale of progress made by an individual, however it is impractical and time consuming in usual learning settings, scientific experiments excluded.

When e-learning *in* architecture, the results are often less important than the process of going through the task solving, teamwork motions, etc. Contrary to that, e-learning *about* architecture and sustainable spatial behaviour strives for the results: the deeper understanding of cause-effect consequences, changing of attitudes, shaping of values and redirecting learners away from future harmful spatial practices. The results however cannot be measured in absolute terms - right or wrong - but can be only compared to the best informed and expert, interdisciplinary opinion what the solution of a given task should be. In a sense this represents also a measure of overlapping views and envisioned steps that experts and non-experts share after going through the learning process.

4.7 E-Learning about architecture cannot offer an answer to every perennial spatial problem: the limitations

Although it seems the (e-) learning *about* architecture is the perfect solution for the prevention of spatial problems and detrimental practices it cannot solve the problems as long as there is a difference between *knowing* and *doing*, different interests of groups and individuals that need to balance priorities that sometimes exclude themselves.

The question about the discrepancy "between words and actions" is certainly an interesting phenomenon of human nature, which is particularly materially expressed in cases of spatial interventions. The reasons for this duality can be found between the awareness of spatial values on a principal level and a different other actual knowledge of every individual, which may differ. One of the view points allows that value formation on a declarative level, including their normative function of what is and is not allowed, is often not related with day-to-day priorities. It is furthermore far from the role of a strong motivation force giving energy, wish and inspiration for action. It may occur that the "trained" society is aware of global environmental issues and also strives to act towards decreasing them, but with simultaneous interventions (unintentionally) harms their local environment. (Verovsek & Juvancic, 2009)

The scope of complex relations and intertwinement of cause-and-effect relationships is daunting and needs to be systematically approached not only with the e-learning tools but also with the curricula on levels of formal education, combining the efforts and means to achieve better understanding of our (cultural and natural) spatial environment that we live in and should act responsively and sustainably within its carrying capacities.

4.8 Showcase example: Educational eco-spatial Interface[3]

The emerging field of architectural educational interfaces presents new opportunities to address younger generations and non-expert public as early as possible. Such systems are only part of a wider selection of means and tools for teaching and transmitting spatial topics to non-experts (other efforts that follow the more traditional path of learning include i.e. Arkki school of architecture for children and youth, Finland, Meskanen, 2007).

The showcased prototypical Educational Eco-spatial Interface (Juvancic & Zupancic, 2008) represents architectural educational interfaces 1) for communicating professional values, issues, problematics, 2) for showing simplified cause-and-effect relationships and 3) for teaching responsible spatial acting through selected cases and learning-by-doing tasks. It acts as the helping hand for teachers who are already besieged with other equally important topics, overcoming the knowledge and time constriction barriers in formal education practices. Being part of the experiment, the elements of interfaces (the contents included) were tested through their use in educational settings in primary schools. Also tested were the independent variables of interface characteristics: ways of navigation, ways of narration and ways of interaction with elements. The system openness rate and rate of immersion were presumed constant (closed system and non-immersive interface) as was the contents (identical in all cases).

4.8.1 Methods and materials

The software application was designed as a collection of five selected tasks - each presented within one screen size (Fig. 2). The screen was divided into several parts: two larger parts were dedicated to education, passing of information and task at hand, the bottom part of the screen was reserved for the title, the top for navigation. The contents of educational part (light-green) – texts and small pictures for reference were visible most of the time, while other multimedia presentations opened on the same page (either automatically or on demand, depending on the variation of interface) and played in bigger quadrant to the right. The same quadrant was also used for presentation of the task solving instructions and tests themselves.

The interface was prepared in 5 different variations, with different levels of interactivity consisting of 3 variables: (i) navigation, (ii) narration/presentation of contents and (iii)

[3] adjective eco-spatial was coined from two adjectives: ecological and spatial to emphasize the interrelation between the two

Fig. 2. Eco-spatial Education Interface (task#3 and the classroom setting).

interactivity of tasks (visual feedback, reversibility of actions, experimenting). Conditions ranged from maximum to minimum interactivity, from traditional face to face (f2f) education method to the test group (which did not receive any information and educational contents, just the task and basic instructions). Several parameters were automatically recorded (i.e. time, user choices, etc) and results of each task graded. The technical requirements for running the application and its IT scope were intentionally scaled down to match the IT equipment in schools (no installation required, application runs even on slow computers).

The educational contents and tasks dealt with eco-spatial topics and most urgent, common and annoying local problems the experts want to warn future generations of-, call to their attention- or change their attitudes toward- were building on sloped grounds, greenery around habitats, unfinished houses and their surroundings, building in the existing environment, adapting to scale, renovation of residential neighbourhoods, etc. The method of learning from (positive) examples, through the analysis of them, and learning by doing in a constructivist manner - simulating everyday considerations and decision making in task contents, was applied and built into the educational interface.

The test group of 9th grade primary school pupils (age 13-15) had 218 units, which were evenly distributed among 5 test settings - 5 variations of interfaces. This population represents the last instant before the whole generation diversifies into different vocational and professional directions, it is mature enough as it has built relatively independent system of abstract, contextual thinking abilities and social responsibility awareness (Marjanovic Umek & Zupancic, 2004; Marjanovic Umek & Svetina, 2004) and not least - the architectural awareness of their parents is still reflected in their way of thinking.

4.8.2 Results

Interactivity has a significant influence on the test results. The traditional f2f teaching with the computerized test solving part at the end still yields the best results. It has the smallest range between the lowest and highest grades. It is closely followed by the maximum interactive version of the interface, with middle and minimum versions trailing behind. In all these versions the range between the lowest and the highest scores extends. The results of the test group were unexpected - it has surprisingly good and focused scores. Nevertheless, the average scores are not as good as in traditional f2f approach, they are lower than the maximum interactivity group average, equalling middle and beating minimal interactive interfaces.

Results also show that (i) navigation has some effect on the results (moving freely among the tasks contributes to effectiveness), while (ii) narration/presentation of contents (or the lack of it) and (iii) interactivity of the task have considerable influence on the final score, but due to test design their individual effect contribution cannot be isolated. Considering (ii) narration: even though the pupils had an opportunity to look at the informative presentations as many times as they wished ('max' version), they mostly did not bother to do that; on the contrary, nobody even looked through the half of all presentations. On the other hand, in the 'mid' interface version all were able to interrupt the automatic presentation at the beginning of each task, but only two did so, with many replaying the presentations (despite this fact the average grade in this group is lower than that of the 'max' version). The visits to each task (where possible) show similar results - the highest average score is achieved in six visits (which means one visit more than there are tasks).

Considering (iii) interactivity of task: while the possibilities to reverse the actions ('undo') do not play a significant role, visual feedback, possibilities to test different elements or situations, visually evaluate and change selection if needed, and significantly contribute to higher score. Evaluating the amount of time spent compared with the grade, the best results were achieved by the users who spent approximately 20 minutes in the interface – the score up to this time gradually rises and then gradually falls. The majority of users spent between 5 and 20 minutes within the interface. The pupils considered task #3 the most interesting one. The same task was also the most complex of all five tasks and most game like, with different architectural elements, their 'value' and 'financial' balance required. The most difficult task was, according to the pupils, task #4, which was also the most abstract and the least liked.

4.8.3 Reflections and lessons learned

With each prototypical test run of software there are plenty of lessons learned and stories to tell but here we would like to focus on the pedagogical, technological and institutional aspects. From the perspective of the learners the interface and this kind of e-learning has been well accepted not least because it was a welcome distraction from the traditional teaching the learners are used to and freshness of topic as the primary education curricula in its span only briefly touches architecture.

While ignoring the provocative question "feedback, multiple-way communication, interaction: luxury or necessity in e-learning?" in the conclusions of that subchapter and dealing there more with the mechanics of the interfaces, we return to it at the conclusion of the subchapter: interactivity by all means is not a luxury any more. It has many aspects in e-learning, beyond traditional interactionist theories (i.e. Haralambos, 1989), the major two: facilitation of interaction between dislocated participants of the learning process (which is of even greater importance in expert architectural e-learning) and in tune with interactionist theories that meaning is constructed in interactive situations through negotiations and discussion (Haralambos, 1989) and interactivity of learners and e-learning tools (contents included). The sustainable topics highlighted through the spatially related activities of groups and individual have been seen as a positive contribution to the curricula by the teachers and the interface a tool that they could use for teaching (among many other tools on offer i.e. R.A.V.E. Space project suggestions: Demsar Mitrovic et al., 2007). They also suggested and insisted on more open system that would allow them to insert their own contents (graphics, photographs, texts) related to local environment and its specifics (which also proves that they understand the notion of acting locally and that understanding/explaining sustainability through the cause-and-effect relationships in our immediate surroundings is of the essence). The time constraint is beyond the topics of the chapter but it has to be emphasized, the range of topics to teach is so vast and the competition of themes so fervid that teachers feel an enormous time pressure, mentioned very often, much more than questioning of their competency to teach so specific topics (Demsar Mitrovic et al., 2007).

At the institutional level - the management of the particular schools involved has been a very understanding and cooperative body to work with on the topics of spatial sustainability, often asking for more contents and pedagogical contributions that we were able to provide. The Ministry of the environment and spatial planning on the yet higher institutional level has expressed an interest to implement the interface nation wide at primary schools but the discussions did so far not progress beyond the agreement that it would be a useful contribution provided it surpasses the prototypical phase. The talks however resulted in discussions about the necessity to look into the spatial sustainability issues, common curricula and education through a project in a Targeted research programme scheme (Zupancic et al., 2009).

From the technological perspective the potential improvements point in the direction of adaptability, networking and wider variety of topics covered with multiple tasks per one topic, offering more possibilities to show complex issues and asses the gained knowledge, more feedback to learners informing them whether they are on the right track, how good have they done and challenging them with the complex game-related tasks.

5. Conclusion

A fundamental consideration is that there are two types of learners when it comes to the field of architecture: the future experts, learning the methods, gaining the knowledge, skills and expertise in the field - *learners in architecture* and the non-experts, lay public, learning to understand cause and effect relationships in space, regarding built, cultural and natural environment, gaining an insight into the field, and into the expert logic - *learners about architecture*. Efforts of one group cannot compensate for the efforts of the other when dealing with built environment and spatial interventions as they more often than not, when not in sync, result in misunderstanding, misinterpretation, contradictions, which arise in response to physical manifestations discernable in spatial problems and unsustainable practices.

Both groups of learners can benefit from architectural e-learning, each group requiring a particular set of e-learning environments, tools, contents for suitable learning settings and positive learning outcomes. While some aspects are shared among the groups, such as blended learning, constructivist principles and project based learning, the use of visual messages, visuospatial multimedia learning principles, and the use of e-learning platforms, other aspects are particular for each group of learners as a whole and yet more particular within the same general group given the specific targeted population (as in the case mentioned: primary education pupils or a group of people who want to build their own dwellings in the near future, or public gathered around a specific spatial interest, etc).

Following the development of e-learning (and distributed learning) *in* and *about* architecture through the literature (i.e. CUMINCAD, a database of resources on the topic of Computer aided architecture and education) and recent publications, it is apparent that the practice has not yet established a foothold in architectural schools' curricula, nor found a place in general education (very few reports and even fewer scientific publications on the topic). However we can still discern two patterns of slow but gradual introduction of e-learning into architectural education: one approaching e-learning in architecture holistically - developing the whole system, including curricula, contents, tools (or concepts of them) and e-platforms (i.e. showcase example in the chapter VIPA: Kipcak, 2007; IMLAB: Gatermann & Czerner, 2003; etc), the other tackling specific and individual issues of e-learning, either developing prototypical tools (i.e. showcase example in the chapter Eco Spatial Interface: Juvancic & Zupancic, 2008; virtual design studios - VDS, etc) or integrating and combining the existing ones into systems. Neither of them is yet in the phase where we could claim that e-learning is institutionalized. It seems that as in other fields, e-learning in architecture is caught between the resistance to curricular change and the established ways of traditional teaching[4]. Mizban & Roberts, (2006) have analyzed e-learning in architectural education and established that a majority of cases in their analysis have been technologically driven - as a 'test bed': trying out the advances in ICT and applying them to architectural teaching or trying out new ways of supporting creativity or simply to develop students' ICT skills - and did not origin from pedagogical needs. On the other hand, some joint projects, due to their nature of distributed partners, teacher, students and teaching involved, introduce e-learning without intentionally emphasizing it. Archi21 is an example of ongoing European project (Hunter et al., 2011) that fosters Content & Language Integrated Learning (CLIL). The content in this case is architecture. The (envisioned and in some cases already executed) learning has all the characteristics of blended learning, with LMS, virtual environment (as a place to learn- and collaborate- in) and other e-communication tools at their core. It seems that such interdisciplinary endeavours are a short-term roundabout to gradual and persistent integration of e-learning in architecture.

In more general, lifelong education the hindrance is not so much avoidance of e-learning practices (the use of Moodle is quite wide spread already, with certain examples of educational interfaces already embraced), but the lack of architectural and spatial sustainability related topics in the learning programmes.

Throughout the chapter we have highlighted the benefits of e-learning *in* and *about* architecture, summing them up as: the ability to promote different types of collaboration, enhance students' set of skills, facilitate a flexible access to multimedia, educational resources anytime and anyplace (Mizban & Roberts, 2006), but also helping teachers introduce topics they are not expert in to non-expert public, enhance the experience of learning, introduce and present complex cause and effect spatial relationships that we are unable to grasp with the traditional teaching tools, simulate and test the processes prior to their physical manifestation, help in efforts for sustainable building practices and support informed decision making.

There are also barriers that hinder the widespread of e-learning *in* and *about* architecture. The main are the lack of pedagogical demand for them as observed by Mizban & Roberts

[4] There are exceptions to this rule in fellow field of design, where the university and consequently also the design programme within is based on the distributed (e-learning) principles that stand at its core of teaching and is thus institutionalized. Such an example would be The Open University, UK

(2006), the rigidity of curricula and inertia – "we have been doing it for years, why change it?" The students themselves often lack the motivation to acquire additional skills required to efficiently work in e-learning environment (students perceive additional learning as extra and non-essential workload). The rest usually consists of variety of technological issues. The systems are staying on the prototypical level, riddled with bugs and technological constraints hindering the usual design process or lacking the functionalities of common tools in use, making expressing oneself more difficult than in traditional learning, lacking the integration, having compatibility issues, problems with communication, bandwidth and simply put: things not working consistently and reliably - in effect, transferring the emphasis from the learning architecture to solving technological problems. All these reduce the motivation of learners and teachers even further. Overcoming the prototypical levels mean also overcoming institutional, investment, ICT barriers and requires a critical mass of teachers and learners seeing the benefits of-, feeling the pedagogical need for- and eventually using the e-learning in architecture.

On the path to maturity, however, there are many opportunities for widening the scope and usefulness of e-learning tools *in* and *about* architecture: introduction of networked learning, adaptive learning systems, extensive usage of graphic capabilities, integration of tools, and more, that the fast technological advance will offer us in the future.

6. References

Abel, C. (1997). *Architecture and identity: towards a global eco-culture,* Architectural Press, ISBN 978-0750607902, Oxford

Bates-Brkljac, N. (2007). Investigating perceptual responses and shared understanding of architectural design ideas when communicated through different forms of visual representations, *Proceedings of Information visualisation 2007 conference,* ISBN- 0-76795-2900-3, Zurich, Switzerland, July 2007

Chou, J. R. & Hsiao, S. W. (2007). A usability study on human-computer interface for middle-aged learnes, *Computers in Human Behavior,* Vol. 23, No. 7, pp. 2040-2063, ISSN 0747-5632

Demsar Mitrovic, P., Miklavcic, T., Resnik Planinc, T., Urbanc, M., Fridl, J., Simoneti, M., Sorn, M. et al. (2007). *R.A.V.E Space: project final report. Raising awareness of values of space through the education process,* Demsar Mitrovic, P. in Rihar, J. (ed), Ministry of the Environment and Spatial Planning, 978-961-6392-56-3, Ljubljana

Dondi, C., Behnn, E. & Moretti, M. (2004). Why Choose a Game for Improving Learning and Teaching Processes? In: *Guidelines for Game-Based Learning,* Pivec, M., Koubek, A. & Dondi, C., pp. 20-76, PABST, ISBN 3899671937, Lengerich, Berlin, etc

Fischman, J. (2011). The Rise of Teaching Machines, In: *The Chronicle of Higher Education, The Digital Campus,* 8.5.2011. Available from http://chronicle.com/article/The-Rise-of-Teaching-Machines/127389/

Fruchter, R. (2006). The Fishbowl™: Degrees of Engagement in Global Teamwork, In: LNAI 4200 *Intelligent Computing in Engineering and Architecture,* I.F.C. Smith, pp. 241-257, Springer Verlag, ISBN 978-3-540-46246-0, Berlin Heidelberg

Gatermann, H. & Czerner, J. (2003). Modular E-Learning-Environment for Architecture, *Proceedings of the 21th eCAADe Conference: Digital Design,* ISBN 0-9541183-1-6, Graz, Austria, September 2003

Gauzin-Müller, D. (2002). *Sustainable architecture and urbanism: concepts, technologies, examples,* Birkhäuser, ISBN 3-7643-6659-1, Basel, Berlin, Boston

Greeno, J.G. (1998). The Situativity of Knowing, Learning, and Research. *American Psychologist,* Vol. 53, No. 1, pp. 5-26, ISSN-0003-066X

Haralambos, M. (1989). *Sociology*, Unwin Hyman, ISBN 9788634303872, London

Hunter, M., Chase, S., Kligerman, B. & Zupancic, T. (2011). ARCHI21: Architectural and Design based Education and Practice through Content & Language Integrated Learning using Immersive Virtual Environments for 21st Century Skills, *Proceedings of the 29th eCAADe Conference: Respecting Fragile Places,* ISBN 978-9491207013, Ljubljana, September 2011

Juvancic, M. & Zupancic-Strojan, T. (2008). Towards effective interfaces for general architectural learning: eco-spatial educational interface for pupils, *Proceedings of the 26th eCAADe Conference: Architecture "in computro : integrating methods and techniques,* ISBN 978-0-9541183-7-2, Antwerpen, Belgium, September 2008

Juvancic, M., Zupancic, T. & Hocevar, M. (2011). Towards effective interfaces for non-professional architectural learning: Architectural educational interface for pupils. *Javnost - The Public,* accepted for publication in 2012

Kipcak, O. (2007). The VIPA Project. What is VIPA? In: *VIPA virtual campus for virtual space design provided for european architects,* Marek, C., Edition mono/monochrom, pp. 6-9, ISBN 3-9500731-8-3, Graz

Manovich, L. (2002). *The language of new media,* reprint ed., MIT Press, ISBN 978-0-262632-55-3, Cambridge, Mass.

Marjanovic, L. & Svetina, M. (2004). Spoznavni in govorni razvoj v srednjem in poznem otroštvu, In: *Razvojna psihologija,* Marjanovic, L. & Zupancic, M., pp. 408-427, Znanstvenoraziskovalni inštitut Filozofske fakultete, ISBN 8672071468, Ljubljana

Marjanovic, L. & Zupancic, M. (2004). Teorije psihičnega razvoja, In: *Razvojna psihologija,* Marjanovic, L. & Zupancic, M., pp. 28-63, Znanstvenoraziskovalni inštitut Filozofske fakultete, ISBN 8672071468, Ljubljana

Mason, R. & Rennie, F. (2006). *E-Learning: the Key Concepts.* Routledge, ISBN 0-415-37307-7, New York

Mayer, E.R. (2005). Multimedia Learning: Guiding Visuospatial Thinking with Instructional Animation, In: *The Cambridge Handbook of Visuospatial Thinking,* P. Shah & A. Miyake, pp. 477-508, Cambridge University Press, ISBN 978-0-521-00173-0, New York

McDonough, W. (1998). Declaration of Interdependence, In: *Dimensions of sustainability: architecture, form, technology, environment, culture,* Scott A., pp. 45-55, E & FN Spon, an imprint of Routledge London, ISBN 0-419-23620-1, New York

Meskanen, P. (2007). Shaping Spaces; Architecture and Children – Teaching the values of space to children and youth. *Presented at R.A.V.E. Space Project Final Conference,* Ljubljana, Slovenia, December 2007.

Mizban, N. & Roberts, A. (2006). The Place of E-learning in Architectural Education - A Critical Review, *Proceedings of the 24th eCAADe Conference: Communicating Space(s),* ISBN 0-9541183-5-9, Volos, Greece, September 2006

Mullins, M., Zupancic-Strojan, T. & Juvancic, M. (2002) Experts and Users Efficiency and Accuracy in the Presentation of Design Ideas Across Networks, *Proceedings of the 20th eCAADe Conference: Connecting the Real and the Virtual - design e-ducation,* ISBN 0-9541183-0-8, Warsaw, September 2002

Neville, A. (1999). The problem-based learning tutor: Teacher? Facilitator? Evaluator? *Medical Teacher,* Vol. 21, No. 4, pp. 393-401, ISSN 0142-159X

Prensky, M. (2001). *Digital Games-Based Learning,* McGraw Hill, ISBN 978-1557788634, New York

Quintana, C., Carra, A., Krajcik, J. & Soloway, E. (2002). Learner-Centered Design: Reflections and New Directions, In: *Human-Computer interaction in the new millennium,* Carroll, J. M., pp. 605-626, ACM Press, ISBN 978-0201704471, New York

Rhee, C., Moon, J. & Choe, Y. (2006). Web Interface Consistency in E-learning. *Online Information Review*, Vol. 30, No. 1, pp. 53-69, ISSN 1468-4527

Severin, W.J. & Thankard, J.W.Jr. (1992). *Communication theories: Origins, Methods, and Uses in Mass Media*. Longman, ISBN 978-0801304637, New York

Sherman, W. R. & Craig, A. B. (2003). *Understanding virtual reality: interface, application and design,* Morgan Kaufmann, ISBN 978-1558603530, San Francisco

Shneiderman, B. (1998). *Designing the user interface: strategies for effective human-computer interaction,* 3. Ed, Addison-Wesley, ISBN 978-0-201694-97-0, Reading

Stager, G. (2005). Towards a Pedagogy of Online Constructionist Learning, *Proceedings of 2005 World Conference on Computers in Education,* Stellenbosch, South Africa, July 2005

Stibbe, A. & Luna, H. (2009). Introduction, In: *The Handbook of Sustainability Literacy: Skills for a changing world,* A. Stibbe, pp. 9-16, Green Books, ISBN 978-1-900322-60-7, Foxhole, Dartington, Totnes, Devon, UK

Strojan, T. Z. & Mullins, M. (2002). The Identity of Place in Virtual Design Studios. *Journal of Architectural Education,* Vol. 56, No. 1, pp. 15-21, ISSN 1046-4883

Svetina, M., Istenic Starcic, A., Juvancic, M. , Novljan, T., Subic Kovac, M., Verovsek, S. & Zupancic, T. (2011). How Children Come to Understand Sustainable Development : a Contribution to Educational Agenda, *Sustainable development*, Vol. 20, No. 20, pp. 1-10, ISSN 0968-0802

Tos, N. et al. (2004). *Vrednote v prehodu III. Slovensko javno mnenje 1999-2004,* Tos, N. (ed), Fakulteta za družbene vede, IDV – CJMMK, ISBN 978-3-901941-23-8, Ljubljana

Ucelli, G., Conti, G. & Klercker, A. J. (1999). Visualisation: The Customer's Perception, *Proceedings of the 17th eCAADe Conference: Computing from Turing to 2000,* ISBN 0-9523687-5-7, Liverpool, September 1999

Verovsek, S. & Juvancic, M. (2009). Identifying spatial values in the opinions of teenagers. *Urbani izziv*, Vol. 20, No. 1, pp. 164-174, ISSN 0353-6483

Verovsek, S., Juvancic, M. & Zupancic, T. (2011). Interpretation Model of Urban Space Coherence, *Proceedings of the 29th eCAADe Conference: Respecting Fragile Places,* ISBN 978-9491207013, Ljubljana, September 2011

von Glaserfield, E. (1991). An exposition of Constructivism: Why some like it radical, In: *Constructivist Views of the Teaching and Learning of Mathematics,* R. B. Davis, C.A. Maher & N. Noddings, pp. 19-29, VA: National Council of Teachers of Mathematics, Reston

Wenger, E. (1998). *Communities of Practice: Learning, Meaning and Identity,* Cambridge University Press, ISBN 0-521-66363-6, Cambridge New York

Zupancic, T., Novljan, T., Juvancic, M., Verovsek, S., Subic Kovac, M., Istenic Starcic, A. & Svetina, M. (2009). The concretization of the term sustainable spatial development for the assessment of child and juvenile awareness. *Urbani izziv*, Vol. 20, No. 1, pp. 153-163, ISSN 0353-6483

Zupancic, T., Verovsek, S., Juvancic, M., Svetina, M., Novljan, T., Subic Kovac, M. & Istenic Starcic, A. (2010). Education for Sustainable Development in the Built Environment in Slovenia, *AR - Architecture, Research,* No. 1, pp. 70-77, ISSN 1580-5573